Gallery of Mirrors

Swedenborg Studies / No. 7
Monographs of the Swedenborg Foundation

Emanuel Swedenborg (1688–1772)

Gallery of Mirrors

REFLECTIONS OF SWEDENBORGIAN THOUGHT

Anders Hallengren

Foreword by Inge Jonsson

SWEDENBORG FOUNDATION PUBLISHERS
WEST CHESTER, PENNSYLVANIA

Swedenborg Studies is a scholarly monograph series published by the Swedenborg Foundation. The primary purpose of the series is to make materials available for understanding the life and thought of Emanuel Swedenborg (1688–1772) and the impact his thought has had on others. The Foundation undertakes to publish original studies and English translations of such studies and to republish primary sources that are otherwise difficult to access. Proposals should be sent to: Senior Editor, Swedenborg Studies, Swedenborg Foundation, 320 North Church Street, West Chester, Pennsylvania 19380.

Library of Congress Cataloging-in-Publication Data

Hallengren, Anders, 1950–
Gallery of mirrors: reflections of Swedenborgian thought/
Anders Hallengren : foreword by Inge Jonsson.
p.   cm.   (Swedenborg studies : no. 7)
Includes bibliographical references and index.
ISBN 0–87785–188–3 (hardcover).
ISBN 0–87785–189–1 (paperback).
1. Swedenborg, Emanuel, 1688–1772—Influence.
2. New Jerusalem Church—Doctrines—History.
I. Title.
II. Series.
BX8721.2.H35 1998
289'.4—dc21   98–23862
CIP

Edited by Mary Lou Bertucci
Designed by Vivian Bradbury
Set in Present and Weiss by Sans Serif, Inc., Saline, Michigan

Printed in the United States of America.

From this infinite variety, the infinity of God the Creator
can be seen as in a mirror.

Emanuel Swedenborg,
True Christian Religion, ¶32 (2b)

For
DALE KUSHNER
and
JOHN CHADWICK

Contents

Foreword by Inge Jonsson • ix
Acknowledgments • xv
Introduction • xvii

Music, Metaphysics, and Modernity • 3

The Secret of Magna Tartaria • 17

The New Church in the West Indies • 43

Revival and Reform in Russia • 61

In Search of Robsahm's Memories • 79

The Code of the Ancients: New Church Spirituality
and New England Transcendentalism • 89

An American Philosophy of Use • 105

The Ancients and the Postmoderns:
Notes on the Currency of a Classic • 115

A Mirror Reflecting a Higher Reality:
Hermetics, Al-Qur'an, and the Crisis of Modern Man • 129

Notes • 137
Bibliography • 163
Index • 197

Foreword

By Inge Jonsson

For almost five hundred years, a great part of Swedish literature was written in Latin. When the first university in Scandinavia was founded in Uppsala in 1477, the Roman Catholic Church had been established in Sweden for more than three centuries and had produced at least two figures of European stature.

One of them, Petrus de Dacia, is usually credited with having been the first Swedish author, although all the writings he has left behind are in Latin. Petrus belonged to the Dominican order and ended his career as prior of the convent at Visby, where he died in 1289. During his years as a student at the Dominican college at Cologne, he made the acquaintance of a female ecstatic, who gave vivid accounts of remarkable mystic experiences: visions, tribulations, and even stigmatization. Petrus wrote a book about her called *Vita Christinae Stumbelensis*, which established his reputation as a hagiographer.

However, Petrus' contribution to that important medieval genre was soon surpassed by the works of a younger compatriot, Saint Bridget. Although she wrote very little herself, Bridget was canonized because of her visions, which she had related to her confessors, who then gave them a proper literary form in Latin. Saint Bridget belonged to the highest circles in society, both through birth and marriage. Her revelations clearly reflect this status, but her experiences as a woman and a mother made the strongest impact on her spiritual message. On divine command she gave severe reprimands to the Swedish king, as if she spoke to a disobedient child; and she even ordered the pope to return to Rome from his humiliating exile in Avignon, which, in fact, he did for a while.

Saint Bridget's *Revelations* contain a strange combination of class interests, including lust for power and humility, but above all an absolute conviction that she was the mouthpiece of the Lord. No doubt, self-confidence on the verge of arrogance was needed to force through the great project of her life, which was to found a new religious order. Things did not turn out exactly the way she had envisaged, but finally the pope accepted her plans and rules as they were represented in Latin, the common European tongue. Bridgettine nuns with their special veils still are found in many countries, holding the memory of the visionary saint from Sweden sacred.

As the language of the learned, Latin lasted much longer than the Middle Ages. It is indeed a remarkable fact that Sweden has produced two prominent religious writers, Saint Bridget and Emanuel Swedenborg, both of whom have given accounts of highly concrete experiences of the world of spirits and angels. They have become parts of what Goethe called *Weltliteratur,* world literature; but, for the two of them, the old observation that no one will be a prophet in his or her native country has proved valid. In the case of Saint Bridget, her relative anonymity in Sweden can be attributed to the Lutheran Reformation in the sixteenth century, which caused a total breach with Roman Catholic Europe for a long period of time. But the fact that rather few Swedes know anything about Swedenborg must have other explanations.

One explanation is probably that Swedenborg almost exclusively used Latin in his many works. A comparison with his younger relative Linnaeus (Carl von Linné) may be telling. Linnaeus published his innovating botanical writings in Latin for a learned audience; but he was also commissioned by the government to investigate the natural resources in various parts of Sweden, and his reports in Swedish have won status as minor classics. Nothing similar is represented in Swedenborg's voluminous *oeuvre.* With the exception of some small treatises and articles written in the 1710s, Swedenborg published everything in Latin both as a scientist and religious thinker. Significantly, the book by him best known among his compatriots was written in a very expressive Swedish although never published by himself (or even meant to be). In the *Journal of Dreams*, Swedenborg made notes of his journey to Holland and England in 1743–1744 and recorded his dreams during a deep religious crisis in these years. This diary was not made public until 1859, when it attracted much attention, not least because of its matter-of-fact descriptions of sexual visions.

But the most important reason that Emanuel Swedenborg is a greater name in world literature than in Swedish culture should be sought elsewhere. He started a career as a scientist and technician in the 1710s and held an influential office in the Royal College of Mining for almost thirty years, most of the time fulfilling a very ambitious research program in addition to his official duties. In the mid-1730s, Swedenborg published his first *magnum opus*, the three-folio volumes called *Opera philosophica et mineralia*. They contain an enormous amount of compiled facts and original observations on the production of iron and copper, and made him highly respected in his profession. But the most momentous volume from a historical point of view was devoted to natural philosophy—what today would perhaps be designated theoretical physics. Here Swedenborg tried to chart the evolution of nature from the mathematical origin created by God to the height represented by our solar system, accomplishing this attempt from a Cartesian basis with considerable originality.

From inorganic nature Swedenborg then proceeded to organic and, finally, to spiritual nature, with the explicit intention of empirically proving the immortality of the soul, or *ipsis sensibus* in his own Latin. This superhuman project resulted in a couple of thousand printed pages and still more manuscript sheets on the structure of the human body and the intercourse between body and soul, until it was finally interrupted by his religious crisis of the mid-1740s. This period of anguish ended in a divine vision, in which he was ordered to abandon his scientific work and start interpreting the Holy Scriptures.

Swedenborg obeyed the command of the Lord; he resigned his office in the Royal College of Mining and devoted the remaining twenty-five years of his long life to writing a series of massive Latin works, in which he alternated pure exegesis with accounts of what he had seen and heard in the world of spirits. The most original quality of Swedenborg's later writings is his claim to living simultaneously in the natural and spiritual worlds. On the basis of what is known as his doctrine of correspondences, he describes how spirits and angels inhabit equivalents of earthly communities. These correspondences are said to be so complete that it is a long while before recently deceased human beings actually realize that they have left life on earth. Like cells in our body, myriads of such spiritual communities form a universal human figure, a *Maximus Homo*, who stands constantly turned to God in the shape of the Sun of Heaven, the eternal Fount of Love and Truth.

Since the clergy had great power in eighteenth-century Sweden, censorship of books was quite rigid in theological matters, so Swedenborg had to print all his exegetical works abroad. Officially he was not allowed to keep any copies in his own house, and until the end of the 1760s, he published his books anonymously. But as a nobleman who had contacts in high places, he could ignore this ban; according to an item in a Stockholm periodical in 1764, he even donated some volumes to the royal library. Literary circles in the capital soon found out who the author was, and opinions of the value of his writings varied from a smiling compassion on a case of misguided enthusiasm as in Carl Gustaf Tessin's famous diary to an attitude of appreciation, even admiration, as in Anders Johan von Höpken's private correspondence.

Swedenborg himself made no other missionary efforts than writing his books; but after his death, small congregations of fascinated readers gathered within the "new church," which had been portended in Swedenborg's works. Such groups arose in many countries, but in Sweden, the New Church was assailed both by zealous clergymen and by radical writers. The most prominent of these opponents was Johan Henric Kellgren, a leading poet and critic, and his devastating attack has made it almost embarrassing for many Swedes until this very day to accept

Swedenborg as part of our cultural heritage. For quite a few of those, to whom he is something more than an age-old name, Swedenborg appears to be the archetypal scientist who lost his grasp on reality while struggling with an impossible research program.

Fortunately, enough people have been less prejudiced in many other countries, even if Swedenborg's reception in Germany was hampered by Kant's scathing 1766 essay *Träume eines Geistersehers* (The Dreams of a Ghost-seer). The most vigorous early follow- ers were to be found in England; and they, in turn, inspired the founding of congregations in the United States. Some of these congregations are still very active. In literature Ralph Waldo Emerson has perhaps played the greatest role in making the name of Swedenborg world-famous, since he elected the vision- ary as one of his *Representative Men* in 1850. But the reception of Swedenborg's achievement in France via Balzac and Baudelaire has probably been of even greater importance within the more exclusive modernist tradition. None of the great authors who read Swedenborg professed themselves his adherents in a reli- gious sense, other than temporarily, for example, Strindberg and Blake; nevertheless, it is quite clear that enough have been fasci- nated by Swedenborg's visions to entitle him a seat on the global Parnassus.

In fact, there are some indications of an increasing interest in Swedenborg in later years, even in Sweden. During the 1990s, two extensive dissertations have been devoted to his early disci- ples, and at least two other theses in preparation will most prob- ably give us new knowledge of essential aspects of his own writings. In 1996, two prominent Swedish writers, Olof Lager- crantz and Lars Bergquist, published highly interesting books, the first of which presented a reading of Swedenborg's visions as a magnificent poem, a personal interpretation to be sure, but well-informed and full of empathy. In the following year, Anders Hallengren alone published two collections of Swedenborg studies, of which a selection has now been chosen for the pres- ent volume together with other material.

Anders Hallengren is a prolific writer indeed, and his

scholarly interests are very broad. In this volume the reader will find two fields that Hallengren has cultivated with particular fervor, the impact of Emanuel Swedenborg and that of Ralph Waldo Emerson as the leading American philosopher. These fields are, of course, closely connected, and Hallengren's profound knowledge of Swedenborg gave a special value to his impressive doctoral thesis *The Code of Concord: Emerson's Search for Universal Laws,* which he defended at Stockholm University in 1994. I had the privilege of being his supervisor, a most rewarding duty from which I learned a great deal. I am sure that the reader will find Hallengren's learned company as agreeable and instructive as I did.

Acknowledgments

The starting point for my inquiry into Swedenborg's global influence was "The importance of Swedenborg to Emerson's Ethics," a lecture delivered at the international Swedenborg Symposium in Bryn Athyn, Pennsylvania, in 1988 and published in the comprehensive volume *Swedenborg and his Influence*. I am particularly grateful to the chair of that great event, Prof. Jane Williams-Hogan, and to the general editor of the proceedings, Prof. Erland J. Brock, for their enthusiasm, encouragement, and support.

During those days in Pennsylvania in February of 1988, I met for the first time with my fellow-countrymen His Excellence Ambassador Lars Bergquist and the New Church reverend Olle Hjern, president of the Scandinavian Swedenborg Society. Both have, in different ways, been essential to my research during the past decade, as sources of knowledge and of inspiration. In Bryn Athyn, I also met with Dr. George F. Dole, as proficient as unpretentious, who would on his own initiative translate some of my texts and who has inspirited the whole book.

In addition, Dr. John Chadwick, another distinguished philologist, has, in other respects, meant very much to my work. My wise and humble friend, the philosopher Georg Henrik von Wright, formerly of Cambridge, has been indispensable in my attempts to understand the forces at work in moral decisions and has remained a source of encouragement.

But I am primarily indebted to the former president of Stockholm University, Dr. Inge Jonsson, who initially introduced me into this field of research and who guided and supported me for many years, as did my teachers and highly esteemed friends at Harvard, Daniel Aaron and David H. Donald.

I also owe many thanks to the Nordenskjöld Fund of the Royal Academy of Sciences, which gave me a substantial grant to write this book, and to other institutions that have supported me in various ways during years of travel, archive studies, lecturing, and writing: The Swedenborg Society in London, Swedenborg Publishers International, Swedenborg Foundation, the Sven and Dagmar Salén Foundation, the Marcus and Amalia Wallenberg Memorial Fund, the Swedish Institute, and Stockholm University.

Among others, I also would like to thank the heroic librarians of the former Lenin Library in Moscow; the Slavist Rev. Göran Appelgren; professors Lars Kleberg, George Cline, Aleksandr Dobrokhotov, and Leonard Fox; and, finally, Dr. Magnus Ljunggren who first gave me the idea to follow Swedenborg's traces in Russian history, but who has no doubt forgotten it by now. I have not.

Furthermore, I am much obliged to Gordon Jacobs, Norman Ryder, and Friedemann Horn for information on pertinent passages in musicological literature and eminent advice in other respects too, when I decided to pilot into the thin air of reverberating celestial music.

My study on the West Indies rests primarily on field interviews and archival studies, since I had no forerunners in that field. I am gratefully indebted to many local historians, archivists, and others with special knowledge or interest in my constantly confusing questions, who were willing to help me in my quest. Foremost among them are the librarian Carol Wakefield of the St. Croix Landmarks Society in Whim, the directors Erik and Frits Lawaetz in Christiansted and Fredriksted, Curator William F. Cissel of Christiansvœrn, all in St. Croix, Virgin Islands; the librarians Louise Woofenden and Jonathan Mitchell of the Swedenborg School of Religion in Newton, Massachusetts; Carroll Odhner of the Swedenborg Library in Bryn Athyn, Pennsylvania; and Nancy Dawson of the Swedenborg Society in London. Last but by no means least I should like to mention the patient and generous staff of the State Archives in Copenhagen, who let me for an extended period freely handle the immense, handwritten *Folketœllinger* of the Virgin Islands for the years of Danish power.

Lastly I wish to thank the reader of this book, without whom all this work had been done in vain.

Introduction

Heaven on Earth:
In Pursuit of Swedenborgian
Reflections in History

The eminent scientist Emanuel Swedenborg (1688–1772) spent the latter part of his life surveying the "beyond." When the heavens at last were opened to him, he perceived the celestial origin of the forces of life. He realized that "there is an influx of the Spiritual world into the Natural world, but not the reverse." He also observed that wisdom and insight "inflow according to the state of the organization of people's minds."

Swedenborg's own influence on people's minds and the spiritual world of humanity—on literature, art, music, philosophy, religion, and politics—was extraordinarily profound and far-reaching; but this vast field of reflected inflow has been only partially investigated. The following essays, based on travels and research in various parts of the world, aim at mapping some hitherto unexplored regions of major moral and historical concern. In this context, I also wish to add something to our understanding of the nature and singular power of Swedenborg's visionary writings and give an idea of their intrinsic international purport in a kaleidoscopic fashion.

To begin with, I would like to draw attention here to the combined poetical, metaphysical, and ideological character of the subject, and to propose that there is an original point of convergence where the variety of influence can be seen as reflecting different facets. To use a related and explanatory analogy, Swedenborg believed, like his forerunner and relative Georg Stiernhielm, in the existence of an original unity of the universe, a primordial being, *ens unum et primum*, from which all reality stems. Again, this would explain that "steady storm of corre-spondences" which the twentieth-century poet Theodore Roethke (1908–1963) perceived "In A Dark Time."

In enchanting prose, the Swedish poet and literary historian Olof Lagercrantz has described the Swedish seer as a poet and his lifework as a poem (*Dikten om livet på den andra sidan*, 1996). To un-derstand such a perspective, which is far from unique in the his-tory of ideas, we should recall Blake's and Yeats' poetical use of Swedenborgian revelation as well as the view, expressed by poets like Samuel Taylor Coleridge, Ralph Waldo Emerson, and Charles Baudelaire, that Swedenborg belonged to the great poets. In this sense Jesus was a poet too, because he saw that he had to communicate in metaphors and parables, and accordingly did so. After all, what is poetry really? According to Aristotle's *Poetics*, it is primarily metaphor-making. Furthermore, during the golden age of Roman culture, the poet was called a *vates*, a seer. The notion of the poet's divine mission was propelled by Plotinus and eventually paved the way for the idea of the poet as creator and inventor, not imitator and discoverer. Renaissance humanism baptized its inspired souls as *poets*, *authors*, and *artists*, using names of God: the Author of the world, *Artifex Mundi*, the Greek verb *poieó* (aorist *epoíesa*) having since the ancient time of the *Septuagint* been associ-ated with the power of the Creator, not the power of humans. *En arkê epoiesen o Theos*, "In the beginning God created," to quote this classic Alexandrian rendering of the opening words of Genesis.

The influential Renaissance humanist and poet Cristoforo Landino (1424–1492) stated, in his *Camaldolenian Discussions* on Virgil's *Aeneid*, that poetry, due to its metaphorical character, has primacy over all forms of knowledge. To Landino, the basis of poetry was the sphere "in which we see the ideas and the images of what God created, as in a mirror." We are here faced by the mystical aspects of the poet and the poetical aspects of the mys-tic in the Western tradition, stemming from this neoplatonic and hermeticist veneration of the poetical power of insight, but also from an even older appreciation of nature as the *liber naturæ*, the Book of Nature, the Creator's magnificent Opus 1 written in metaphor, that may eventually serve to explain and interpret

Opus 2, the Holy Scripture, and vice versa. In this stereoscopic field of hermeneutics, Swedenborg's work appears.

In Ralph Waldo Emerson's lecture "The Poet," Swedenborg's writings are referred to as "prose poems." And in one of his early lectures, Emerson found that Swedenborg's major design was to exhibit "the poem of the world." Thus, Emerson's world-historical perspective included a future aspect as well. In his historic address on the Emancipation Proclamation, delivered in 1862, Emerson merges a Swedenborgian vision with Shakespeare's sonnet No. 107 in the jubilant "message to other spiritual societies, announcing the melioration of our planet":

> Incertainties now crown themselves assured,
> And Peace proclaims olives of endless age.

Swedenborg was, in fact, lauded as a successor to Shakespeare. We should then recall the dictum of Emerson's cogent lecture on "The Poet" in "The Times" series delivered in Boston, Providence, and New York in 1841–42, with the young journalist Walt[er] Whitman in the stalls, taking notes: "After Dante, and Shakespeare, and Milton, there came no grand poet until Swedenborg."

Edward Young, another of Emerson's favorite poets, remarked in his *Conjectures on Original Composition* (1759) that Shakespeare, though not an erudite man, knew the Book of Nature and the Book of Man. There is ample reason to return to that complex connection between man and nature, words and things, the language of thinking and our perception of external reality as well as of our own situation on earth, even more so since "America's Singer," Walt Whitman, and his gospel of the new man and the new world can be understood in full only from this hermeneutic angle of vision of ancient origin. The same can be said of Swedenborg himself, as I explain in the essay entitled "The Code of the Ancients."

Of course, Swedenborg's writings are hardly poetical in the ordinary sense of the word. In his youth he wrote poems, epics, and allegories; but most of his mature works on natural and spiritual matters are heavily prosaic, systematizing observations in minute order, both of this world and of the world beyond, in the style of Linnaeus and eighteenth-century empirical science. Nor was Swedenborg a poet in the sense of Shaftesbury and romantic imagination, and even less in the modern usage of a second originator, creating a world of his own. On the contrary, he looked upon his mission as that of an explorer of hidden regions, a re-discoverer rather than renewer or artisan. Swedenborg never thought he presented anything new, nor anything that was born out of himself. His identity in the latter part of his life is that of a lonely *ángelos*, a messenger. He is always afraid of distorting the communication by his own mental and rational shortcoming. Late in his life he seems to have regarded the message of his theological writings as the Second Advent of the Lord: *"hic liber est adventus Domini,"* he wrote in two of his books, one of which is now in the British Museum in London. This pretentiousness set, on the other hand, an unbeatable record in the literary history of copyright claims, including those maintained by the prophet Mohammed, some of whose devoted followers will be given the last word in this book.

Swedenborg's constant concern was temptations, especially those arising from avarice and self-love. His life as a theosophist started in a fight against gluttony and carnality, as is revealed by his remarkable dream journal, recorded in 1743–1744, and in Carl Robsahm's famous account of Swedenborg's "call" vision, which he experienced in England. That crucial experience opened up a sphere of new resolution and revelation to the Swedish seer. Sometime around Easter 1745, while dining alone in his favorite restaurant in London, Swedenborg suddenly was confronted by the words of the Unknown Friend whom he had seen at night almost exactly a year earlier, the unrecognizable Resurrect: "Don't eat so much!"

There is a great deal of symbolic truth in the well-known witness reports on the aging seer's ascetic bill of fare: buns of wheat, with milk from his cow, and coffee. The importance of the initial, or initiatory, vision in London—be it spurious or not, its influence was real—is outlined in this collection in the essay on Robsahm's contemporary reminiscences, where we also catch glimpses of distant reception and refraction in different historical contexts.

The reception of Swedenborgian thought has not only been vast but also varied. From the outset, Swedenborg's religious writings were met with suspicion and mixed feelings. I am not going to address the unproductive question of whether Swedenborg was a lunatic or a mystic, since most theologians today seem to agree that he was neither. However, I remind the reader of an elementary rule in traditional Roman Catholic estimation of religious experiences—how to tell a divine inflow from a diabolic. The reason for this reminder is that the rule is simple and natural, so similar to distinguishing that which promotes growth from that which ruins it. The basic criterion of how to recognize a revelation from God is that the epiphany is elevating, improving, and constructive. And these qualities apply both to the receiver and to the aftermath.

The comprehensive *Documents concerning the Life and Character of Emanuel Swedenborg*, collected by Rudolf Leonard Tafel and published in three volumes in the nineteenth century, testifies to the gentle, sincere, and cheerful character of the Swedish seer. His visions, and accordingly his mental health, have been questioned, but hardly ever his character. A similar standard could certainly be set up in any evaluation of faith: if religion does not improve humanity and society, it is just private magic, a vehicle of egotism, of success or inaction, be it illusive or not. In this respect the history of world religions is assuredly equivocal. Viewed from the other direction, as it were, the myth of an ancient "secret" kept among the summits of the Far East highlights Swedenborg's idea of the nature of the truths of faith, at the same time as it shows the global aspects of Swedenborg's concern. His musical interests and metaphysical awareness reveal his deep communication with different worlds in the universe of the human mind. Thus, he could inspire his disciple Charles Bonney to establish the ecumenical World Parliament of Religions in 1893, as well as inspirit the founders of modern music. These two apparently different miens of message are considered in the first two essays of this book, "Music, Metaphysics, and Modernity" and "The Secret of Magna Tartaria."

This expansion of the perspective of human awareness forms a significant part of the Swedenborgian patrimony and is visible everywhere. I will provide a few examples here, from the East as well as from the West, which will be treated more closely and from other aspects in later essays. It is of especial importance here to see the complexity of the influence and gradually realize the reason it has to be of such nature. Finally, I will discuss the problem of "influence" in general.

Disciplines of Dispensation

The well-known Russian philosopher Vladimir Solovyov, in an article on Swedenborg, written for the 1900 edition of the Brockhaus-Ephron Russian encyclopedia shortly before he died, focused on three different aspects of Swedenborg's achievements: first, his contributions to natural science; second, those to theology or theosophy as a visionary; and third, his importance as a source of inspiration to writers. There is an old Russian tradition of reading and interpreting Swedenborg's writings, which embraces all three aspects mentioned by Solovyov; but these are not sufficient as categories of influence, nor can they be completely distinguished from one another. The literary tradition, in which Swedenborg is viewed as "a source of inspiration to writers," also addresses philosophical, moral, and political problems of profound significance, as does the theological or theosophical outgrowth.

The first Swedenborgian work to be translated into Russian was a memorandum on the decimal system; in 1725, the translator, the Russian historian and scientist Vassily Nikitich Tatishchev (1686–1750) presented the work to the cabinet in St. Petersburg. As a member of the Russian Board of Mines, Tatishchev had gone to Sweden and met with his colleague in Stockholm, Emanuel Swedenborg, member of the Swedish Board of Mines. Tatishchev's incidental introduction of Swedenborg in Russia foreshadowed the remarkable reception of

Swedenborg's comprehensive work *Opera Philosophica et Mineralia*, for which he was nominated in 1734 as a corresponding member of the Imperial Academy of Sciences in St. Petersburg.

In Russian literary circles, Swedenborg became a household name, for better or worse. In 1808, Gavrila Romanovich Derzhavin, one of the first echoes of Swedenborg in Russian literature, jubilantly recalled Swedenborg's accounts of the delights of the heavens and wrote an exalted ode on ballet with the recurring refrain *Prav ty, prav ty, Shvedenburg* (You are right, Swedenborg!). Aleksandr Pushkin cited Swedenborg, and Pushkin's father was delighted when his daughter Olga Pavlishchev turned to the Christian piety of the Swedish mystic. On the other hand, Maksim Gorky read Swedenborg and dismissed him as *erunda*, nonsense. More important, Vasily Mikhailovich Drozdov (1782–1867), who became famous as the Metropolitan Filaret instrumental in the emancipation of the serfs, early had observed that nothing in Swedenborg's writings contradicted the views of the Orthodox church. Princess Kleopatra Mikhailovna Shakhovskaya, one of Swedenborg's most devoted Russian followers, felt the world approached a new and peaceful era of integration and understanding through the "new dispensation." In 1872, she enthused, "The ferment is cast in, the impulse is given, and freedom of thought, speech, and conscience—that true and powerful companion of this new era—opens the very depths of the human mind for the reception of regenerative truth." (However, in that same year, in *Diary of a Censor*, Aleksandr Nikitenko recorded a laconic note: "A new censorship law. Finis press!" Even Shakhovskaya's Russian rendering of the Decalogue, drawn from Swedenborg's *True Christian Religion*, had to be printed abroad, in London 1872). The princess passed away in Moscow in 1883, a year that was in a way a centennial, since the first society of Swedenborg readers in Moscow was formed as early as 1783.

Leonid Petrovich Grossman, and after him Dmitry Ivanovich Chizhevsky and Czeslaw Milosz, all tried to understand Dostoevsky's brooding on good and evil, on heaven and hell, from a Swedenborgian angle. And the protagonist Dar'jal'skij in Andrei Bély's novel *Serebryanyi golub'* (1910), the second volume of which grew into the famous *Peterburg*, reads as a young student utopists and revolutionaries like Lassalle and Marx along with the visionaries Boehme and Swedenborg, a rather representative combination for young reformers and radicals of the time. Indeed, Bély helped prepare for publication the last volume of Swedenborg's works published in Russia before the revolution, *Uveseleniya premudrosti o liubvi supruzhestvennoi*, a work on marital love, published in a small St. Petersburg edition in 1914.

Swedenborg's major importance in this historical context was moral, and among his followers we find the most radical humanitarian reformers, as is shown in the essay "Revival and Reform in Russia." The moral aspect is, so to speak, the ideological side of his obvious literary and unrecognized theological influences; seen in a wider perspective, it is the more important and even more controversial one, and confronts us with major issues like the relation between religion and politics in history as well as in the contemporary world.

In the 1860s Swedenborgians played an active part in the emancipation of the serfs in Russia and in the abolishment of slavery in the United States and, much earlier, in West Africa and the West Indies, Swedenborgians had been active in establishing equal rights of Africans. In fact, the international New Church was built on that political stand, as can be seen from the earliest documents of the organization, such as the British *New Jerusalem Magazine* of 1790. Even on the island of Mauritius in the Indian Ocean, resident Swedenborgians observed the reform movement in Russia and set a good example of ethnical and religious liberalism in their multiracial society.

How was all this possible? When we try to find the basic reason for Swedenborg's influence on social issues, we face the incessant conflict between faith and charity in Swedenborg's protest against Protestantism. The crucial point is his reaction against the belief in *iustificatio sola fide*, justification by faith alone, and his introduction of a universal doctrine of "uses," which states that everything is made to serve. In practice, this doctrine means that truth is inseparable from use, and accordingly faith from love. Thus *caritas*, love of one's neighbor, is primary and belief secondary: without *active* goodness, the truths of faith are closed. There can be no divine grace reserved for mere worshippers. Nor has God the power of punishment: man makes heaven and hell in freedom. And besides, Swedenborg asserted that the Last Judgment had already occurred, having witnessed that great spiritual event in the heavenly realm in 1757.

Far from being utilitarian, Swedenborg's philosophy of uses was *pragmatic*. In his vivid introduction to the Swedenborgian thought of J.J.G. Wilkinson, Frederick Evans observed that the doctrine of uses was less a gray theory than a daily meal—the truth was its practicality: "no theory is of any good to us unless it can be put to Use; knowledge is merely dead power, Wisdom is the living power." The attraction of post-doomsday Swedenborgian radical optimism is apparent. In its symbolism, straightforward individualism and pious communitarianism could be reconciled. Wilkinson summarized the Swedenborgian picture of humanity in the following way:

> The human race is practically and really One Man. . . . Each individual man is separately conscious, and is sufficiently alone to be himself, but in that very soleness he is also conscious that he is part of a greater Manship, and that without being in it he would perish. . . . At death every member of it enters a corresponding spiritual world; and carries along with him, so to speak, his own spiritual world. He is still part of the One Man, but on new conditions; he is member of some one of the vast societies of the spiritual world. . . . There are ways for all the virtues there. . . . There are ways for all the vices; paved ways, smooth with the granite of the customs and habits of the Will in the life-time.[1]

To declare oneself a Christian was not a sufficient reaction against that monument of Western racism, the enslavement of Africans. That is obvious, indeed, since chattel slavery, of time-

---

[1] Frederick H. Evans, *James John Garth Wilkinsson: An Introduction*, reprinted by Dr. Garth Wilkinson's youngest daughter Mrs. Frank Claughton Mathews, Edinburgh 1936 (1912), pp. 71–72, 81. Wilkinson's letters to Emerson, an interesting collection, are stored in the archives of the Swedenborg House in Bloomsbury, London.

less origin, was an institution that was developed with ingenious skill and reached its acme of organization within the framework of Christian civilization, in the New World especially. Persuasive and consistent thinkers of the South, like John Caldwell Calhoun and others, more often and more efficaciously referred to the Bible than did their adversaries in the pre-Civil War era. Swedenborg's admirer Emerson, who has been called by Irving Howe "one of the most political of Americans," observed: "What is more rare in Christendom than a Christian?" Emerson shared the theologian Theodore Parker's view that not believing in a higher law, which declared slave laws and other corrupt acts, rules, and regulations void, was indeed atheism. Not by mere coincidence we find Ralph Waldo Emerson and Theodore Parker together on a lecture platform at a New Church chapel before the Civil War. To both men "revival" meant practical ideals—such as the correction of unlawful legislation, the abolition of immoral institutions.

Due to the emphasis on good works, the primacy of ethics, Swedenborg, and later his followers, spoke for a kind of universality in religion. The basis is a central New Church doctrine, as stated in *The New Jerusalem and Its Heavenly Doctrine*, ¶246: "The Lord's Church is with all in the whole world, who live in good according to their religious system." The Swedenborgian focus is on fraternity and sociality, which are the basis of faith, since the truths of faith cannot be received without goodness, that is, social action. In the Swedenborgian system, faith without good works is unthinkable, a fraudulent bigotry, even a contradiction, like a sun without warmth. The main point of Swedenborg's theological criticism in his time—the contended *solifidianism* of the contemporary churches—was a major protest against this legacy, and its consequences were profoundly practical and political.

In his introduction to the modern critical edition of *Representative Men*, which contains the influential essay "Swedenborg, or the Mystic," Wallace E. Williams summarizes: The Swedenborgians "had much influence in the United States throughout the nineteenth century—an oddly disproportionate influence considering the small number of formal adherents (perhaps about a thousand by 1845)," and most historians today agree with this point. Similarly, if we turn south, the situation in the West Indies shows the remarkable moral power of the Swedenborgian message in a transitory stage of nineteenth-century history. The more we magnify and narrow the field we are studying here, the more strange and the more complex connections we discover, as we see in the story of the American diplomat John Bigelow (1817–1911), who was of such political importance to the North in the Civil War. Bigelow's fortuitous encounters during a voyage to the West Indies show the extent of Swedenborgian influence on the island societies.

In the winter of 1854, John Bigelow sailed for Haiti to study African self-government. But Port-au-Prince was desolated by yellow fever and cholera. Of the entire crew of the bark that brought him to Haiti, all but two were in the cemetery within four days of his arrival. Having nowhere to go and nowhere to live, Bigelow took lodgings with a merchant named Benjamin Peter Hunt. Hunt was a native of Massachusetts, a graduate of Harvard, in the same class with Ralph Waldo Emerson with whom he had shared an early interest in Swedenborg's writings. Hunt had much to tell about Haiti and its history. The town where they were had earlier been called Port Henri, named for King Henri I (Henri Christophe, 1767–1820), a black man who had fought in the liberation war of the 1790s. During his few years as king, Henri tried in vain to introduce peace, law, and order in Haiti with a compromise bill, a fundamental law called Code Henri, and by introducing Swedenborgianism as the state religion. That was the true creed of African Christians, he believed. When John Bigelow arrived in the infected Haiti, King Henri had committed suicide thirty-four years earlier.

In his search for a ship to New York, Bigelow was driven afar to the island of St. Thomas to wait for a steamer. But even that island was isolated due to a cholera epidemic that had already killed more than ten percent of the population. Thus, Bigelow found himself staying in the hotel in the harbor of Charlotte

Amalie for an uncertain length of time, being one of two guests in the large house.

One morning Bigelow and the other guest chanced to be seated in the spacious but deserted dining hall, Bigelow at one end and the stranger at the other. They were both reading a book. Like many other people desolated at hotels, Bigelow read the Bible, since he had nothing else to read. He read the account of Abram driven by a famine into Egypt. The more he read about the holy Abram, the less sympathetic the patriarch appeared. The low moral standards of the biblical figure, who commands his wife to tell a falsehood, apparently with the sole purpose of saving himself, agitated Bigelow heartily.

"Is it not extraordinary that this book should be accepted by the most civilized nations of the earth as the Word of God?," he blurted out to the stranger in the hall.

"Does not the Egyptian, whom the Bible represents as the oppressor of God's people, appear, according to our standards at least, to have been the better of the two?"

The stranger answered after a little while: "Well, yes, it does appear so *at first.*" Then he referred to a passage in the first volume of Emanuel Swedenborg's exegetic work *Arcana Coelestia*, where this is explained in detail according to the spiritual sense of the Word. He lent his copy to Bigelow who read it with growing interest. The new friend then lent Bigelow more of the works.

Later, on the voyage back to New Orleans, prolonged by storms and calms for twenty days, Bigelow read his friend's Swedenborg books at least ten hours a day.

The man Bigelow had encountered in Charlotte Amalie was Procurator Niels Andreas Vibe Kierulff (1796–1874), one of the leading New Churchmen of the secret and disperse Swedenborgian congregations in the Virgin Islands, where white and black men and women had worshipped together for many years; this topic is the subject of a central chapter of this book, "The New Church in the West Indies." But before then, we will be confronted with a great mystery that occupied Bigelow's thoughts on Swedenborgian exegetics: the inexplicable references in the

Word of God to even older scriptures—some of which were said to be preserved only in Magna Tartaria.

What Is Influence?

Bigelow also thought about all the apparent circumstances or coincidences that determined his life, all that influenced his decisions. What, or rather, *why* is influence, then? What is the nature of influence in general? Why are heliotropes drawn to the sun, the flies to the ceiling lamp? Why do cows avoid the lady's mantle, the nocturnal animal light? Why was Dr. Johnson repelled by Voltaire, and Spinoza ambivalent to Hobbes? Why did Lucretius summarize Epicur and Karl Marx choose the Greek materialists as the subject for his doctoral dissertation? Why was Goethe attracted by Spinoza and Whitman by Emerson? Why did Jesus go to see John the Baptist and Emerson call on Colderidge, Wordsworth, and Carlyle? Why did Emerson make excerpts from Swedenborg, and Swedenborg from Christian Wolff, Wolff from Leibniz, Leibniz from Spinoza, Spinoza from Descartes, etc.? The purpose and the momentary attraction, as well as the fruitful reaction, are innate in the receiver and have a long background somewhere. Traditional research on "influences" often is an end in itself, a collection for an antiquity's cabinet or a curio cupboard of the copyright owners, something to pay a visit to on rainy Sundays. However, savants are no sleepwalkers, and writers are no savanna zombies. One-sided impact would be such a miracle as unisexual fecundation or a bolt of lightning without any electrical charge of the ground. Reception is an active process, with several determining factors, such as seed, season, soil, and sower. Perhaps first of all climate determines the rise.

The eclectic yet original Emerson sometimes seems to have accepted sayings of Socrates, Montaigne, or Swedenborg in the same manner as a cook at his wit's end may embrace an unexpected fishmonger coming by: the so-called influence is a kind of satisfaction stemming from the fact that one has found something one was looking for, something that one needed at the moment and could make use of. The discerning Emerson observed that invention means to adopt ingeniously: "the greatest genius is the most indebted man," and among the greatest geniuses he counted Swedenborg. Very few elements in Swedenborg's doctrines are new, not even in the forerunners or in their sources; in fact, Swedenborg himself, still less than Montaigne or Socrates in his maieutics, laid claim to patents in these matters. Through him, old wisdom was restored, himself acting as a servant. *Pregnancy of thought disproves primogeniture.*

Receptivity is a necessary condition for influence, but is not enough for effect. The ground must be prepared for the seed. But the human being is not mere soil, nor is the mind a pistil. Man is both the garden and the gardener. "Influence" implies that you open yourself up to receive an effect, since there is an imminent attraction or an immanent affinity: it belongs to you and has already domiciliary rights in the world of your mind. In another way this may also be explained in Jacques Derrida's words in "Cogito and the History of Madness": "The disciple must break the glass, or better the mirror, the reflection, his infinite speculation on the master. And start to speak." The essays in this collection show that the disciples of Swedenborg, after reflecting on the words of the master, did indeed start to speak and honestly tried to contribute to a finer and more just world.

Gallery of Mirrors

Music,
Metaphysics,
and
Modernity

A single note or tone does not tell us anything about the tune; it could be all or nothing. Melody, rhythm, and expression, like the meaning of anything around us, are totally dependent upon setting and interaction, invisible forms and affinities. And the same is manifest in the human condition as a whole.

At the Skansen open-air museum in Stockholm, Emanuel Swedenborg's little summer house is preserved. It is almost empty. Belongings were dispersed and are gone, except for a few items; but, even in its owner's lifetime, it was never cluttered. Only necessities were kept in the cell of the seer, such as the Bible in Hebrew and Latin, books of excerpts, and diaries of experiences. There is a small chamber organ in the corner. It was saved for posterity by Swedenborg's first followers in Sweden, and eventually was included in the sparse collection of Sweden-

This essay was originally presented as a lecture at the Swedenborg House, London, on September 30, 1993. It was first published in Swedish as "Swedenborg och Musiken: Från Barockharmoni till Tolvton" in Världarnas Möte 2 (1994): 74–90; and in English as "Music—Celestial and Mundane: From Baroque Harmony to Dodecaphony," Arcana 1, no. 2 (1995): 55–68.

borgiana.[1] Now the small organ, technically an eighteenth-century barrel-organ with wooden pipes and keys, is displayed in the corner, silent; but it is placed where it once was when Swedenborg was sitting in his pavilion over two centuries ago, in the bosom of the symphony of birds and the odors and colors of his rose garden. Why is the organ standing there in the corner? What is it really—furniture or instrument or emblem? A collector's adornment? An object unearthed from the dust of ages? Were the bellows blown? What does this instrument signify; what is its context? Has it any relation to his revelations, to the books on the table? We have no scores, no keys, no records. In the following pages, we will find our way through the constellation of Baroque metaphysics and music where, from one specific angle, the full meaning and vast significance of the quiet keyboard in the shady corner at times may be heard and seen.

Young Swedenborg and Music

Swedenborg was a lover of music. A student of many disciplines, he received a good musical education as well, and his early musical training seems to have been partly a matter of his own choice. His father, Jesper Svedberg, was a famous hymnwriter and the controversial driving force of the commission for the Swedish *Book of Hymns* in the early 1690s.[2] Svedberg created a stir with a hymn book of his own that was banned and confiscated when the official version was issued and recognized in 1695.[3] His son Emanuel certainly learned very early in his life many of the hymns he came to love.[4] He learned to play harpsichord or clavichord as a student at Uppsala University, where he probably took organ lessons from a faculty professor who was an enthusiastic musician. Eventually, he became a skilled organist.

Jesper Svedberg encouraged his gifted son's desire for foreign travel and study. After his graduation in classics from Uppsala University in 1709, the young Emanuel Svedberg accompanied his father and stepmother to Skara where the family settled at the Brunsbo episcopal mansion, Jesper having been appointed bishop of the diocese. Emanuel had planned to go to England as soon as possible, but the voyage was delayed a year because of a maritime war between Sweden and Denmark. He spent that year at the old vicarage writing poetry, some of which was published. He also practiced his music.[5] In a letter written from Brunsbo on March 6, 1710, he writes to his mentor and brother-in-law Eric Benzelius the younger: "I have little desire to remain here much longer; for I am wasting almost my whole time. Still, I have made such progress in music, that I have been able several times to replace our organist; but for all my other studies this place affords me little opportunity."[6]

Years of Travel

When he later obtained such an opportunity and could begin his travels, Swedenborg was absorbed by scientific investigations. But his love for music always had a share of his passion. His poem to the Swedish poetess Sophia Brenner, submitted from London in October 1710, addressing "the only poetic singer of our age, when she sang her songs anew" (*unicam ætatis nostæ camœnam cum carmina sua de novo caneret*), connects her art with playing the lyre and singing. In a letter to Eric Benzelius, written from Rostock in 1714, he mentions some of his projects and lists fourteen proposed inventions. Besides a submarine, a water clock, a mechanical carriage, a drawbridge, and other things, we find a "universal musical instrument," an instrument "whereby the most inexperienced player can produce all kinds of melodies, these being found marked on paper and in notes."[7] He obviously thought such an invention would be as useful and important as the other, more practical mechanisms. In 1715, on composing a funeral ode upon the death of the dowager queen, he writes: "Comes now unto thee the sad hour/ when words must be sung/ Alone without chords."[8] That year he also wrote the poetic allegory *Camena Borea*, on the Northern Muse, which shows that the scientist had not left the field of the arts and the humanities.

In Germany, the traveler would later move within distinguished circles of natural philosophy and Baroque art; and he visited many cities, among them, Leipzig, Dresden, Berlin, and

Hamburg. Duke Ludwig Rudolph, father-in-law of the emperor's son and himself a son of the tsar, became Swedenborg's patron and defrayed all his expenses, and, among other honors, presented Swedenborg with a gold medal.[9] Swedenborg dedicated a part of his *Miscellanea Observata* to the duke, as well as the first volume of *Opera Philosophica et Mineralia*, published at Leipzig in 1734.[10] Swedenborg calls Ludwig Rudolph a great patron of the arts and sciences.

Johann Sebastian Bach, who was the same age as Swedenborg, lived and played in Leipzig at this time, as well as traveling and presenting concerts in other cities Swedenborg visited. The duke appears to have taken a special interest in Bach also, having presented him too with an award; and Bach and Swedenborg seem to have had both friends and enemies in common, the theologian Johann August Ernesti (1707–1781) being the most famous among the latter. Ernesti was Swedenborg's adversary, as well as being the principal of the Thomas School in Leipzig from 1734 to 1759, where Bach had been the cantor since 1723. There is no evidence to prove that Swedenborg and Bach ever met, but it is highly unlikely that Swedenborg did not know of Bach. In any case, Swedenborg had strong doses of Baroque music at its summit during those years, which, in a way, is significant. At this period, Bach was a famous organist, but not as famous as a composer. He was recognized much later: he marks the fulfillment and perfection of Baroque polyphony, especially the fugue, at a time when that music was giving way to the more homophonic and gallant style of the Rococo. Similarly, Swedenborg remained with the Baroque—its metaphysics, its poetics, its style, and its visions—and in his way also marks a late summit of the era. He, too, would not be recognized or widely known before the next century. The more light-hearted, easy-going, sensual, and wanton style of the Rococo, which paved the way for the subjectivity, intimacy, and sentimentalism of the Romantic era, culminating in a dissolution of classical harmony, certainly was very alien to Swedenborg, who, all his life, remained an empiricist, documenting and producing evidence of irrefutable laws of life and of the universe. Finally, like Bach,

Swedenborg dedicated his work "to the greater glory of God," as Bach did his music.[11]

Traveling the continent during his long periods abroad, Swedenborg often listened to music, both sacred and secular. He heard church music, writing a long exalted passage in his "Itineraria" on the elevating mass in the cathedral in Brussels, with its "beautiful music, instrumental as well as vocal."[12] In Turin he heard a castrato singing in the presence of the king and queen in the Royal Chapel.[13] And he notes the fine music played at a consecration of seven nuns in Florence.[14] He went to the opera in Italy and France, but he preferred the Italian opera, especially that of Verona: "Concerning the singing and dancing, they surpass the French opera to such a degree, that it seems to be mere child's play in comparison with them."[15] These are the words of a connoisseur of music, who later was to travel in his coach to attend famous concerts in Stockholm where orchestral works by his friend and colleague at the Royal Academy of Sciences, Johan Helmich Roman (1694–1758), were often performed.[16]

Spectral Sonority

In Swedenborg's 1742 work *De Anima*, posthumously published as "Rational Psychology," an important theme is harmony and disharmony, concord and discord, answering to love and hate, where the usefulness of the individual is described in terms of an existence in love and harmony with others, being part of a whole, a context, without which the single constituent is nothing.

Swedenborg's knowledge of music theory, and his interest in the physics and physiology of music, is evident from numerous references in his scientific works, especially in his book on the five senses, *De sensu communi*, written in 1744, a work intended for, and partly used in, the *Animal Kingdom* series.

The composition of these works comes at a time that Swedenborg was experiencing a life crisis, his "dark night of the soul." During this period (1743–1744), he experienced his first mystical epiphanies. He did not really know what to do about these revelations. He prayed and sang hymns that he had probably learned at home, a favorite one being "Jesus is my best of friends."[17]

When the spiritual worlds were opened to him and he was permitted to enter into these dimensions, there were sounds, yet everything was quite different—like the silent language of the angels. When the meaning of the Word was opened to him, and likewise the correspondence of the material world to the heavenly, there was also music. He entered into a higher dimension of musical instruments, in which the signification of drums, flutes, harps, organs, voices, lutes, lyres, zithers, clavichords, strings, timbrels, violins, horns, choirs, and entire orchestras was revealed. He also realized the deep significance of melody, song, tone, tune, notes, keys, symphony, and harmony.[18]

Celestial choirs of harmony moved him, as expressions of a unity in love, and he observed that the angels, at a distance, may appear as a song. The pillar of cloud was a choir. He learned that music derives from affection, not from the understanding: it may be true or false, good or evil. To play the organ signifies an expression of the goodness and truths of faith. He also finds that an influx into the spirit has a correspondence in the wind instruments, which are celestial, whereas the string instruments are spiritual.[19] Love, he discovered, is like a melody. A harp, as well as an orchestra, is like a city where the parts form the whole, as individual angels form the heavens, which, in their entirety, have the appearance of a single angel. Music, in our world, is of spiritual and celestial origin; and earthly music can elevate the listener to the heavens and also has an impact in the beyond.[20] Hymns have an effect on spirits. Of such reactions in the spiritual world Swedenborg provides accounts—for instance, in *The Doctrine of the Sacred Scripture* ¶108, where some spirits hear a psalm being sung in a place of worship in our world. This affects them with such delight that they sing along with the congregation, and after their ears are closed, they experience an illumination.

In *Arcana Coelestia* ¶8261 and *Apocalypse Revealed* ¶279, Swedenborg writes that song exists for the exaltation of life, for a holy and blessed celestial influx. Moreover, the Bible is song, the "song of Moses and the song of the lamb." Faith itself is revealed to be a sound. Thus, there is a connection between music and religion, and just as the ear becomes deaf by hearing only one tone for a long time, polyphony and symphony are the sounds of truth and goodness. He finds that there is a human tone like the sound of the lyre and one like that of a heavy drum; affections of thoughts and the sounds of the discourse of angels, from different angles, are heard as the sound of harps, of trumpets, or as thunder; and an answer, as well as our life, can be like a single note, without meaning. The laws of the ear and those of the universe correspond. Discord has many meanings; there is spellbinding and bewitching music on earth as in the heavens; earthly songs and tunes continue after death. We can thus imagine that there was even Baroque music in the heavens, but Swedenborg describes the harmonies of the heavens as ineffable.

If music has a celestial origin and connection, then what is the role of the composer? The answer is that he or she is virtually inspired, influenced by spirit. This fact has also given music its Greek name, being protected by deities or spirits, the Muses, as everything external corresponds to something internal and the human mind may serve as a channel. The greatest of all "New Songs" is the recognition and glorification of the Lord, as explained in *Apocalypse Revealed* ¶279, since a song signifies glorification and singing elevates the mind. This song expresses itself in sound as well as in life and is the summit of joy, the elevation of the life of love. Despite the possibility of reaching supreme happiness, even some angels stay within dangerous boundaries "by the sea of glass, having the harps of God," which Swedenborg interprets as their having religion and worship, but not the goodness of love (*Apocalypse Revealed* ¶661). Each spirit chooses his or her mode or key. Each morning, in a certain angelic society, beautiful singing expresses some particular affection. This singing, "delightfully exalted," sets the tone for an angel's day. The Word can set the tone of mundane lives by the reception of the celestial music within.[21]

Swedenborg's exegesis of music influenced many musicians and composers, as well as writers, who brought the theory to life in musical and literary works.

Music in the New Church

Turning to the wisdom of Albion, as Swedenborg did, we observe that the first Swedenborg Society, which developed in 1784 from the early Theosophical Society, was constituted primarily by artists, the eminent musician Francis Hippolythe Barthélémon among them.[22] Being a founder of the first society, Barthélémon was, appropriately enough, also the first New Church composer.[23] In the *New Jerusalem Magazine* of 1790, there are several pieces of music by Barthélémon—settings of the Psalms and other texts. One of his followers was Carl J. Wittington, the man behind a book of genuine New Church music, *A Psalmody for the New Church, containing the First Fifty Psalms and Other Selections from the Word*, published by the Academy of the New Church in Bryn Athyn, Pennsylvania, in 1898.[24] Another work, written in England, was A. Vale's oratorio entitled *Nunc Licet*, written for two soloists, organ, and orchestra, and published by F. Pitman Hart & Co. in London in 1930. Crossing the ocean again, we have the recent oratorio by Donald Dillard, "The New Jerusalem."[25]

Similarly, the founders of the first Swedenborgian church in Sweden, in 1874 (made possible because the Dissenter Law was passed the year before), were the composer Jöns Peter Cronhamn (1803–1875), a member of the Royal Musical Academy, and Carl Oscar Tyboni, a member of the Royal Opera House Orchestra, who would set the tone of church life for years to come.[26]

These musicians have had numerous successors among New Church people, such as George James Webb, J.B. Dykes, John Worcester, William Wallace Gilchrist, Rollo F. Maitland, Clarence and Mary Lathbury, Frank and Maude Sewall, Harry Barnitz, and Brian Kingslake, to name only a few eminent musicians who created a firm basis for worship, as well as the renowned composer Richard Yardumian (1917–1985), about whom Rachel Odhner Longstaff and Ethelwyn Worden have written.[27] We should also remember the composer Max Sinzheimer, organist of the Sheridan Road New Church in

Chicago, who wrote a piece for mixed chorus and organ based on some well-known words from *Heaven and Hell* ¶228.[28]

In this context we should perhaps also mention Eric Coates (1886–1957), who touched upon his religion and his New Church connections several times, as in his *Doxology* for voice and organ and his *Song of Loyalty*.[29] A number of Swedish composers also were inspired by Swedenborg, from Carl Jonas Love Almqvist to Sven-Eric Johanson (1919–1997) and Tommie Haglund (1959–) and up to the recent oratorio *Ovum mundanum* by Björn Linnman (1998).[30] These few examples demonstrate the presence of a living tradition of Swedenborgian music.

We turn now to another historical line, a main current in modern music and music theory, which is a little more difficult to grasp than the musical heritage of the New Church.

From Baroque Harmony to Dodecaphony

The most prominent figures in modern atonal music, especially those who invented and developed the twelve-tone technique, have testified to the importance of Swedenborg: Arnold Schönberg (1874–1951), Alban Berg (1885–1935), and Anton Webern (1883–1945). Among their contemporaries, we may also mention Wilhelm Furtwängler (1886–1954); among their numerous followers, the Swiss music theoretician Max Adam (1901–1995); and among their precursors, Richard Strauss (1864–1949).[31] Why is that? There is no similar interest or inspiration to be found in Romantic musicians and composers of the nineteenth century, except perhaps Hector Berlioz, who adopted themes from Swedenborg for some of his texts. The answer may lie in an intertextual counterpart in nineteenth-century literature, which served as a bridge between Swedenborgian thought and the world of modern music.

A reading of Swedenborg's universe as a world of music, and an interpretation in musical terms, was introduced in France by Gérard de Nerval (1808–1855) and by Honoré de Balzac. In his short novel *Aurélia*, completed by Nerval shortly before his suicide, there is a concluding section called "Memorabilia," a title borrowed from Swedenborg's visions of the other world. Here, the universe is conceived as music, and so is the moment of creation:

> From the bosom of the silent darkness, two notes sounded forth—one low, the other high—and the eternal globe began forthwith to turn. Blessed be thou, O first octave which begins the divine hymn. . . . Hosanna on Earth! Hosanna in Heaven! The air vibrates, and the light harmoniously opens the nascent flowers. A sigh, a shiver of love, comes from the swollen bosom of the earth, and the choir of stars unfolds into infinity; it swerves and turns back on itself, contracts and expands, and sows far and wide the germs of new creations.[32]

The philosophical novel *Séraphîta* by Balzac—who studied Swedenborg and once declared that Swedenborgianism was his religion—is permeated by music in a similar way, from the sound of the Creative Word, the solitary hymns of spirits, and the apocalyptic trumpets of angels, to the living melody of cosmic cycles, and the harmonies of heaven, vaguely audible on earth. The characters Wilfrid and Minna feel the world shrink under their feet:

> On a sudden, the trumpets sounded for the victory of the Angel . . . their music filled space, like a sound met by an echo; it rang through it, making the universe tremble. . . . They heard the various parts of the infinite forming a living melody; and at each beat, when the concord made itself felt as a deep expiration, the world, carried on by this unanimous motion, bowed to the Omnipotent One, who in His unapproachable center made all things issue from Him and return to Him. This ceaseless alternation of voices and silence seemed to be the rhythm of the holy hymn that was echoed and sustained from age to age. . . . Light gave birth to melody, and melody to light; colors were both light and melody; motion was number endowed by the Word; in short, everything was at once sonorous, diaphanous, and mobile; so that, everything existing in everything else, extension knew no limits, and the angels could traverse it everywhere to the utmost

depths of the infinite. . . . They understood the invisible bonds
by which material worlds are attached to the spiritual worlds. . . .
they discerned the principle of melody as they heard the songs
of heaven which gave them all the sensations of color, perfume,
and thought, and reminded them of the innumerable details of
all the creations, as an earthly song can revive the slenderest
memories of love.[33]

Arnold Schönberg was a great lover of Balzac's *Séraphîta* and
drew upon it for his *Four Orchestral Songs* of 1913–1916. In an
essay written in 1941, published in the posthumous collection of
essays *Style and Form*—in large part an outcome of his flight from
the Nazis—he explains to his new American audience the
essence of the art of dodecaphony. In "Composition with Twelve
Notes," he explains that "the unity of musical space demands an
absolute and unitary perception. In this space, as in Swedenborg's heaven (described in Balzac's *Séraphîta*), there is no absolute down, no right or left, forward or backward."[34]
Schönberg and other composers have drawn on Swedenborg
for ideas and structure, instead of using text fragments for lyrics or
setting passages from Swedenborg to music. This is a remarkable
fact. Webern wrote to his teacher Schönberg in 1913: "I am now
reading Swedenborg. It takes my breath away. . . . I had expected
something colossal, but it is even more." For some time Swedenborg's writings constituted Alban Berg's favorite reading. Schönberg himself often referred to the religious aspect of music; and
his unfinished magnum opus, *Moses and Aaron*, is deeply imbued
with the spirit of Swedenborg's *Arcana Coelestia*. In 1991, commem-
orating the fortieth anniversary of Schönberg's death, Radio RIAS
Berlin broadcasted a program in which were quoted passages from
Swedenborg as Schönberg's credo. Schönberg seems to have occupied himself with Swedenborg up to his death in 1951.[35]
In the novel *Doktor Faustus*, Thomas Mann describes a point of
crisis in Western music, the Devil struggling for power in the
mind of the composer/protagonist Adrian Leverkühn, for whom
Schönberg served as a model. Schönberg did not appreciate that
portrait but admitted that the twelve-tone technique had made

his task immensely more difficult. He indicated, however, that the development of the technique was unavoidable; it was the logical outcome of tradition and marked the beginning of a new epoch. Yet, in a way, the twelve-tone technique was a return in a new key. It had been foreshadowed in Bach, in the inverted fugues of *Kunst der Fuge* as well as in the B-minor fugue in *Das Wohltemperierte Klavier*, where the theme is, in fact, comprised by the twelve tones of the chromatic scale. Richard Wagner too had found possibilities in the chromatic twelve-tone scale that had been explored in the seventeenth century by Gesualdo.[36] The new turn was prepared for—at the end of the Baroque—in the chromatic tension that finally culminated in Wagner, Gustav Mahler, and Richard Strauss, a tension leading to disintegration and chaos, out of which the creation of a new structure was the logical consequence. Schönberg returned to a system of law, which he thought had a universal significance and foundation. He felt that he had a mission. At the basis of a musical composition was an Idea, a structure of totality, which was eternal, in his view.

Webern, who, like Schönberg, had to fight the Devil in the form of the Nazis and was among the last people shot in World War II, composed music that is similarly sacral in character, never profane. We hear a universal polyphony, parts crossing one another in a perpetual flow, light and darkness, waves, harmony, anxiety, a presence of invisible forces; we are confronted with an organic monism that is basically spiritual. In an unfinished stage play, *Dead*, Webern turned to Swedenborg's last work, *True Christian Religion*, as a source of inspiration.

The Swedenborgian composer Richard Yardumian, like Schönberg, stressed that "it is not the forms; it is the ideas" that make up the secret pattern of the whole, the eternal. In the idea of the four choirs of the heavens, of the cardinal points, as developed in his *Oratorio on the Story of Adam*, the mystical space referred to by Schönberg is enveloped, vast as the universe.[37] Harmonious concords or consonances have universal meaning; they are qualities of nature, pure mathematics—tones whose vibrations have a common denominator (such as the series 2, 4, 8, 16 of the octavo). Harmony is a quality that is as physical as it is

mental and universal, and the same applies to discord or dissonance; these opposite forms of vibrations can be traced from the
world of the atoms to distant galaxies. In this way, two tones can
interact as harmony and disharmony, attraction and repulsion,
love and hate; and, as in Nerval's vision of the Word of Creation,
two tones generate the movement of the whole. This also explains the reason that dissonance is as important as consonance
to Schönberg; they form a dynamic equilibrium between heaven
and hell, as in Swedenborg's universal picture of life. That is
Schönberg's "realism."[38]

Atonal music and the twelve-tone technique in a way represent a return to pure music—in some cases, to pure mathematics
(in Berg, Schönberg, and Xenakis as in Bach and Handel)—a reaction against subjectivity, arbitrariness, the dissolution of the
norms of predecessors. In a way, too, it is a return to "other-
worldly" music, the freely flowing rhythm and tones of the early
Gregorian period up to the Baroque. It is music in its own right,
a return to *Ton-spiele*.[39] Such music is not personal as in
Beethoven, Brahms, and Bartók, but based upon fundamental
principles, in Buxtehude as in Boulez and Babbit. There is an inherent relationship between the twelve-tone technique and the
strict laws and patterns that make up the order of the canon,
madrigal, motet, ricercar, conductus, canzone, and fugue.

The works of Schönberg, Webern, and Berg are remarkably
rich in allusion to earlier music. There is a dialogue with tradition, a struggle, out of which a post-tonal structure subsumes the
conflicting traditional elements. In Schönberg's orchestration of
works by Bach, the circle is somehow completed, yet open.
Something new is emerging, which is also a renaissance.[40]

For these reasons Swedenborg was relevant to composers of
modern music in an age of transition. He served as a bridge-
builder between the old world and the new.

Finale

Now, here we are, in that intersection between past and future
called "now," perpetually moving onwards, the moment when we

have access to reality. Nothing is gone, history is with us, alive and present; there is no distance between past and future. This is, spiritually, what Swedenborg experienced in the state of the beings in the beyond—beyond time. And this is the Space referred to by Schönberg, the Moment in Webern's very short whispering pieces of timelessness, and, finally, the Minimalism of John Cage, where the music suddenly becomes silent, completely inward, and the musicians sit still, motionless, quiet, the composer writing four minutes, thirty-three seconds of nothing, and a score of profound signification.[41]

The Secret of Magna Tartaria

When August Strindberg was honored as a countryman of Swedenborg in the French occult magazine *L'Initiation* (1896), his fascination with Honoré de Balzac was kindled. Without delay he purchased Balzac's Swedenborg-inspired novel *Séraphîta* (1835). Enchanted, Strindberg suddenly found himself face to face with "this angel-like giant, interpreted by the most profound of the French geniuses." In his account of his own personal crisis, *Inferno* (1897), Strindberg recounts that he felt he had received *Séraphîta* in the form of a gospel. It was, he writes, a time when heaven drew him to itself with an irresistible longing; a connection with a higher world had been re-established.[1] As the psychiatrist Johan Cullberg has shown in his study *Skaparkriser* (Crises of Creative People), this turning point became the purgatory of Strindberg's soul. Through his studies of Swedenborg, Strindberg found secret connections that gradually made possible an orientation in the darkest caverns and

This essay first appeared as "Magna Tartarias Hemlighet," in *Världarnas Möte* 3 (1992): 104–122. An English version, "The Secret of Great Tartary," appeared in *Arcana* 1, no. 1 (1995): 35–54.

convolutions of life, and at last gave a new meaning to existence. These were texts written especially for him.

In an earlier novel, *Louis Lambert* (1832), Balzac presents Swedenborg's religion as the lodestar of the protagonist, as a synthesis of all the world's religions, presented by the "Buddha of the North." In the years following, Balzac carried this universalist tone through in the philosophy of nature as portrayed in *Séraphîta:* a voice in the whirlwind whispers that Swedenborg's advances in innumerable sciences placed him in a position to detect the ancient sources of the biblical scriptures in the distant regions of Tartary.

As the sagacious Paul Valéry (1871–1945) reminded us, it may be that Europe is just a *cape d'Asie* and the Bible itself a collection of writings from the Near East, but the rumors about an earlier Word originating in Mongolia or in the vast expanses of the Himalayas were amazing news, especially since those rumors were quite old. In the 1890s, knowledge based on wisdom from the "elevated masters" of the Orient, from Egypt to India and Tibet, was current theosophical teaching in England and the United States as well as in France and Russia. As legend has it, the Russian-born writer Yelena Petrovna Blavatsky (1831–1891), a friend of the spiritualist Aleksander Aksakov and the eclectic philosopher Vladimir Solovyov, founded modern western theosophy after being initiated into the secret wisdom of the Ancients during visits to Egypt, India, and, primarily, Tibet.[2] However, it was the eighteenth-century information about sacred writings in Tartary that roused the orientalist Strindberg's fervor. Where were these ancient biblical books to be found?

Strindberg's reading of Swedenborg during the existential crisis described in *Inferno* took form as a theosophical belief in reincarnation, according to which the earthly life was conceived of as a purification process. When Strindberg read about hell, he recognized himself and realized that he was already there. The deadly struggles that broke forth in *Inferno* and *Legender* (1898) were hardly Swedenborgian. The New Churchman and publisher Albert Björck reacted against Strindberg's interpretation in a short book published in Stockholm in 1898, *Emanuel Swedenborg,*

August Strindberg och det ondas problem ["Emanuel Swedenborg, August Strindberg, and the Problem of Evil"]. Strindberg, who respected only worthy opponents, developed an acquaintance with Björck, as we can see from his letters to Björck at the beginning of the twentieth century. Björck became the publisher of Strindberg's most comprehensive prose work, *En Blå Bok* (A Blue Book [1907–1912]), which was dedicated "to the teacher Swedenborg from his disciple." A few of Strindberg's letters to the publishing house of Björck & Börjesson are particularly interesting. They provide the background for the important section on *"Bibelns källskrifter"* (The Sources of the Bible) in the second part of *En Blå Bok.*

In a letter dated December 4, 1907, where he writes about his own studies concerning Philip Johan von Stralenberg's map of Asia, and about Lorens Lange and other eighteenth-century Swedish predecessors of Sven Hedin, Strindberg mentions Kalmuck and Tibetan manuscripts he had earlier found in Linköping and asks for help in obtaining information about any Mongolian manuscripts Hedin might have discovered:

> At the same time, will you ask Pastor Björck if he remembers where Swedenborg says that in 'Greater Tartary' will be found manuscripts that constitute sources of the Old Testament? I have read this but forgotten where. Swedenborg's relative, Peter Schönström (captive in Siberia) is mentioned in connection with these manuscripts.

Perhaps it is still his reading of Balzac that haunts him here: he could never forget *Séraphîta's* beauteous light. The next day, December 5, he writes again to Björck & Börjesson, and notes that in the *Biografiskt lexicon* (Biographical Dictionary) he had learned that "it was in the *Apocalypse Revealed* that Swedenborg mentions the sources of the Books of Moses." After this he looks for all kinds of literature on ancient writing, from hieroglyphics to the Mongolian alphabet, "for I have found a trail that begins in Egypt and ends in Great Tartary."[3] In the legends about Great Tartary an old fascination combines with a new one, and they mutually ignite each other. The interests in Sinology and cultural history that Strindberg had kept alive since his younger days—when he was an amanuensis at the Royal Library and sorted a portion of its East Asian manuscripts—were revived by contact with Swedenborg.

The Pre-Biblical Word in Asia

In 1766, in the opening chapter of *Apocalypse Revealed* (¶11), Swedenborg first writes about the hidden Word in the Far East. In his exposition of John's letter to the seven churches in Asia, found in the first chapter of the Book of Revelation, Swedenborg explains that by "Asia" is understood those who are in the light of truth from the Word:

> The Most Ancient Church, and after it the Ancient, and after this the Israelitish, was in Asia . . . because with them was the Ancient Word and afterwards the Israelitish; and from the Word is all the light of truth.

Swedenborg had advanced this idea some years earlier in *The Doctrine of the New Jerusalem Concerning the Sacred Scripture* (1763), another book published in Amsterdam. But in *Apocalypse Revealed* he continues:

> Concerning the Ancient Word that had been in Asia before the Israelitish Word, this new thing deserves to be mentioned: It has till now been preserved among peoples who dwell in Great Tartary. In the spiritual world I have spoken with spirits and angels who were from there, and they said that they possess a Word, that they have had it in their possession since ancient times, that they perform their Divine worship in accordance with that Word, and that it consists of nothing but pure correspondences.

Swedenborg then notes that some of the books of the Old Testament refer to still older writings that are lost to us, such as "The Book of the Upright," "The Wars of Jehovah," and "The Book of Prophecies" (*Enuntiata*). The quotations in the Holy

Scripture from these ancient writings are obscure and unintelligible to us, and evidence for them cannot be found in older literature; but after looking into the matter, Swedenborg finds that these texts are known in the spiritual lore of Tartary. By this Swedenborg is convinced that the Ancient Word is preserved there. In a conversation with spirits, he is told that in Great Tartary people believe in God, who "is worshiped by some as an invisible God, by others as a visible God." They tell him further "that they do not allow foreigners to enter, other than the Chinese," with whom they have peaceful relations, because they belong to their own people. Aside from this, it emerges "that they believe no region in the world to be more populous." Swedenborg says that it is likely that this is the reason for the Great Wall of China, that it was built as a protection against these neighboring people.

Swedenborg's statements on the whereabouts of the Ancient Word appear contradictory: "Search for it in China, and perhaps you will find it there among the Tartars" (*Apocalypse Revealed*, ¶11). Of course, in Swedenborg's time, both "China" and "Tartary" were anything but definite concepts—they merged into each other. Tartary comprised the whole eastern portion of Asia, including Mongolia, Manchuria, and Tibet. Magna Sina was, practically speaking, the whole east-Asian continent, including Indochina.[4]

In his next comprehensive book, *Conjugial Love* (1767), in which he makes known the wisdom of the angels regarding love between man and woman, in marriage and otherwise, Swedenborg returns to the subject of the special grace of the Asians, as presented in a vision from the other world. As he describes in ¶77, from a vantage point in the westerly parts of the heavenly kingdom:

> We saw a mountain high as the clouds, and between us and the mountain were villages, interspersed with gardens, groves, and fields. And going through the villages all the way to the mountain, we ascended, and behold, its top was not a peak, but a plateau, and stretched out upon it, a city.

The houses were made of wood, even the temples:

> and in their center is a sanctuary where, in an ark, is preserved
> the Word which was given to the Asiatic people before the Is-
> raelitish Word. . . . Today, this Word is lost in Asia's regions and
> is preserved only in Great Tartary.

In his spiritual testament, the theological work of his old age,
True Christian Religion (1771), Swedenborg returns to the same experience in a significant account that he appends to an outline of
the spread of the Word in the world from the regions of India
and east Asia to as far as Egypt and Ethiopia. He gives the same
picture as in the *Apocalypse Revealed*, but he adds, in ¶279:

> I have, moreover, heard that the first chapters of the first books
> of Moses—on the creation of the world, on Adam and Eve and
> the paradise of Eden, and on their descendants down to the
> Flood, and on Noah and his sons—all this is in this Word, and
> that consequently Moses quotes from it.

Regarding the abode in heaven of the souls from Tartary,
Swedenborg also notes:

> They are to be seen in the southern quarter towards the East.
> They are separated from others by living on a higher level. They
> do not allow anyone from Christian countries to visit them, and
> if any do go up, they put them under guard to prevent them leav-
> ing. The reason for this isolation is that they possess a different
> Word.

Besides this, "tigers and lions in Tartary's forests" are spoken of in
¶515, which is not a report from the other world, but gives a
possible clue as to what kingdoms Swedenborg had in mind. If
this information, provided in passing, on the flora and fauna of
that time, or of past times, has anything to do with the Asiatic
abode of the Ancient Word, then this would seem immediately
to exclude the Asiatic highlands, including Tibet, where one
would more probably encounter a bear.

In the text that concludes his life's work, the *Coronis* (an appendix to *True Christian Religion*, 1771), Swedenborg explains that the Ancient Church was in Greater Tartary because it had been "spread over the whole of Asia." The Word of Tartary seems to be a relic, a divinely inspired remnant from older times. By divine providence, the pre-Israelitish Word had been preserved in Great Tartary (¶ 39). Why?

Hidden Sources

In 1762 or thereabout, Swedenborg first made notes on the secret of Greater Tartary in his private journal of spiritual experiences, which he began in 1747 and stopped in 1765 and which was posthumously published as the *Spiritual Diary*:

> Several inhabitants of Tartary close to China—Lesser Tartary— were with me. . . . They said that they knew nothing about war. They knew of China and Siberia. They said that, with them, only he who is able to govern is put in power, and if he does not tend to his affairs, he is deposed and punished.[5]

They reported that they are all engaged in working in the fields and

> wondered how God could be understood as being anything other than a man. They likewise understand the precepts of the Decalogue and have only one wife. . . . They reported that they have houses, where they are taught about life and about the commandments of God. They said that they possessed a book, which people elsewhere do not know that they have. This they call the *Divine Book* [the Sacred Scripture], which they read and are instructed by, and which they understand. Upon further inquiry, this book was found to be the Psalms of David. They told me that strangers are indeed admitted among them, but they are not given the opportunity to leave: they are given all the necessities of life, and if they are willing to work, they are accepted. They have the Decalogue. They call the Chinese their friends,

because they are of the same nation. . . . But they have some fear of Siberia.[6]

Swedenborg immediately includes this new information in his work *The Last Judgment*, written in 1762 but published posthumously. This is the first work in which Swedenborg writes of these "peaceable and peaceful" people who dwelt somewhere beyond the Wall of China.[7]

Where, more precisely, did they live, in this kingdom of peace and rectitude? Where is this treasure of Great Tartary, the Word from the past, hidden? And in juxtaposition to these geographical questions, were there contemporary sources? Are confirmations to be found elsewhere regarding these statements about secret wisdom among the Mongols? Finally, from this space/time dimension arises the question of research in comparative religion: can supporting parallels be found in the Far East? In what follows, we shall take these routes in approaching the riddle of the Tartars.

Strindberg postulated a number of viewpoints after extensive investigations into the matter; few have been as ingenious as he. For a long time he had been obsessed with related problems. After having closely scrutinized the passages referred to in both *Apocalypse Revealed* and *True Christian Religion*, to which his quotations bear witness, he draws the following conclusions about the chosen people of Tartary in his essay on "The Sources of the Bible:"

> The populous people against whom the Great Wall was built were the Mongolians. The fact that the emperor of China is their friend, since he is of the same nation, points to the Manchurians, the founders of China's last dynasty of emperors; but Swedenborg's information that these people who preserve the source of the biblical texts live on a plateau and do not admit Christians into their land points to Tibet.

However, continues Strindberg, there is

another way to explain what Swedenborg means. He himself has stated in another of his writings that unknown places exist on earth where mighty beings dwell who serve the Lord and govern men's destinies. This reminds us of Plato's *Phaedo*, where the same thing is said, and also of the theosophist doctrine regarding the Mahatmas, or teachers, who live in the Himalayas.

Further, as a particularly strange fact in this connection, Strindberg goes on:

> all who travel in southern Siberia and Mongolia find handwritten documents in the desert, in the sand, in heaps of ruins, and all of these that have been translated have a religious content. Swedenborg's cousin, Peter Schönström, and Stralenberg say that they have brought back a hundred.

Strindberg believed that the documents he himself had rediscovered in Linköping belong to this group. "I sent the Mongolian one to Paris to be translated, and it was found to be a prayer." Finally, he summarizes: "Perhaps the old sagas about Prester John and about the Old Man of the Mountain contain some truth, and there do exist undiscovered lands beyond the poles."[8]

We do not know the result of Strindberg's inquiry into Sven Hedin's contacts with Mongolian manuscripts. However, Hedin, like a number of subsequent travelers to Asia, tells of lamaseries that contain ancient wisdom, esoterically preserved in sealed chambers. Nonetheless, this need not be interpreted as being any more remarkable than the self-evident fact that in monasteries, as in libraries around the world, people are fearfully protective of their rarities, most especially the oldest source documents (which are, therefore, used only in the form of copies).[9] In the Far East, too, there was indeed reason to safeguard precious manuscripts in the presence of traveling researchers, who often took their discoveries home with them. But we shall return to the sacred scriptures of the lamaseries when we have found the key.

Strindberg had been working in this direction for a long time.

And it is interesting to see that Inge Jonsson of Stockholm University, the scholar who tried to clarify the mystery of Tartary after Strindberg—although now from the viewpoint of the history of ideas—tried the same paths that Strindberg had staked out. Jonsson did not get much further that did Strindberg, but found some interesting sidetracks, which we shall eventually explore.[10]

This is not to cast suspicion on the guide of *En Blå Bok*. It could just as well mean that Strindberg was correct on several points, but that the observations are too few to enable us to see the lay of the land. Swedenborg's statements can be construed as bizarre and Strindberg's speculations as quasi-scientific, but we perhaps touch on a problem here about which the most one can say is that the data are insufficient.

The Missionaries' Discovery

That we do not have all the facts does not mean that they are all missing. There are a great many factual bases. Strindberg seeks to approach Great Tartary from several directions in his *Kulturhistoriska Studier* (Studies in Cultural History [1881]). In that book, he maintains that there have been contacts between China and Sweden ever since the seventeenth century, despite the great distance between these two countries. In the seventeenth century, this information moved in both directions, primarily through military and diplomatic personnel on journeys to and from the East and West. A significant connection with the East came about through the thousands of Swedish officers who became prisoners in Siberia after Charles XII's military campaigns, some of whom were assigned advanced research tasks. Tobolsk seems for a time to have been an important area of contact between leading scientists and traveling explorers, among them Philip Johan von Stralenberg, who would come to be famous through his map of Asia and his historical overview, printed in 1730 and published in many languages—*An Account of Travels in Russia, Siberia, and Great Tartary*. During this period of Swedish exile, knowledge about Asia was also gathered from travelers and researchers, as well as from Jesuit missionaries. When Tsar Peter the Great died in 1725, Bernard Le Bovier de Fontenelle declared in his well-known memorial address to the French Academy of Science that, through his three-thousand enterprising Swedish prisoners, the Tsar had provided himself with an eastern center of culture, one which lacked neither mathematicians nor linguistic geniuses. Carl Jonas Love Almqvist, in his history of the world, *Människoslägtets Saga* (The Saga of the Human Race [1839]), would claim that the prisoners of war in Russia "civilized their guards," as in the familiar quotation from Horace to the effect that the conquered Greeks overpowered their masters and brought culture to the rustic Roman Empire.

Among these cultured members of the Carolinian line were Stralenberg and Swedenborg's cousin Peter Schönström (1682–1746), both keen collectors of manuscripts and artifacts. Both devoted themselves to the question of the faith and philosophy of life among the Tartars. Schönström, among other pursuits, gathered information on the religious ideas and customs in the hinterlands of southeast Siberia, which he interpreted as being of a primitive Christian and ancient Nordic character in a Rudbeckian spirit: in some sense, they stood near the source of prehistoric Eden. In addition, Strindberg provides examples of the fact that the Pietist movement, especially, seems to have been a living force within the circle of exiled Swedes in Tobolsk. By revolting against orthodoxy, the Pietists cultivated an individualistic and subjective piety that paved the way for the new spiritual currents of the eighteenth century.

Regarding significant experiences of missionaries in the East, these were sometimes quite remarkable. The Nestorians had already introduced Christianity into China in 635, and centuries earlier followers of St. Thomas the Apostle had founded a church in India. Indeed, Buddhism itself could, from time to time, be misapprehended as a form of Christianity:

In the year 1246 Innocent IV sent the monk Giovanni Carpani to win the Tartars and the Chinese for Christendom, whereupon

27

the striking similarity that exists between the religious customs of Buddhism and Catholicism delighted the apostle greatly, because he assumed that Christianity had already been introduced. The same mistake was made, moreover, by Rubricus [Ruysbroeck], who had been sent out in 1253 by Ludwig the Holy.[11]

Inge Jonsson, too, has interesting things to report from the missionary world. During the latter half of the eighteenth century, interest in China reached its zenith, as is evidenced by the decoration of the courts, porcelain tea services, and formal gardens. The Swedish aristocracy was heavily involved in chinoiserie, a fad that reached its peak just when Swedenborg turned his eyes toward the reaches of Great Tartary. The fascination with China was the result of the Swedish East India Company's world trade. As we know, this internationalization coincided with the awakening of interest in Swedenborg's free-thinking, and this occurred precisely with the men of the great ships in the port of Gothenburg.[12]

As for Swedenborg, the springtime of his interest in China had already taken place upon his discovery of the philosophy of Leibniz, which he drew on especially through the volumes of Leibniz's disciple, Christian von Wolff.[13] Swedenborg received his first dose of Wolff's and Leibniz's strong fascination with the China of old when he read Wolff's Empirical Psychology (1732).[14] Leibniz regarded China as Europe's equal counterpart in Asia and argued for cultural exchange. He was of the opinion that, ethically and politically, China had reached levels Europe had not dreamed of.

With the particular assistance of a knowledgeable dissertation on these German contacts with China, written by a Chinese researcher in Switzerland and printed in Hong Kong, Inge Jonsson made an important assertion: Leibniz had acquired his concept of China through Jesuit missionaries with whom he had exchanged letters. This correspondence also attests to the interest in the "hieroglyphic" character of Chinese writing, as containing a singular, archaic symbol-power. According to Jonsson, "The French Jesuit Joachim Bouvet presented a thorough analysis of this writing from the conviction that the Chinese had already found the true God by the time Fu Hsi had established the oldest kingdom."[15]

Leibniz, who, among other things, pleaded for a European edition of a Tartar–Chinese dictionary, refers in his *Nouveaux essais sur l'entendement humain* (new edition, Amsterdam, 1765) to the idea held by the missionaries to China that the true religion was alive in ancient China. Leibniz's book was thus published the year before (and in the same city as) *Apocalypse Revealed*, which contains Swedenborg's best known descriptions of the Word in Great Tartary. His possible reading of this edition of Leibniz's book could have served, at most, as a confirmation or recollection for Swedenborg, who had indeed written the same thing earlier in his private diary. This whole investigation shows clearly the direction in which the thought of the time was moving and what kind of reports from East Asia were in circulation.

After Poltava

The news that spread to Sweden from Asia's interior, often of a Rudbeckian and fantastic nature, with echoes of Eden and Atlantis—that is to say, in resonance with the academic atmosphere of the young Swedenborg's Uppsala—originated, as we have seen, not least from the Carolinians in Russian Asia. When we look to Tartary, a great deal more can be found in Swedish–Russian relations of the times. In addition, when we return to the remarkable Stralenberg and his map, we meet a previously overlooked link: the versatile Russian historian Vassiliy Tatishchev, best known for his theories on the ancient Nordic past of the Russians.

As for Schönström, he was regarded as the Swedenborg family's genealogist, and his collection of historical material included everything from lists of rulers in Tartary to the family trees of the Svedberg and Behm families, Behm being Swedenborg's mother's name. Contacts between Swedenborg and Schönström are well documented, and the former's faith in his cousin is evident from IOU's that have been preserved, which show that Schönström was loaned considerable sums by his well-to-do cousin.[16] Swedenborg certainly kept himself informed about Schönström's interests and research projects. His intimate friendships with travelers, to Russia in particular (e.g., later in life with Edvard Carleson and Carl Reinhold Berch), strengthen the picture of information from the East that he received. At dinner with Carleson and Berch in the mid-1760's, approximately at the time of the publication of *Apocalypse Revealed*, the newly inducted priest of Stockholm's Russian congregation Yoaniki Goroneskul was moved to tears while listening to Swedenborg's words about the realm of the blessed.[17] We know very little about the direction taken over the decades in this enormous area of eastward contact, but can surely conjecture that, interwoven with historical and geographical material, spiritual and abstract things came up during various conversation.

The efforts at inquiry by the prisoners in Siberia during the first half of the eighteenth century had the significant result that knowledge reached the West about areas that had hitherto been largely unknown in Europe. Here the Tartar vein is opened.

A remarkable and highly noteworthy consequence of the defeats at Poltava and Perevolotyna in 1709 was an internationalization of the Swedish perspective. Tobolsk, Siberia's chief city, became for a time a center of cultural activity where East and West met. Tartary became known. In reality this was due to Tsar Peter's imperial plans, which were carried out by others: Russia was to grow to a sixth of the world's surface. The prisoners of war were put to work exploring and mapping unknown territories; in this way, the conquered enemies became pathfinders for the Russians. Corporal Heinrich Busch rode with the Cossacks to Okhotsk and sailed to Kamchatka. After his return home to Sweden in July 1718, having been on other assignments in the same general area, Lieutenant Ambjörn Molin reported on the Tartars, whom "one meets far to the northeast in Asia." Captain Johan Bernhard Müller journeyed to the pagan eastern Yakuts and wrote a book about them. The cornet officer Christopher Schnitzker escorted a Chinese legation through Siberia to the Kalmuck khan Ayuka and wrote an account of his travels. At the same time, the German explorer Daniel Gottlieb Messerschmidt and Captain Philip von Stralenberg, both devoted Pietists, began an intensive cooperative effort in Tobolsk, and went on an exploratory trip in the company of Quartermaster Daniel Capell and the artist Carl Gustaf Schulman. Stralenberg continued the whole time to work on his map, with the assistance of Fortifications Officer Johan Anton Matérn, as well as that of Schönström.[18] As Strindberg very particularly pointed out, Lorens Lange, a prisoner of war who, like many others, remained in the service of Russia when peace with Sweden was concluded, became St. Petersburg's emissary to Beijing, and he traveled there as often as possible.[19]

Other works also explored the East. Friedrich Christian Weber's *Das veränderte Russland* (Russia Transformed [Frankfurt, 1721]), manifestly Strindberg's chief source, tells especially about cavalry Captain Peter Schönström, who, during ten years in Soliamsk, gathered all kinds of material and information, not least from travelers and caravan drivers who passed through the city. The encyclopedic work *Der allerneueste Staat von Sibirien* (Siberia's Newest State), which swarms with Carolinian information, was published in Nürenburg in 1724–1726. The *Histoire Généalogique des Tartars* (Historical Genealogy of the Tartars), printed in Leiden in 1726, builds on the above-mentioned manuscript, and particularly engaged the attention of the Rudbeckians, Stralenberg and Schönström. It is a story about the dynasty of Genghis Khan, written by the Tartar khan Abu'l-Ghazi Bahadur (1605–1665) and completed by his son. Schönström seems to have been working on having a Russian version of this work translated into German. This illustrates the direction of scholarly interest at the time. The enthusiasm could have been sparked by the legend of Prester John, the Mongolian empire's priest-king. Here is a link between the fanciful search for a hidden, inner origin of things and a world-embracing interrelationship, pursued by Olof Rudbeck, Sr., and Johannes Bureus, and, in looking for an interrelationship of the same breadth, the tradition passed on from Marco Polo and the Franciscan nuncio Ruysbroeck.

Before the experiences of the prisoners of war in Siberia, the interior of Asia glimmered only through the mysterious pictures of the missionaries and from the remarkable stories of Marco Polo's time. Where facts were lacking, imagination filled in. Through the collecting of facts and the drawing of maps the East became more real. That which was foreign came ever closer, became more concrete, but at the same time its mystery grew ever more complex. The worship of the Land of the Rising Sun, which reached its peak in Europe in the nineteenth century, was gradually fanned by the wind from the East, which had been stirred up by the eighteenth-century explorers of Asia. In this way Swedenborg's reference to Great Tartary in the 1760s presages the romantic and theosophical orientalism of the coming century.

Vassily Tatishchev

In the 1720s Swedenborg met several times with the Russian historian Vassily Tatishchev (1686–1759), who was active in many fields. Tatishchev was also a collector of note; at Uppsala, where he enjoyed the company of Eric Benzelius, Jr., he took an interest in, among other things, an old Church Slavonic text that relates the story of Barlaam and Josaphat, originally an Indian tale, in which legends about the life of the Buddha are clothed in Christian dress—a transference very much in tune with the times.

Tatishchev, acting on the orders of his tsar, also studied the geography of the Russian Empire and was well acquainted with the Swedes who worked on similar tasks. As assessor in the St. Petersburg College of Mines, he conferred closely with his colleague in Stockholm, the assessor in the Swedish College of Mines, Emanuel Swedenborg. Tatishchev was the first to present a document by Swedenborg in Russia, namely, a report on the decimal system, which in its way heralded renown for Swedenborg in St. Petersburg during the following decade, when he was nominated as a corresponding member of the tsarist St. Petersburg Academy of Sciences.

Thanks to Juri Küttner's exploration of earlier, unresearched material, we now have a new Swedenborg document available to us.[20] Tatishchev was also among those who had participated in the battle of Poltava. After the battle he had marched with the Russian army against the Turkish empire, and upon his return to St. Petersburg in 1719, set to work mapping the kingdom. He also devoted himself to Turkish history, a broad study that begins with the legends of the ancient Russian chronicles of Nestor. So we find him on a journey far to the east—in Kazan, where he joins Johan Berglin from Falun; in Soliamsk, where he begins a cooperative effort with Peter Schönström, an important source of history for him; and further, to Tobolsk and the circle around Stralenberg. Directly after returning from an expedition to the Kalmucks, he travels to Sweden, where not only does he see Stralenberg again, and meet Polhem, Anders Swab, and Lars Benzelstierna, but he also meets Swedenborg.[21] Tatishchev had an ongoing communication with the Orientalists of the time, among them the learned and far-seeking Henrik Brenner, who had been a captive in Russia after visiting Persia. One can perhaps even sense an affinity in Tatishchev's special interest in the Russia-oriented poetess Sophia Brenner, to whom Swedenborg had written the most devoted poem of his youth.

When Tatishchev met with Eric Benzelius in Stockholm, Stralenberg traveled up from his base in Eskilstuna to give Tatishchev "a Kalmuck document" (now unknown) that he had obtained from the Sinologist Gottlieb Siegfried Beyer in Königsberg. From the Rudbeckian historian of ancient times, Eric Julius Biörner, he received an overview of the oldest annals of the kingdom of Russia—which embraced ancient Magog and Scythia—a manuscript that has since been lost.

The mode and mood of these lines of thought can be sensed from the excitement manifested over many other findings of the Russian prisoners, for example, the discovery of a mammoth tusk in Siberia—which was taken to be either the remains of the biblical monster Behemoth, mentioned in the Book of Enoch, or the horn of a unicorn. In this intellectual milieu, ancient biblical and mystical discoveries in the East were the topic of the day.

From Lake Baikal to Tenduk

Vilhelm van Ruysbroeck and Marco Polo, the earliest travelers to Tartary from Europe, mention a prince in Asia called Naiman, or Un Kan, who was identified with Prester John. This figure was a legendary priest-king who had been reported in European sources since the twelfth century. Because the pope wanted to have contact with this distant ally in Great Tartary, the legend gave rise to delegations eastward during the thirteenth century. He was not found. Instead, the legend of Prester John was transferred to Africa—more explicitly, to the old Abyssinian empire, which in the seventeenth century was still called the Kingdom of John the Presbyter. Inge Jonsson tried to see in this wandering tale a parallel to Swedenborg's teaching about the Ancient Word and how it "wandered" from Asia to Africa. He even sought in this story an explanation for the high esteem in which Swedenborg held the Africans—a view remarkable for that time. Perhaps, he suggests, there is also a connection here to the fact that, when this subject arises, Swedenborg's primary study is the Apocalypse, the Revelation of John.[22]

Here we touch upon a quality even more fleeting and fragile than the colors of a butterfly's wings. The plausible parallels are scarcely in line with what Swedenborg meant by either the "Ancient Church" or *verbum vetustum*, the Ancient Word. Those who come closest to Swedenborg's conception of the original church are perhaps Wilhelm Schmidt, in his colossal work *Ursprung der Gottesidee* (Origin of the Idea of God), summarized in his lectures at Uppsala entitled *Religionen hos Urkulturens folk* (The Religion of the People of the Original Culture [1926]), and Sir Arthur Drews in his *History of Monotheism in Ancient Times* (1913).

As regards Great Tartary, however, we can find our way with the help of worldly and fairly well-known facts in the tradition stemming from Marco Polo. In his journey within the Great Khan's empire in Tartary in the thirteenth century, Marco Polo went to Tanguth. The name comes from the "Tangut" people, who are related to the Tibetans and who founded a kingdom in the eleventh century in northwest China, more specifically, in the province of Gansu.

This region included a number of places visited by Marco Polo, each one quite different from the other, and here and there he met Nestorian Christians. Subsequently, when passing the city of Karakorum in Outer Mongolia, the place where the Tartars had located their residence, he wrote a brief description of a few essentials of Tartar history and customs. Heading in a north-easterly direction from Tanguth, Marco Polo arrived at the Province of Tenduk, "the kingdom of John the Priest. . . . The present king is one of his descendants and is named George. He is also a Christian and a priest." In this land of great beauty the Christian populace is occupied with "agriculture, trade, and mechanical work." It is known that the Christian Öngut king George died in 1298, thus only a few years after Polo passed through. The king had been a Nestorian, but died a Catholic, converted by the missionary Giovanni de Monte Corvino.

Of the people's origin, Marco Polo reports that "the Tartars dwelt in the northern lands Jorza and Bargu." Consequently, it is most likely that this area lies in tracts east of the Baikal Sea. Even today one can visit the city of Barguzin on the Barguzino River, near the "Barguzinskiy Khrebet" mountain chain, after an Aeroflot flight from Moscow to Ulan-Ude. Thus, it is in the Siberian region of the Mongolian domains, in that region which at the present day is the Buryat Republic, and possibly in the Trans-Baikal area bordering on Manchuria. Within this region "are wide plains, good pasture, great rivers and an abundance of water. The people had no sovereign among them. But they were bound to pay tribute to a great lord whose name in their language was, according to what I have heard, Un Khan, which name has the same meaning as Prester John (Preste Giovanni) in ours." Herein lies the explanation of the mighty hopes that Schönström and others pinned to the Mongolian chronicle that had been found. But who was this "Ioan Khan"?

The Christian contribution to Asia was not entirely unknown. We also know that Kublai Khan sent Marco Polo to Jerusalem to procure some holy oil and that the great khan's own mother was

a Christian. According to the legend, Genghis Khan had succeeded John the Priest. But what was it that Marco Polo wrote?
His actual words were: "In the course of time the tribe multiplied
so quickly that Un Kan, or Prester John, began to fear that it
would become mightier than he." Many generations are being
telescoped here. How could John the Priest govern so long? The
priest "John" (Ioan-han) is a priest-king's title. It reads *Wang-Han*
in Chinese documents, referring to the ruler of Christian Mongolian peoples living near the Great Wall. Every new such ruler
of the Nestorian Keraits was called *Wang* (king). "John the
Priest" existed as a legal person, and the title reflected old Christian traditions in central Asia before the rule of Genghis Khan.

When Marco Polo describes the customs and practices of the
Tartars, the parallels to Swedenborg's writings are again immediately recognizable:

> Unfaithfulness in marriage is considered by this people to be a
> dishonorable, vile practice. . . . The most praiseworthy peace
> and unity prevails among them. . . . They devote themselves to
> trade and household duties, such as care for their family's daily
> needs. . . . The faith and doctrine of the Tartars are as follows.
> They say that there is one god, great, noble, and heavenly. They
> burn incense in bowls daily for him, and they send their prayers
> for spiritual and physical health up to him. They worship an-
> other god, too. He is called Nitigai (Nacigai), and his image,
> covered in a blanket or cloth, is found in every home. . . . They
> think that he is the god who rules over their earthly existence,
> and at their mealtimes they never forget to grease the god's
> mouth with a fat piece of meat.[23]

The visible and the invisible God? The manifest conception
of God as Man? The similarities between Marco Polo's and
Swedenborg's descriptions of the same—at least in name—harmonious and domestic people in the Mongolian territory outside
the Great Wall of China, in the land between Tibet and Siberia,
lie on the rim of chance. Why do such similarities exist at all?

In De-yúng's World of Symbols

Similarities arise more frequently the closer one approaches the source. In the voyage to distant regions, all the way from the shores of the Baikal, we move upstream through the waters of the Mongolian fountainhead.

Strindberg had come to think of Tibet when he examined Swedenborg's statements. Stralenberg in his 1730 book had identified John the Priest with the Dalai Lama.[24] No such Tibetan connection is mentioned by Marco Polo, the first European to give a detailed description of Tibet. Nor was there yet a Dalai Lama in Polo's time (the first Dalai Lama ruled in the fifteenth century), which makes Stralenberg's coupling anachronistic. But since the Mongolians and Tibetans have the same world of religious concepts in most respects, we shall seek the promised land with them.

The same documents are there to be read in both Tibetan and Mongolian—among others, the two hundred and twenty volumes of commentary on the Buddha's teaching. These were on the program in 1978, when there was a Buddhist Congress in Ivolginsk, southwest of the Baikal Sea in the Buryat-Mongolian Soviet Republic.

The report by Christian Schmidt-Häuer in 1978 gave a wondrous picture of the mood emanating from this gathering of Buddhist Buryats, Kalmucks, Tuvinians, and Yakuts:

From the twenty wooden buildings of the lamasery, each housing thirty lamas, streams warm light. . . . In spite of the industrious preparations, a solemn, almost uncanny stillness lies over the Datsan. The impression of a special stillness comes from the light-spirited, monotonic chanting of a group of pilgrims, spinning their prayer wheels in the dusk, and the delicate striking of a little bell, which, with its ethereal ringing, shall keep all evil away, and the soft crunching of snow at every step—the average temperature in winter is minus 25°.[25]

The place could just as well have been Tibet, in both inward and outward respects. In the same way, the present Dalai Lama, the fourteenth, has told how interesting it has been for him while in exile to visit these same Mongolian and Turkic peoples, peoples of the same faith, but with somewhat different customs. Since the distant past, they have read the same scriptures. To a certain extent, this has actually been done in the same language, due to the introduction of the lamaist hierarchy into Mongolia at the beginning of the seventeenth century, which produced a large number of translations of Buddhist texts into Tibetan.

During World War II, when people wondered where General Doolittle's air attacks against Japan originated, American President Franklin Roosevelt answered, diplomatically, "From Shangri-la!" This was, in fact, the name he had given to his own secret aerie in the mountains of Maryland. The concept of "Shangri-la" is a modern literary invention of James Hilton, who, in his novel *Lost Horizon* (1933), describes a Tibetan lamasery hidden somewhere among the snow-covered Kunlun mountains, where people live in an idyllic valley, century after century, without aging, a place no one can find except he who becomes lost.[26]

A similar tale is found in the Tibetan Buddhist canon, a series of more than three-hundred volumes called *Kangyur* and *Tengyur*. This work is the bible of the Tibetans. It contains the Buddha's teachings together with commentaries by later saints and learned men. In the oldest writings are accounts of the land *Béyú*, the "Hidden Country," also called *De-yúng*, the "Wellspring of Happiness." The corresponding word in Sanskrit is *Shambhala*. That name, of unknown origin, is also used among the Buddhists of the North.

The Tibetans have not sought this kingdom in their own land. It has been placed in, among other places, the tracts of the Gobi desert in Mongolia, or in the mountains and forests of Siberia. In the same way, Hindu mythology looks northward beyond the Himalayan wall to Mount Meru, the center of the world, where the king of the gods, Indra, has his jewel-encrusted palace. Chinese Taoist legends about Lao Tzu (Laozi) recount that he has retreated forever to the Jade Mountain, somewhere in the west, beyond Kunlun.[27]

Modern researchers seeking the "original religion" have frequently turned their sights in the same direction, toward central
Asian "shamanism." While inquiring theosophists in the West
during the last century were fascinated by Tibet, the Tibetans in
turn have searched for the holy land in other directions, "somewhere north of Tibet." The stories about Shambhala have never
been particularly well known outside of Tibet and Mongolia,
even though rumors and fragments of information have reached
us through missionaries and travelers ever since the seventeenth
century.[28] A scholar who has seriously taken up the question is
Edwin Bernbaum. Some of his observations have a burning rele-
vance for us. Here we can glimpse Swedenborg's depictions as in
a distant mirror.[29]

The holy scriptures in the Tibetan canon depict Shambhala as
a kingdom where an enlightened royal family guards the most
secret doctrines of religion. According to the apocalyptic
Shambhala literature, a future king of Shambhala will ride forth
with his mounted hosts, conquer the evil ruler of the world, and
finally restore a Golden Age. In Shambhala heavenly arcana are
protected and preserved in order that, after the final devastation,
they may maintain the world and guide it to future glory. This is
the final connecting link. Therefore, these secrets had to be
saved from destruction.

Can one, then, come to Shambhala before this happens? The
texts add that a long and mystical journey through mountains
and deserts leads to Shambhala. Those who succeed in overcom-
ing all the hardships along the way and reach that distant holy
place come to find secret wisdom that can give them power to
master the temporal life and free the self from its slavery. The
texts, which warn against any weaknesses along the way, also
say that only those who are spiritually prepared can reach
Shambhala.

Many of the old manuscripts on Shambhala have been added
to through the ages; but many have also disappeared, carried
away, perhaps *en route* from lamaseries; and some have left Tibet.
Many people have set out to find Shambhala and have become
lost. Four guide books, however, have been preserved among the

Tibetans. The oldest of these travel guides is from the time of Genghis Khan and describes journeys through mountainous lands, forests, vast expanses, and bodies of water.

The oldest volumes that mention Shambhala were written in the twelfth century, translations from Sanskrit. This older, north Indian, Sanskrit literature about the Kalachakra was lost when Islam pushed aside the remnants of Buddhism in India. However, many Western researchers agree that the teachings of Sanskrit literature about Shambhala had their ancient origin in central Asia. The traditions had come from there to India in the tenth century, sometime around 960; from India, they were brought to Tibet by a teacher named Somanantha. According to the Tibetan calendar, that occurred in the year 1—the year 1026 A.D. in our chronology. Shambhala had preserved this *kalachakra* wisdom for thousands of years before it trickled out into the world. Much of this wisdom had never been written down because of its esoteric character, but was passed on orally and transcribed only later. The difficulty is that the texts are written in a language of symbols that can be understood only by those who have been specially initiated.

Kalapa is the capital of Shambhala. It is surrounded by lakes and groves. The king's temple is adorned with jewels and shines in the night. The roof gleams with the purest gold, and emeralds and sapphires frame the gates—reminiscent of the oriental splendor of the New Jerusalem in the Apocalypse and that of Swedenborg's vision of the Temple of Wisdom in *True Christian Religion* ¶387. The inhabitants live in peace and harmony, free from all sickness. They cultivate the earth, and the harvests never fail. They go about dressed in mantles of fine, white cloth. Again, this may remind us of the saving hosts in the Apocalypse (19:14), who, with the mounted Lord at their head, "followed Him upon white horses, clothed in fine white linen," as described in Swedenborg's book *The White Horse* (1758). The laws that govern the people of Shambhala are just and gentle. Immorality does not exist. The very words "war" and "animosity" are unknown. The people have a positive attitude to the things of this world. Life is active; their philosophy of life emphasizes good works; but to be liberated one must also receive the insight of wisdom. The Ten Commandments are in the Tibetan-Mongolian canon. The commandment to love is fundamental, the great commandment, found in the ten commandments of Realization, as in the Eightfold Path, etc. In addition, there are also the Tibetan "Holy Ten," words of wisdom that are a part of the Kalachakra.

According to the records, Shambhala has existed since the dawn of mankind; "the religion was not Buddhist."

Kalachakra, "the Wheel of Time," is the most sacred of lamaist doctrines; it is the one that comes from Shambhala. Therefore, it may not come into the hands of the uninitiated, and besides, the symbolism requires such a deep degree of initiation that few outside Shambhala can ever understand this literature. For Tibetans, there is a special message for the future of all mankind in this, and its practices open the spirit to a great inner unity. Therefore, and in the face of all sectarianism, which he regards as a poison for the world, the present Dalai Lama has given the initiation into Kalachakra in several countries "in order to promote world peace." The way to Shambhala is first and foremost an inner journey. The Dalai Lama, who in younger years was much taken up with the question of the location of Shambhala, affirms in his book *Freedom in Exile* that the land of Shambhala is a reality, that it actually exists, although not in the conventional sense.[30]

Like Balzac and Strindberg, I have listened to what Swedenborg, the "Buddha of the North," declared and have, perhaps a bit superficially, taken him at his word. However, there is substantial scholarly evidence that Swedenborg's vision of the Ancient Word in China's outer provinces and bordering lands, within the Sino-Tibetan language family, may derive from historical and contemporary sources. Perhaps "the Ancient Word" itself has been found among the Tartars, among the Turkic-Mongolian peoples.

The New Church in the West Indies

What *attention,* what astonishment would it prompt if a cabinet member stated today that Swedenborgianism was an appropriate doctrine to be taught in communities abroad, or in the multiracial domestic parishes, crowded by immigrants of various creeds. This is about what occurred when Councillor Anders Johan von Höpken (1712–1789) suggested to King Gustav III that Swedenborgianism was an appropriate religion out in the colonies. The reaction was predictable.

In his correspondence with New Church people, von Höpken justified this proposal not only because he believed that Swedenborgianism attenuated a fear of death, but because it emphasized morality, thus establishing a perfect social doctrine and creating honest subjects "inasmuch as it taught that piety was a matter of life and manners."

Höpken was a member of the first Swedenborgian society, the Exegetical-Philanthropic Society, and, in later times, others have sometimes read a defensive tone into his proposal. The one

This essay was first published as "Västindien, slaveriet, och swedenborgianismen," *Världarnas Möte* 4 (1994): 128–142. Translated from Swedish by George F. Dole.

question that persists is why he stressed the importance of Swedenborgian doctrine overseas, in the colonies.

A remarkable historical fact is that the first Scandinavian Swedenborgian group was not founded in Sweden, or in Norway or Denmark, but on the island of St. Croix in the West Indies, a hundred and fifty years ago. When we search through the earliest history of the New Church in the Nordic countries, we find ourselves exploring the Danish Virgin Islands, a group of islands in the Lesser Antilles in the Caribbean.[1]

The Leeward Islands

The island of Santa Cruz was named by Columbus on his second journey, who thought of himself as a crusader. Later, under French control, it came to be known as St. Croix, and it has kept this name even today, with an English pronunciation (ever since Danish times, actually, when the official language became English). The Danish West Indies also included St. Thomas and St. John. The principal city for most of Danish occupation was Charlotte Amalie on St. Thomas, named after the Danish queen, but the formation of Swedenborgian societies took place on St. Croix, where the towns also bore (and still bear today) names from the Danish court, Christiansted amd Fredriksted.

When Columbus reached the Virgin Islands in 1493, the multitude of little islands made him think of the legend of Saint Ursula, who, to atone for having thought of marrying a heathen, went on a pilgrimage to Rome followed by 11,000 virgins. On November 14, 1493, Columbus' fleet anchored in a bay near St. Croix, later known as Krause Bay after a famous German-Danish family; the name turns up later among followers of Swedenborg in the area. In 1850, Swedenborgians in Christiansted included a bookkeeper named Gustavus Adolphus Krause, named after Sweden's most famous king, a man living in a simple house on Fiskare Gade, Fisher Street. This area is called Free Gut, the free "colored" section of the city since 1747, bounded by Fisher Street, East Street, New Street, Queen Cross Street, and Little Hospital Street.

The Danish family names are misleading, since most of the people who bore them were people of color, as is still the case in the West Indies. This phenomenon goes back to the days of slavery. Slaves were named after their masters; some were adopted; there were many illegitimate children; and freed slaves carried on the family names. Marriages eventually increased the number of mulattos in the West Indian colonies. The blacks, the mixed race known as "colored," and the whites constituted three social classes, with the middle group showing the most growth over time and coming to constitute a rising middle class.[2]

The New Church in the Virgin Islands

On June 28, 1846, a group gathered at the home of lawyer Carl Andreas Kierulff, at 31 Strand Gade in Christiansted, for the first official Swedenborgian worship service. However, twenty years earlier, individuals interested in Swedenborg had gathered privately and secretly here and there in the Virgin Islands. The first adherents were Vibe Kierulff on St. Thomas and Henning Gotfried Linberg on St. John.

Swedenborgian activity began as early as 1826 on the three islands. Adherents tried to win acceptance in particular for *True Christian Religion*, the work in which Swedenborg summarized his "true Christianity" and one in which the special spirituality of Africans was emphasized. In a letter from the island of St. John, Henning Gotfried Linberg wrote to John Hargrove, pastor of the New Jerusalem Church in Boston, that Carl Kierulff on St. Croix had also succeeded in interesting the pastor of an English Episcopal church on the island in this book. Linberg was spreading the writings among interested people on the island of St. John, and would soon move to Christiansted, St. Croix, to serve as judge of the court where Carl Kierulff was a lawyer. Vibe Kierulff was gathering an interested circle on St. Thomas and was to become procurator, and later sheriff, on St. Thomas. These were influential people.

The bookkeeper Andreas Birch joined this circle and began a collection for the publication of Swedenborg's works, a drive that was particularly successful among plantation owners, first and foremost the shopkeeper John Meyer Johnson and later also Dr. William Henry Ruan, both of whom would come to belong to Swedenborgianism's inner circle on the islands. Birch, who on a trip to London had contacted the Swedenborg Society there, saw to it that people in the islands of the West Indies had access to Swedenborg's writings. In 1831, Birch wrote from St. Croix to the London Society that, in the preceding year, he had distributed letters of information to six hundred interested individuals. And, indeed, records show that, during the 1830s, islanders ordered Swedenborgian books and pamphlets from publishing houses in London, Manchester, and Boston. Linberg traveled to Boston, Carl and Vibe Kierulff to Boston and New York, where they loaded up with as many books as they could carry. None of these individuals, though, was a foreign missionary. They were lifelong residents of the islands, none of them coming from England or America. But like many who sparked enthusiasm in the islands, they became well known abroad, since they sought theological instruction and had acquired leadership within a fledgling religious community.

From 1846 on, we can follow the course of events in a series of letters from the New Churchman Elijah Bryan, who functioned as the Swedenborgians' official minister in the Virgin Islands, officiating at worship, baptism, and communion, leading a Sunday school for many years, generally making a beginning without authorization from any quarter. Bryan worked as a dentist. His name can be found in the American *New Church Almanac* for 1889. There we learn that he had been ordained by Pastor Solyman Brown in the Swedenborgian church in 1850, that he was connected with the General Convention from 1856 to 1867, and that he was active in the West Indies until his death in 1867.

When Bryan first came to St. Croix in 1846, he was surprised to find well-versed Swedenborgians there, one of them being Andreas Birch, whom he described as a "thorough New Church Man." Henning Gotfried Linberg had died by that time, but his work was being carried on by his widow Mary Linberg, who lived in the colored district.[3] In Christiansted, Carl Kierulff was still a central figure, with a circle of some two dozen active Swedenborgian adherents around him. Andreas Birch kept in touch with the eminent Swedenborgian James John Garth Wilkinson in England. Bryan corresponded with Ralph Waldo Emerson's New Church reviewer, Professor George Bush of Boston.

Carl Kierulff and his four children had already been baptized into the New Church while on a journey to Boston and New York. Indeed, a young man named Emanuel Swedenborg Kierulff, Carl's youngest son (1827–1881), now strolled the streets of Christiansted, and he had been baptized into the New Church. Jakob Elias Kierulff (1794–1842), a resident of St. Thomas like his brother Vibe, also named a son Emanuel.

An effort to arrange public lectures and worship was soon made. Andreas Birch and Elijah Bryan went to the police chief in Christiansted to request permission, but met with a summary re-fusal: the chief said, "No new doctrines." Carl Kierulff and ten prominent Christiansted individuals, including plantation owners Johnson and Ruan, wrote to the governor; but, although a liberal thinker, Governor Peter von Scholten could not assent because it was against the law and the decision of the Danish government. Kierulff decided to go further, to the seat of government in Copenhagen. His letters to Danish authorities turn up a number of times in the ensuing years, but no one would ever grant public authorization for meeting. In the meantime, Peter von Scholten tacitly allowed private meetings to be held without interference over the years until the emancipation of the island's slave popula-tion in 1848, after which he was recalled to Denmark.

On the island of St. Croix, which, in 1848, had a population of approximately 30,000 inhabitants, there were, by custom, five established religions. There were historical reasons for this fact, resting in the different nationalities on the island. When the Danes took control of the islands from the French, Catholicism had predominated. With the arrival of the Danes, Lutheranism, the state religion of Denmark, was introduced. The Anglican or Episcopal church came in with the English, the core of the island's well-endowed plantation owners. Then there was the Moravian church, originally from Germany, and the Jewish community, both of which had been sanctioned since the end of the eighteenth century.

Bryan provides in passing a remarkable bit of information. He notes in his diary that a majority of St. Croix's Jewish population was converting to Christianity, largely because of New Church pamphlets. He reports this on the basis of a conversation on religious questions with several Jews in Christiansted. At the same time Swedenborgians had won some sympathy among both Anglicans and Protestants, and were beginning to make an impression even among Catholics. Among Swedenborg's works, it was especially *True Christian Religion* that made it clear that the paradox of the trinity was of no benefit for a rational religion, an argument that favorably impressed rationalists. However, the inroads that were made occurred before the emancipation, the abolition of slavery, in 1848. Thereafter there was a reaction against the rising tide of proselytes, of Protestants and Anglicans who more and more associated themselves with the New Church. One of the leading Swedenborgians who worked energetically for the official approval of the New Church, the plantation owner William Henry Ruan, was attacked on the street and knocked down for his "treachery," his "subversive" activity, by F. L. Hawley, pastor of the Episcopal church.

The year 1846 saw the death of Andreas Birch, who, although born in Denmark like the Kierulff brothers, had been a resident of the Virgin Islands since his early childhood. Carl Kierulff died in 1849. New names come forward. The influential Wright family on St. Thomas comes into the picture, the Dawson family, and German-born Johannes Zimmermann. In Christiansted, more and more families turn up with a mixed racial ancestry, with names like Carty, Benners, Moorhead, Rogiers, Hatchett, Muller, Canvane, and Heyliger. The influential adherent Claudius von Beverhoudt, who married a woman of mixed ancestry, also named his son Emanuel. Emanuel Swedenborg emerged more and more as a bridge between cultures.

A Voyage to Other Islands

Toward the end of the 1840s, Swedenborgianism had spread to several of the islands in the West Indies. On a voyage to Trinidad, Bryan met a Swedenborgian named Thomas Shirley Warner from the island of Cedros near Port of Spain, and another, Francis Burke from the island of Montserrat. However, outside the Danish Virgin Islands, the one lone organized Swedenborgian society was on Jamaica, where there was a group of a dozen individuals who met in the coastal town of Lucea. The activity of this society culminated about 1846, the same year in which the association was founded on St. Croix.

The Jamaican circle had sprung up around Alexander Chambers, who died in 1842, and his son John Carr Chambers, who died in 1870. Meetings were held in their house in Lucea from 1840 on, a small group of adherents and preachers, mostly of African descent. It is clear from letters found in the archives of the Swedenborg School of Religion in Newton, Massachusetts, that this was and remained an important religion among the black population of Jamaica.

The Chambers family, which had settled in Jamaica as early as 1640, was among the world's first Swedenborgians, but also had early connections with freemasonry. In 1789, they participated in the Swedenborgians' foundational General Conference in London; eight delegates were from Jamaica. This New Church activity can be understood as a parallel to that in the Virgin Islands, but apart from Elijah Bryan's visit to Lucea in 1841, the two island groups went on without contact with each other. The New Church movement in Jamaica had its roots in England, while the movement in the Virgin Islands drew its inspiration from both England and the United States, even though its initial leaders— the Kierulffs, Linberg, and Birch—had Scandinavian ancestry. In neither instance was there a question of direct missionary effort, but rather of the islanders' contacts with overseas countries.

A trace of Swedenborgianism in the New World can be seen in the colony of New Sweden and in the rest of Swedish North America, from Delaware to Minnesota. Nicholas Collijn, pastor of the Swedish church in Philadelphia, had met Swedenborg personally. On the Swedish island of the West Indies, St. Barthélemy (a Swedish possession from 1784 to 1877), the first two governors, Salomon Mauritz von Rajalin (1757–1825) and his adjutant and successor Pehr Herman Rosén von Rosenstein, both very religious men, had Swedenborgian connections. Rajalin resigned his position in 1787; later he served as governor of another Swedish island, Gotland, and as organizer of a Swedenborg society there as well as member of the Swedenborgian foundation *Pro Fide et Caritate* in 1796.[4] Rosenstein, equally religious-minded, ended his days in 1799 among Freemasons in Finland, in the upper St. Andreas Phoenix Lodge. We know from Christopher Carlander's published travel diary (1788) that Rosenstein had Swedenborgian visitors in St. Barthélemy. As the late bishop Jan Arvid Hellström showed in his excellent study of religious institutions in the Swedish colony (*Åt alla christliga förvanter*, 1987), there developed on the initiative of these first two governors a religious freedom without parallel in their native Sweden. When Rajalin prematurely left St. Barthélemy in 1787, never to return, the abolition of the slave trade already stood first on the agenda of Swedenborgians worldwide, owing especially to the Norrköping meeting of 1779, and it is probable that a connection was made here with the trade in the free harbor of Gustavia, which was encouraged by the king's order.

Here our primary source material is wanting, and we must be careful about drawing conclusions *e silentio*. The exiled Swedish priest Carl Andreas Kierrulf's intensive activity as pastor of the Swedish church on St. Barthélemy in 1795–1796, for instance, has no connection whatever with the many West Indian Swedenborgians named Kierulff (with various spellings) who came along later, other than a remote family relationship (an ancestor from Jylland, a different branch of the family). During the decade from 1792 to 1802, our sources are particularly poor as regards St. Barthélemy; most of them, unfortunately, have been destroyed or lost.

We find Swedenborg also in Haiti, the island of Hispaniola, in the 1810s, where King Henri Christophe, a black man who

fought in the slave rebellion of 1794, tried to introduce Swedenborgianism as the state religion after having received a consign-
ment of the writings from the extensive book distribution
program of the American New Churchman William Schlatter.
The king's religious reform, like his own life, came to an abrupt
end in 1820. His fate is described in a play by the modern
French author Aimé Césaire of Martinique, *La tragedie du roi
Christophe,* in which the tragic hero Christophe dies as a passionate champion for the downtrodden blacks' deliverance from
their oppression and for the dignity of their country.[5]

Finally, we run across Swedenborgianism on three other islands in the West Indies. Trinidad and Tobago was the target of
one of the earliest Swedish colonization projects in the West Indies, and the religion found a foothold there, although there is
little information available about its history.[6] Swedenborgianism
is also represented in the old sugar island of Cuba up to the
1950s, especially under American influence, but disappears
when that influence does.

In the West Indies, Swedenborgianism was introduced by
white immigrants from the United States, Denmark, Sweden,
and Germany. But in most quarters, adherents were drawn from
the black or mixed-blood population. On St. Croix in the 1860s,
as in Jamaica at the same time, black Swedenborgian preachers
crop up.

West Africans of the West Indies

When we look at this historical development in its global
context, we find obvious points of connection with the war over
slavery. The whole economy of the West Indies was based on
West Africa, a fact that was also underscored by the people who
opposed slavery, among them the Swedenborgian philanthropist
Carl Bernhard Wadström. The latter's vast project in West Africa
in the 1780s, the idea of a free state for freed slaves, the foundation of the city of Freetown, resulted in his being regarded as the
spiritual father of Liberia and Sierra Leone; and his involvement
rested initially in his reading of Swedenborg's writings. This can

be seen in the remarkable volume of the *New Jerusalem Magazine* for 1790, where the situation in West Africa is the dominant subject. New Church pioneers, among them August Nordenskiöld and Anders Johansén, colored Swedenborgianism's reputation from the outset and gave it a distinctive direction. This is reflected not only in work for Africans in Africa and the West Indies but also in American history leading up to the abolition of slavery in 1861 and in Russia leading up to the abolition of serfdom in the same year.[7]

The background is historical, and the grounds are theological. How did all this happen? What was it in particular that human-rights reformers and people of African ancestry noted in Swedenborg and were inspired by?

The theological grounds for this pragmatic-political reform effort can be summarized under several main points stressed throughout Swedenborg's writings:

- the emphasis on freedom as an inalienable human quality, with free will as the foundation of morality
- the notion that all human beings are equal before God and there is neither predestination nor punishment
- The supreme importance of ethics, with the emphasis on goodness, love of the neighbor, and action being more significant than belief
- the concept that the "neighbor" is society, the country, the human race in its entirety
- the teaching of the profound spirituality of Africans
- the doctrine of spirit that connected with African primal religion and readily appealed to its people.

Persecution on the Island of Holy Cross

Carl Kierulff's house at 31 Strand Gade in St. Croix had become too cramped to serve as a meeting place for the growing group of Swedenborgians and was sold toward the end of his life. In their private quarters, the members could make arrangements for meeting places that, at most, accommodated assemblies and worship of seventy persons, and many were turned away for lack of space and remained standing outside. The Swedenborgians looked for new quarters, but everywhere met resistance from the churches and from the authorities. After the 1840s, the number of members increased sharply. The original nucleus of idealists and humanists of European ancestry was succeeded by people of African origin. These adherents held large meetings in secret in a school.

In a letter to Thomas Worcester of Boston, written on August 17, 1852, Elijah Bryan reported that it was the New Church Society on St. Croix that wanted Worcester to ordain him so that he could return and function fully as a minister there. Ever since the first organizational meeting on June 28, 1846, Bryan had at Kierulff's behest conducted worship according to the liturgy of the English New Church and the principles of the General Conference. The society was poor, he wrote: of the fifty who were baptized, only three were well to do. These were plantation owners—primarily Ruan, Henderson, and Johnson. Further, he wrote, there is a growing number of families of color, with simple artisans, seamstresses, cobblers, and firemen. New Swedenborgian names step to the front.

In addition to the influx of blacks after the emancipation, a growing number of Protestants began to show interest in Swedenborg's teachings, as was previously mentioned. This met with resistance from the traditional churches on the island. It was not just adult baptism, communion, and Sunday schools that Swedenborgians were involved in. They had also begun to hold funeral services. Many Swedenborgians were buried on plantations in the countryside, not in churchyards. Elijah Bryan's burial of Mary Johnson, a convert from an Anglican family, led to an overt schism with the English church.

The Danish pastor of the Lutheran church, Hother Hänschell of Church Street, also called the New Church activity into question, as is evidenced by letters dating from 1851. Bryan's lay spiritual activity came under attack, with greater determination to put a stop to it.

Pastor F. L. Hawley roused the Anglicans against the Swedenborgians and said that he needed only a sign to tear Bryan into ten thousand pieces![8] "I warn you," he shouted to Bryan, "never more to set foot on St. Croix, for if you do, I cannot answer for your safety," and he incited his flock against the Swedenborgians, whom he called wolves in sheep's clothing.

The businessman Johannes Zimmermann was driven from his shop and had to leave the island after the man who held his loan became aware that he was a Swedenborgian and, therefore, had no right to take out a loan. It was clear that the Anglican church lay behind this eviction, and a member of the church council warned anyone who converted to Swedenborgianism that "if they wish to have nothing to do with us, we will have nothing to do with them."

Under Hawley's leadership, the Episcopal church even attacked Bryan physically, but after protests from members of the society who increasingly turned against their leader's aggressiveness, he began to cast suspicion on Swedenborgianism, stressing its illegality, wrongfulness, and destructive immorality—and here the Anglican pastor made use of quotations from Swedenborg's book *Marital Love* as proof. Opponents, it seems, were also reading Swedenborg's writings, albeit with hostile intent. This is still another indication of how accessible Swedenborg's works were to people living in the Virgin Islands. Books like *True Christian Religion, Divine Providence,* and *Divine Love and Wisdom* had a wide circulation and were for some time common reading. Indeed, this reading included also the tomes of *Arcana Coelestia,* as is evident from John Bigelow's story, referred to in my introduction. Thus, when Swedenborgianism was attacked, the adversaries encountered a well-read enemy.

Bryan wrote in his reports published in *The Intellectual Repository* and *New Jerusalem Magazine* that New Church meetings were both public and private at one and the same time. Official permission to hold services had never been granted; however, the group's activities were not hindered by authorities. Indeed, this situation continued until the middle of the 1850s. After that, the enclave on St. Croix withdrew more and more. In spite of the new Danish constitution of 1849, with its decree of religious freedom,

Swedenborgians never received approval. The opposition in their surroundings did not relax, and little by little the whole meeting program collapsed. The only church with which the Swedenborgians were in good standing was the Hutterite Moravian church, which paid particular attention to schools and spiritual care for the black population. Like Swedenborg himself during his period of spiritual upheaval, the Swedenborgian church had friends among the Hutterites. In a sermon at the Central Moravian Church, Pastor Hartine preached to his congregation of black working folk, "There is a New religion come into the Island, but it is a Good religion."

As we have seen, the Swedenborgian congregation was formed on St. Croix in 1846 and met on a regular basis in spite of the fact that it was forbidden. Why would this group disregard the authorities? The answer may lie in the fact that, at this time, slavery had become a burning issue on the island and the public temper was near the boiling point. In 1847, slavery was abolished on St. Barthélemy. In 1848, slavery was abolished in the Virgin Islands. Meetings of Swedenborgians attracted more and more participants. On St. Croix there were as many African Swedenborgians as there were European, and on St. Thomas Swedenborgians were, in large measure, black. The original little white group had grown to a society that was predominantly black.

In the Eye of the Hurricane

We move ahead to the 1860s. The Swedenborgians had never gained official permission to secure themselves a site for public meetings. And after the climax surrounding the emancipation year 1848 and for a few years thereafter in the 1850s, activity to secure official recognition for the religion seemed gradually to fade away, partly because of opposition, partly to lighten the load. Elijah Bryan had moved his activity to St. Thomas. His health was declining.

This period ushered in social and economic upheaval. A time of frustration had begun that culminated in riots in the 1870s.

The sugar plantations were no longer profitable with a decently paid working force. The whole sugar economy, which had begun when Columbus brought sugar cane to the West Indies on his second voyage presupposed slavery. At the same time, in the middle of the nineteenth century, the price of sugar was gradually falling on the world market. The sugar beet, which was increasingly cultivated in Europe, heated up the competition. The West Indies would never recover: today there is still the debris of welfare in the slums, of devastated nature and expensive imports, with the primary source of income being periodic tourism. Voltaire in *Candide,* and after him Esaias Tegnér in his poem on "England and France," summed up the economy of the preceding epoch in a few words. As Tegnér wrote in 1828:

> The negroes are lashed to death, alas!
> To sugar your tea.

When I was searching through archival material in the Whim plantation on St. Croix, I found remarkable reminiscences in a tattered diary written by an active, radical, humanitarian advocate of equality of the 1860s, Rachel Wilson Moore. She and her husband, J. Wilson Moore, were acquainted with the Henderson family of planters, known in Swedenborgian circles and numbered among the friends of Governor Scholten. The plantation owner James G. Henderson was among those who signed letters both to the governor (concerning the official recognition of the New Church) and to the king, requesting Scholten's pardon and return to the island.[9]

Rachel Wilson Moore was a Quaker, a pastor in the Philadelphia Society of Friends, who organized public meetings in which she discussed social issues. In these papers, Moore recounts a meeting with R.G. Knight, owner of the Whim plantation where I sat and read her diary. During her period of lectures and revival meetings, she looked for suitable quarters for her talks, but she met everywhere with excuses. The governor had heard that she was touring around and talking about religion as well as about justice, politics, and morality and was arousing in-

terest among people with her strong social and spiritual message. Acting Governor Sharston warned her against holding
meetings out in the open, to keep the crowds from becoming
impossible to control, and he warned her against talking about
wages, since wages had to be determined by circumstances.

Moore turned to the liberal Hutterites, the Brethren, Zinzen-
dorf's oldest church in America, which had for a long time carried on humanitarian work among the black population and was
concerned with spiritual (but not social) liberation. She re-
quested space for her lectures, but the Hutterite pastor refused,
advising her that permission from the authorities was not to be
had. Ultimately, she received help from an unexpected source,
from a black man who led a Swedenborgian circle. Among Swedenborgians, Moore writes, she was considered neither subversive nor strange. The Swedenborgian remnant among the blacks
seemed still to be active on St. Croix at this time. She writes of a
family named Aarenstrup, a Danish name, but the family circle
she encountered was black. The Aarenstrups lived in Christiansted at 22 Kings Cross Street, that is, in the neighborhood
called Free Gut or Neger Gotted.

With the friendship of the Swedenborgians, Moore could
arrange her own meetings. She comments, "Our ideas about liberation rouse opposition among some, whereas for others they
are the most uplifting ideas in the world." Further, she began to
attend their meetings, as she did on February 21, 1864. She
writes, "They are a little company, the master of which was the
kind man who invited us to hold a meeting in his commodious
parlor, when we could obtain a place nowhere else. I felt it a
duty, and gave them, at the close some suitable counsel, which
was kindly received."

This meeting occurred almost forty years after Swedenborgianism first began to spread on the island, and this is the last
trace I have found of organized activity. By 1880, it all seems to
have faded away.

Despite good will from many quarters, the economic conditions on the islands precluded social reform. The Moores were
witnesses of the general decline both on the plantations and in

the towns where the destitute black population now began to gather. Then came several years of drought in the 1870s, which eventually triggered revolt and looting. When one of the Kierulff family was dispossessed of his house and shop in 1878 and the house was set ablaze on the night between October 1 and 2, along with large sections of the city of Fredriksted, a historical silence fell over the past years of struggle. Moore visited the Hanna's Rest plantation in Fredriksted, where the Swedenborgian Ruan family lived and where the workers were paid, but she saw decline there as well. In Christiansted and Fredriksted, Moore paints a picture of "poverty, distress, and wretchedness," a situation that continues into our own times and can be termed the poorhouse of the United States, where the hope of countless black families on the islands rests on vouchers.

In the course of the revolution of 1878, Vibe Kierulff's widow died, the beautiful Susanna Kerney Yackes, born in Bermuda in 1802. She was buried with her husband in the Lutheran churchyard on St. Croix, who had died in 1874. Their many children (fifteen or sixteen, of whom seven reached adult age) make it clear how the inheritance had been scattered, and the Swedenborgian tradition has now disappeared from the islands. Their daughter Rosamunde Vibe Kierulff died in 1900 in Colorado Springs, unmarried. Their daughter Cathrine Rebekka Kierulff died in California in 1901.

Emanuel Swedenborg Kierulff and his son Emanuel had long since been deceased. However, through the Kierulff family, we have been able to follow the traces of Swedenborgianism for three generations. Emanuel Swedenborg Kierulff's birth year, 1827, gives an indication of how early this current reached the islands.

The Lindberg (Linberg) family can also be traced back to the islands. Supreme Court Justice Jacob Lindberg (1745–1791) married Anna Caroline Heyliger (Krause), born in St. Eustasius, died in 1788. They lived on the Annaberg plantation on St. Croix, owned by the Krause family of King's Quarter, where Jacob Lindberg is also buried. His son was Henning Gottfried Lindberg (born in 1784), married to Mary Lindberg, née Mary

Mac Lachland. This couple became the first generation Sweden-borgians who were born in the Virgin Islands; their conviction is obvious from their collaboration with Sampson Reed of the New Jerusalem Church in Massachusetts. In the 1830s, "Henning Gotfried Linberg" was a widely known intellectual, known even to Ralph Waldo Emerson, who, with appreciation, read Lind-berg's translations of the lectures of the eclectic French philoso-pher Victor Cousin.

Persecution in the Virgin Islands led to Swedenborgianism on St. Croix gradually going underground and disappearing. When the Danish era ended in 1917, its time was wholly past. In the American Virgin Islands, one Swedenborgian or another has sur-faced from time to time.[10] But there is no more collective activ-ity among the resident population, and all the books and writings have vanished as individuals emigrated, or have been blown away by the roaring hurricanes that invade this quarter of the world at regular intervals, sinking boats and destroying houses, blowing hummingbirds with their nests into the sea, and shattering human destinies for ever. Not one full year of any of the old newspapers has come to light in the libraries.

Swedenborgianism in the West Indies is intimately bound up with one era in this turbulent history.

The Linberg, Kierulff, and Birch families, originally of Swedish, Norwegian, and Danish stock, who were at the head of New Church activity in the Danish West Indies, did not import their faith from Scandinavia but had received it indirectly from the New Church abroad. August Nordenskiöld had published his religious proclamation, *Församlingsformen i det Nya Jerusalem* in Copenhagen a half century earlier. But the Danish New Church Society, with its center in Copenhagen, goes back no further than 1871, and is therefore coeval with the New Church in Swe-den. The first Danish New Church Society—the first among Scandinavians—was the one that was founded in the West In-dies and that began its official activity on June 28, 1846, in the house of Carl Kierulff at 31 Strand Street in Christansted.

From a long historical distance, we can now glimpse the revolutionary spiritual and social power and meaning that

Swedenborgianism had among people of various backgrounds in a period of transition; we sense this in its life of destiny in the remote West Indies, far from the sites of their forefather's earthly homes.

In his 1852 history of the New Church, the Lund theologian and Swedenborgian Achatius Kahl remarked about Anders Johan von Höpken that "it was worth noting that the great statesman did not suggest Swedenborg's religious doctrines as appropriate for the state church in Sweden, but only as suitable for the colonies of émigrés from the motherland." The reason was, Kahl thought, that Höpken recognized "the obstacles which in the eighteenth century lay in the way of any dogmatic or liturgical improvement, however slight, in our church constitution."

Against the background of what we now know, Counsellor Höpken's proposal to the king of Sweden two centuries ago appears in a new light.

Revival and Reform in Russia

> *East is East, and West is West, and never the twain shall meet,*
> *Till Earth and Sky stand presently at God's great Judgment Seat.*
> RUDYARD KIPLING, *The Ballad of East and West*

As we move through time, our picture of the world changes, since the perspectives move with us, and reality is in a state of flux. And sometimes things take a different turn than one expected and hoped for.

Turning back to the English *New Church Magazine* of 1917 and 1918, we find that the Russian revolution was met with great expectations. Some of the Russian revolutionaries, in their turn, looked back and discovered that they had nineteenth-century forerunners. In 1925 the centenary of the Decembrist uprising was celebrated in the Soviet Union, and several books and documents were published that revealed that many of these revolutionary precursors were pious Christians, freemasons, theosophists, and Swedenborgians. In addition, these sources revealed that the radical reform of 1861, the Emancipation of the Serfs, was propelled and inspired by Russian Swedenborgians.

"Revival and Reform in Russia: Notes on Radical Humanism and New Church Spirituality from the Decembrist Conspiracy to the Emancipation of the Serfs" was first delivered as a lecture in St. Petersburg and Moscow in September 1991. It was first published in English in *The New Philosophy* 43, no. 4 (Oct.–Dec. 1990: 391–407; and has appeared in German: "Russland, Swedenborg und der Geist des Ostens," *Offen Tore* 3 (1991): 94–107.

This story hints that human history is not written in the stars, but perpetually is passing crossroads. Another—perhaps a better and more beneficial—path could have been chosen in the past, but somewhere the track was lost.

The Meeting between East and West

Peter the Great once breached the wall of Greek Orthodoxy and Russian isolation, but even before his time, Western European literature had entered Russia, often via Poland and the Ukraine. For instance, Thomas a Kempis' *De Imitatio Christi* and the writings of Jakob Boehme were translated and circulated as early as the seventeenth century. Toward the end of the eighteenth century, many translations of religious literature came from a circle led by the publisher Nikolai Ivanovich Novikov— works such as those by Angelus Silesius and the Swabian mysticist Friedrich Christoph Oetinger (1702–1782), the well-known German correspondent and translator of Emanuel Swedenborg. In the beginning of the nineteenth century, Aleksandr I became interested in the writings of Johann Heinrich Jung-Stilling (1740–1817), who was published in various Russian editions.[1] Western transcendental philosophy and mysticism increasingly attracted influential writers, philosophers, theologians, scholars, and critics—the Aksakovs, Bakunin, Herzen, Belinsky. Interest focused on writers like Kant, Schelling, Fourier, and Hegel, but no less upon Franz von Baader, G.H. von Schubert, Boehme, Saint-Martin, Jung-Stilling, and Swedenborg. There were numerous circles, societies, and movements. A member of the westernist circle around Semyon Egorovich Raich (Amfiteatrov), who was also a member of the radical Decembrist society known as the Union of Welfare (founded and led by Aleksandr Muravyov) and president of the Society of Wisdom Lovers (1823–1825) was Prince Vladímir Odóevsky (1803–1869). This central figure in Russian philosophical romanticism and humanism was especially drawn to science and mysticism, and studied Swedenborg, Saint-Martin, Boehme, and Baader. After the Decembrist uprising in 1825, the members of the Society of

Wisdom Lovers destroyed the protocols of the society and partly became a dispersed underground movement. Odóevsky moved to St. Petersburg and would, as a public servant, contribute to public education and musical culture in Russia. He is also known for stories with a mystical bent, such as "Cosmorama"(1840), "The Possessed"(1842), and his utopian vision "The Year 4338." Other influential figures of the westernist currents of the century were Nikolai Strakhov, a philosophical mentor of Dostoevsky and Tolstoí; the spiritualist Aleksandr Aksakov, who translated Swedenborg into Russian;[2] and the great Ukrainian philosopher Pamphil Danilovich Yurkevich, who called Boehme, Leibniz, and Swedenborg the last great philosophers of the West.

Yurkevich was the teacher of Vladimir Solovyov (1853–1900), who is said to be fictionalized as Alyosha in *The Brothers Karamazov*. The visionary eclectic philosophy of Solovyov is reflected not only in Dostoevsky but as much in the religious thinking of the twentieth-century anti-utilitarian Russian exile Nikolai Aleksandrovich Berdyaev (1874–1948); in the modern symbolism of Bulgákov, Bély, and Blok; in the essays of Dmitry Merezhkovsky; and in the variety of the modern religious revival, in such figures as Pavel Florensky and Evgeny Trubetskóy. Solovyov drew much from Boehme, Paracelsus, Swedenborg, Gnosticism, and the Kabbalah for his organicist dualism, where the material is conceived as a reflection of an eternal reality and where love is perceived as the prime force of being.

The supernatural and spiritual elements in the writings of the "national poet" Aleksandr Sergeevich Pushkin are obvious. Pushkin actually quotes and cites Swedenborg as early as 1833, in his prose work *The Queen of Spades*. That short story impressed Dostoyevsky deeply; to him the protagonist Hermann was a "colossal figure" who later inspired him in his creation of Raskolnikov.

If Solovyov served as model for Dostoevsky's Alyosha (and echoes from him perhaps are audible also in Ivan's trenchant debates with the Grand Inquisitor), Emanuel Swedenborg partly seems to have been a prototype for another leading figure in *The*

Brothers Karamazov, Alyosha's holy mentor Zosíma. The profound influence of Swedenborg on Dostoevsky has been shown in essays by Nobel laureate Czeslaw Milosz, one of Swedenborg's many perceptive academic readers in Poland, where Swedenborg's influence on romantics and symbolists ranges from the mysticist Andrzéj Towiański to the national poet Adam Mickiewicz.[3]

Dostoevsky, like many of his contemporaries at home and abroad, was interested in all the mystical literature he could get his hands on, and his library included the Russian translations of Swedenborg, Aleksandr Aksakov's classic work on spiritualism, and studies on animal magnetism and other psychic and spiritual phenomena. For example, at one of Aleksandr Aksakov's seances, we find Dostoevsky and Solovyov attending. Yet Dostoevsky saw himself as a realist in literature and an orthodox Christian in belief. To him, that was no contradiction.

Religion and Politics

When Aleksandr Herzen died in 1870, Dostoevsky wrote in a letter to Nikolai Strakhov that Herzen was "a poet without peer."[4] Dostoevsky also mentions Tolstoí and Leóntiev among those who were influenced by Herzen's ideas. Until his departure from Russia in 1847, Herzen belonged to a group of young writers that included Dostoevsky, Turgenev, and Ivan Aleksandrovich Goncharóv. Their education combined Western and Russian culture. At Moscow University, Herzen became a member of the radical circle of students inspired by Fourier, Saint-Simon, and other utopian philosophers. These students were arrested in 1833, and Herzen served a sentence of internal exile in the cities of Perm and Vyatka in Siberia. In the next decade a similar fate befell Dostoevsky, who also had gone through a phase of admiration for Fourier and membership in an underground organization. One of Herzen's friends in the exile was the architect and mysticist Aleksandr Lavrentevich Vitberg. A Swedish national, Vitberg was born in Russia. His artistic talent and the mystic tinge of his convictions impressed Tsar Aleksandr Vitberg inspired Herzen with the visionary symbolism of

Swedenborg, Paracelsus, and masonic literature. Thus, in Siberia too, convicts pondered upon Swedenborg, as can be seen from Herzen's memoirs.[5] Underground movements and *samizdat* literature have ancient roots in Russia.

Among the insurgent Decembrists were members of the Muravyov family, a prominent *dvorianstvo* family of nobles and landed gentry that had roots in Russian Swedenborgianism. The Decembrist leader Nikita Mikhailovich Muravyov, one of those commemorated in 1925 and later memorialized in an official biography,[6] was a member of the supreme *duma* and early on had drafted the constitution of the future Russian state; he also wrote a tract, *Curious Conversation*, in which he used quotations from the Bible, from the Gospels especially, to argue the need for an uprising against despotism. After the Decembrist uprising, he (like Dostoevsky later on) was imprisoned in the Peter and Paul Fortress in St. Petersburg and sentenced to death—reprieved to twenty years of hard labor in work camps, during which time he died (in Irkutsk in 1835). Sergei Ivanovich Muravyov-Apostol, another radical born in the early 1790s, was among the five leaders of the Decembrist uprising who were hanged in 1826. Nikolai Nikolaevich Muravyov (later remembered as the heroic "Karskii") supported the emancipation of peasants and protected Decembrist exiles; later he was discharged from the army and fell into disgrace.

Nikolai's brother, Aleksandr Nikoláevich Muravyov (1792–1863), an acquaintance of Herzen, also spent years of his life in Siberia. Muravyov was the most prominent and active New Churchman in Russia. He was graduated from Moscow University in 1810, served in the War of 1812 and in the military campaigns of the following years, became a colonel, and was a founder of the Union of Salvation in 1816. More and more turning to radical and humanitarian political activism, he was one of the founders of the Union of Welfare in 1818 and became leader of the union's Moscow branch. This secret society was the fire's center in the Decembrist uprising of 1825. In 1826 Muravyov was sentenced to exile in Siberia in the aftermath of the revolt. From 1828 on he held a succession of administrative posts in

different parts of the country, and under supervision of Aleksandr II was actively involved in the drafting of the peasant reform of 1861, which abolished serfdom and allotted land to
country people and farm workers. The "losers" were the gentry,
among them many of the reformers themselves (the Muravyovs,
for instance, had maintained ancient boyar traditions). This radical humanism is a central theme in Dostoevsky and Tolstoí. The
English New Churchman Jonathan Bayley, a personal friend of
Aleksandr Nikolaevich Muravyov, compared the events in Russia
to the contemporary Civil War in the United States:

> How grand is the contrast of Russia freeing her 25 millions of
> serfs peaceably, bearing the burden and patiently working to
> make the glorious effort successful, to the frantic efforts of the
> slave-holders of America, by rebellion, by war, by universal
> wreck,[. . .] Nothing could surpass the joy of Mouravieff on the
> glorious morning of the emancipation day, though it took away
> probably half his property.[7]

Jonathan Bailey wrote a memoir and obituary of Aleksandr
Muravyov in 1865.[8] From this article, we learn much about Muravyov's love for the principles of the New Church, which Muravyov had cherished for thirty years. Muravyov had first read
Swedenborg's *Doctrine of Life* in French (*Doctrine de la Vie pour la
Nouvelle Jérusalem*, Paris 1822), which he bought in a bookseller's
shop in Moscow, had become profoundly interested, and afterwards read all of Swedenborg's works in French or in Latin. His
attraction to the principles of the New Church was in harmony
with his love of freedom and rights of all people. Bayley thought
that was a natural result of Swedenborg's teachings, which declare "that man should act from liberty according to reason" and
that, without these two faculties, a human being "cannot be reformed and regenerated." This is indeed a point of consequence,
since there is no place for any natural right at all unless the
moral value of individual freedom is recognized. Freedom was
accordingly conceived as a condition for amelioration. Consequently, the serfdom of so many of his countrymen was most

repugnant to people like Muravyov, who urged full freedom to ensure progress and perfection among a people. He was fully aware that the transition to full social freedom would entail loss upon the landowners, and he did not hide that fact when he tried to persuade others. On the contrary he felt and urged upon all the conviction that, in due time, all would reap a rich reward—as the result of doing right!

First having been met by contempt and hatred by the powerful classes, gradually the cause of Muravyov and like-minded persons had at heart commended itself to other earnest and pious minds, then to more, and, finally, to the tsar himself. In 1858 a committee was appointed in Nizhniy Novgorod (called Gorky during the Soviet era) to prepare for emancipation. Muravyov, the governor of the province, presided over the committee. In his opening speech, delivered on February 19, 1858, Muravyov urged the members "to enter fully into the spirit of your exalted mission," making the following statement, which Bayley quotes in its entirety.

> You have been chosen to be the messengers of Him in whose hands are the hearts of kings, that you may realize those divine words pronounced by Himself: "Bind up the broken-hearted: proclaim deliverance to the captives" (St. Luke IV,18,19). Since such is your mission, think of the august part you have been called upon to fill among men. Show yourself not unworthy of it. Do not permit your personal or your material interests to sway you in the work you have to accomplish. Permit not, I say, these interests to weigh with you over the well-being of those who have been confided to your generous cares. Surely material interests ought to yield to moral interests! Ought you not to prove this by your own acts? I have said moral interests: yes, gentlemen, the solution of the question which occupies us will raise us assuredly to a higher degree of moral civilization, it will elevate the glory and raise higher the moral dignity of the class called to accomplish this work with self-denial based upon a consciousness of the rights of man. . . .
>
> But we shall not succeed so long as we regard man as a mere producing animal. We can only succeed by restoring human

dignity, so long stifled, and invoking the aid of free labour. It can only be when an intelligent and equitable appeal, derived of all arbitrary command, shall call forth the living forces of the nation, and breathe new life into what now appears so dead. Now, then, separate from your calculations, however material, a respect for the rights of man. Render to man what belongs to man, and you will justify the confidence of the sovereign and the hope of the nation. . . . History will rank you amongst the promoters of justice, and of the love of the neighbour.

This committee, among others, paved the way for emancipation, and on the same day three years later, February 19, 1861, the peasant reform was an accomplished fact—perhaps less radical, though, than Muravyov had hoped for.

By the time of the emancipation of the serfs, Muravyov was nearly seventy years old; two years later he died, after having been seriously ill for a couple of months. Bayley recounts that Muravyov used to hear the Gospel and the Psalms every day, in the translation he himself had made twenty-seven years ago. He received the Holy Sacrament three times during his illness, and the priest who assisted him is said to have been edified by his pious and enlightened conversation. Bayley, who was a close friend of the family, states that the general was satisfied that he would not recover; on the border of death he had glimpses of angelic joy: "Some days before his departure he experienced so delightful a state of mind that he said it was just as if he had been conveyed to a brighter region, where all within and around him was sweetness and blessedness." Aleksandr Muravyov died on December 18, 1863, at 2 P.M., at the age of 71.[9]

Muravyov had devoted himself to the history of the Russian church after his exile to Siberia, and had resumed, quietly but persistently, his activity for the heavenly doctrines of Swedenborg, employing two persons in producing *samizdat* copies of Swedenborg's writings, which he distributed among family members, relatives, and friends. For that reason the name Muravyov is paramount to the history of Russian Swedenborgianism and New Jerusalem humanism. At the same time, Muravyov held an administrative post as a layman in the orthodox church. To him this dual allegiance was not a contradiction. On the contrary, he felt strongly that the creeds supported each other, a fact that can be seen from the pamphlet *Introduction au Journal: "Orient et Swedenborg,"* printed in London for distribution among Russian readers. There were no indications as to the author or any year of publication. It was humbly signed a *"Lecteur Orthodoxe des Écrits de Swédenborg."* While the journal never actually appeared, the pamphlet was printed and distributed. An annotated translation of that introduction appeared in *The Intellectual Repository* (London) in 1872, and the same year a translation was also published in the Swedish journal *Ett Kristligt Sändebud* (A New Church Messenger, [Uppsala]), edited by Anna Fredrika Ehrenborg. As can be seen from a communication published earlier the same year under the heading "Miscellaneous" in the *Repository*, it is obvious that the author of the pamphlet was the Princess Kleopatra Mikhailovna Shakhovskaya (1809–1883).[10] Kleopatra's father was the brigadier Prince Mikhail Aleksandrovitj Shakhovskoí (1758–1817), and she was General Aleksandr Muravyov's devoted sister-in-law, one of numerous Swedenborgians among his relatives.

The Ecumenical Power of AGAPE

In the pamphlet, Kleopatra Shakhovskaya regards Swedenborg from an Eastern point of view, *ex oriente*, perceiving a convergency between New Church and Orthodox theology. She points out that to study the writings of Swedenborg

that protest, as sublime as it is profound, against the West, may show the East precisely in what the corruption of the Western world consists. . . . If regarded from a point of view neither Protestant nor Catholic, Swedenborg would be a real acquisition to the whole Christian world. He would conjoin that which is still new in the West with that which is already old in the East. This manner of considering Swedenborg would revive the languishing life of brotherly love amongst Christians, divided as they are by all kinds of religious disputes, polemics, and hostilities. There would arise from the East and from the West worthy representatives of this new Christian love, not from the narrow official and despotic forms of an impossible union amongst religious professions, but in the spirit of mutual and universal love—that beneficent and overflowing love without which all languishes and dies. . . . The West has turned away from the ancient Christian simplicity and clearness, and confirmed this deviation by every species of casuistic and scholastic argument. The man of the West, be he Catholic or Protestant, brought up in these vitiated principles, sucks in with his mother's milk this destructive leaven. . . . This incurable evil of the spirit, not having given away to the offered remedies of science, and advancing with frightful rapidity, first reached on the one hand the so-called Œcumenical Council of Nice, and on the other moved onwards towards destruction in *faith without works*, free inquiry, predestination. In this last extremity, the West lost all true faith, retaining only a blind faith, a belief in rationalism, that negation of all faith. . . . Swedenborg is, as the East itself, a high protest against the West. . . . The principles of the New Church, as it is so called by Swedenborg, are entirely the same as those of the Eastern Orthodoxy, with the difference only of the particular tinge which these principles borrowed in passing through the mind. . . . (1) That Eastern orthodoxy is as far from being inclined in favor of Tritheism as in favor of that incredulity [*incrédulité*] which denies the tri-hypostatic unity of the Incarnate Divinity, with which Swedenborg so vehemently reproaches the West. (2) That Eastern orthodoxy has never separated faith from love, more especially as it has never made a blind faith the leading principle of the church. (3) That active repentance and amendment of life have always been considered as forming the fundamental basis of salvation, according to the two great commandments of the law of love manifested in good works, without which all faith is dead. (4) That the Holy Scriptures, as well as the two Commandments on which hang all the law and the prophets, were always considered by the Eastern orthodoxy as divine revelation, containing a high and divine meaning deeply concealed under the letter, which the Lord alone from time to time reveals to some just and holy men, and it is precisely on this knowledge that the whole tradition of the church reposes. . . . The false Western interpretation of the Œcumenical Symbol, explained in the sense of Tritheism, was condemned in the East as early as in the fourth century, in the anathema pronounced upon the heresy of John Philopone, who came from Athens to the West at the time of Boethius. . . . (5) That eternal blessedness or eternal misery is the lot of those who live conformably or contrary to the precepts of orthodoxy, as stated above, and without which there is no salvation for the Christian—is it not in effect what the New Church of Swedenborg teaches? . . . If any one desires to refute the doctrine of Swedenborg in its very basis, he must begin by destroying the very fundamental principles of the orthodox doctrine.

Now, she proclaims, "the ferment is cast in, the impulse is given, and freedom of thought, speech, and conscience—that true and powerful companion of this new era—opens the very depths of the human mind for the reception of regenerative truth."

Kleopatra Mikhailovna Shakhovskaya's words represent a current of the age, where reform was tantamount to revival. Focusing, like Dostoevsky and other contemporaries, on fraternity, Christian love or *agape* was the bond of union and the order of the day. August Tholander, a Swedish artist and philanthropist who had settled in Russia in 1861, when "the great hour struck," picked up something of the spirit of the age in his essays published in Moscow: "The revealed light of Christ has liberated you from the villenage of laws, and made you into a slave under love."[11] Freemasons, spiritualists and Swedenborgians among the reform movements had referred to Christ's gospel of love, which unified and called for active amendment. The Swedenborgian impact seems to have served as a catalyst for a revivifying of orthodox doctrines. Swedenborg was actually received as an anti-westernist.

At the age of seventy-five, in 1883, the Princess Shakhovskaya died in Moscow. That year was in reality a centennial, since the first circle of Swedenborg readers in Moscow was formed as early as 1783. Information on that circle was first given in the Swedish Swedenborgian journal *Samlingar för Philantroper* (The Philantropist's Library) in 1787, the source probably being Bénédict Chastanier. The *New Jerusalem Magazine* (London) reported in 1790 that "a society of the friends of the New Doctrine had begun about the year 1783 to meet at Moscow, but the tyrannical and impious principles of the Empress have given rise to some persecution." The journal continued, however: "Certain accounts are received from Poland, that a great number of professors of the New Doctrine are to be found in that country, and some also in Constantinople. . . ."

The "oriental" church, with its original center in the old Byzantium (today Istanbul), had gradually parted from Western Christianity when the Roman Empire was divided into a western and an eastern part. The divorce became final, resulting in mutual anathemas, at the close of the first millennium. The Orthodox Church keeps firmly to its own interpretation of the first theological extension of the Apostolic Church, the *symbolum nicæno-constantinopolitanum;* this church is rather built on tradition and cult than on sophisticated theology. The name "Orthodox" indicates its ancient character, its roots in primitive Christianity. In concord with that attitude, Swedenborg, in his outline of a new church history in 1770, aimed at showing how the creed of the "Ancient Church" had gradually been corrupted by theological dogma. To one of his closest contemporary followers among theologians, Gabriel Beyer, he declared: "I keep to the Apostolic church."

The Russian Orthodox monk "Oronoskow"—whom Swedenborg met according to the extant documents concerning Swedenborg's life—was in reality Ioaniki Goroneskul, the influential pastor of the Russian Orthodox Church in Stockholm from 1764 to 1769. In his memoirs, Carl Robsahm recalls a dinner with the French-speaking Goroneskul, Swedenborg, and the Swedish diplomats Edvard Carleson and Carl Reinhold Berch, who had both traveled widely in Russia. Goroneskul had read Swedenborg's works and was moved to tears when Swedenborg reported to him on the celestial state of the late Empress Elizaveta Petrovna, so dear to this imperial representative. Goroneskul was not only an Orthodox reader of Swedenborg in

Latin; he obviously believed in Swedenborg. Indeed, Goroneskul may be considered the first Russian Swedenborgian.

In 1769 Goroneskul returned to St. Petersburg, where Swedenborg's *Opera Philosophica et Mineralia* had long ago been met with academic enthusiasm—for that reason the *Bolshaya sovetskaya entsiklopediya* pointed out in its entry on Swedenborg, that "in 1734 he was elected an honorary member of the St. Petersburg Academy of Sciences." In that capital, a circle of readers, something of a society, was in existence in the beginning of the nineteenth century. This is known since these readers ordered as many of the works in French that were obtainable.

A few years afterwards, about 1809, St. Petersburg was visited by the Metropolitan Filaret (1782–1867), who is well known for his fight against serfdom and for his works in defense of the Eastern Church. In the holy synod, people approached him and asked him to read Swedenborg. In fact, he did read Swedenborg's writings, and said that he could not find anything in them that contradicted Greek Orthodox views.

Kleopatra Shakhovskaya never separated herself from the Russian Orthodox church, nor did Muravyov or any other readers of Swedenborg's writings in Russia. Shakhovskaya deplored the increase of sects. To her English friend William Mather, who met her during his repeated visits to Moscow from the 1860s and onwards, she often expressed the opinion that New Church truths would be stifled within the walls of a sectarian organization. "Her conviction was," Mather recalls in retrospect, "that all forms of religious worship were capable of being filled with the 'Spirit which giveth life,' and she certainly never experienced any antagonism between her entire belief in the truths propounded by Swedenborg (whose writings she knew almost by heart) and the forms of worship she joined in, of the Greek Church."[12]

In fact, the very essence of Swedenborgianism is ecumenical or universalist, since its emphasis is on morality, not on creed. In one of the texts that in different ways reached Russian readers, *Of the New Jerusalem and Its Heavenly Doctrine*, it is stated: "The Lord's Church is with all in the whole world, who live in good according to their own faith." Doing right means living in truth. To Mather, Shakhovskaya's own moral commitment was evident from the fact that she gave her whole heart and mind to the work for equality reforms. Concerning the Shakhovskoi family, Mather wrote, "The seeds of truth never fell on better ground or brought forth more blessed fruit." Though full emancipation of the serfs would mean impoverishment to these noble people,

> they pursued their object with the utmost enthusiasm and self-sacrifice. They were joined by others who were inspired by their zeal. The Emperor Alexander gained courage and firmness by such support, and finally within a space of two years granted freedom to millions of human beings, whose class had for centuries been bondsmen and slaves. I made the acquaintance of this distinguished family in the midst of these events, and saw the old General with his whole family circle, and the Princess Schahoffskoy, relinquish the luxury of the high estate in which they had been born and lived, for the humble dwelling and simplest habits of life. . . . It was my happy lot after this to spend many Sundays in the family circle from year to year during my visits to Moscow. The sphere of the household was heavenly. The princess, though physically a great sufferer, was the centre and moving spirit of it. Her remarkable spiritual insight touched everything with its charm. Her conversational powers were so rare, that she could expound the Scripture by the science of Correspondences with a force and vividness I have never heard excelled. . .—the all-encircling love with which she soothed, comforted, and cheered—the goodness that shone on her countenance . . . rendered visible and real to all around her the Beatitude: "Blessed are the pure in heart, for they shall see God."

Mather further describes the princess as "distinguished for those accomplishments which not unfrequently grace the highest society in that country, particularly in the knowledge of languages and the literature of all European countries." When she was still wealthy, the princess "had travelled much in Italy, France, and Germany; and though never having been in England, her knowledge of the language and profound admiration of English institutions [such as the Parliament] caused her ever to regard our country with the deepest interest." Kleopatra Shakhovskaya, Mather concluded in his obituary, "became a patriot in the highest sense of the word, in advocating reforms which she felt to be absolutely essential to the progress and civilization of the Russian people."

The mobility, geographical as well as cultural, described by Mather in his tribute, is the reason that Swedenborg's writings, which were not available in Russian editions until the late-nineteenth century, first of all were received among the aristocracy; they certainly did not serve as an "opium" for the people. On his visit to Russia in 1866, Jonathan Bayley met with five Swedenborgian princesses. At the same time he observed that Swedenborgians had induced the tsar to consider the abolition of serfdom and had advocated many other reforms; he also noted that there was at that time a commission for instituting just laws, of which an unidentified New Churchman was a principal proponent and another New Churchman in St. Petersburg was one of the commission's judges. The basic ideology of his Russian friends, Bayley believed, could be summarized by the words of the Lord to the faithful: "All of you are brethren."

Having such New Church friends in Russia, some of whom were well known to the bishops, Bayley on his visit to St. Petersburg in 1866 was admitted to the holiest place of St. Isaac's Cathedral, behind the Iconostasis, and procured admittance to every part of the imperial palace, which was closed to the public. However, he also reported that Swedenborg's works were still mostly read in French. "They cannot yet print them there, but while I was at Moscow it was announced that a Russian translation of the 'Heaven and Hell' had arrived in Russia, having been printed at Leipzig, in Germany; copies of it were on sale in St. Petersburg."[13]

That translation was made by the Russian spiritualist Aleksandr Aksakov. It was a copy of that book Aksakov's interested friend, Fyodor Dostoevsky, procured for his library.

Russian Apocalypse

In an extensive article on Swedenborg, written for the 1900 edition of the *Brockhaus-Ephron Encyclopedia* [Russian], Vladimir Solovyov mentioned the writer Vladimir Ivanovich Dal' (1801–1872) as an example of Swedenborg's literary influence.

Aleksandr Vasilievich Nikitenko, in his well-known *Dnevnik* (Diary) also noted Vladimir Dal's mystical inclination and his passion for spiritualism, remarking that, since the early 1850s, Dal' had been a follower of Swedenborg. In 1852, in Niznij-Novgorod, Dal' had unriddled the apocalypse with the help of Swedenborgian hermeneutics. In his *Razoblacheniya* (1883), Aksakov recalled Dal's presence at his seances in 1876 and 1877, as well as the presence of Dostoevsky and Solovyov, as has been already mentioned.

From the papers and collections of the historian and editor Mikhail Petrovich Pogodin, we know that Dal' some time after his move to Moscow in 1859 had left his Swedenborgian manuscript on the apocalypse with Pogodin; it was to remain unpublished in the archives of Pogodin, who died in 1875, a few years after the death of Dal'.

Swedenborg's works could not be published in Russia, due to the censorship, nor could Dal's Swedenborgian inquiry into the deeper meaning of the Apocalypse. Aksakov's translation of *Heaven and Hell* was published in Leipzig. Kleopatra Mikhailovna Shakhovskaya's Russian translation of parts of *True Christian Religion* was printed, at her own expense, in London 1872. Dal's fascination with Swedenborgian revelation and piety was only indirectly reflected in his published writings.[14]

But where did Dal's unpublished manuscript go?

A fair copy, intended for reading or publication, was offered to the Swedenborg Society in London by a private person in 1888. We can see a report on this in the Swedenborg Society minutes of that year. Among other manuscripts we find "the Apocalypse interpreted according to the spiritual sense by Vladimir Dal'." This manuscript is still buried in the archives. I happened to recognize the anonymous text when I was looking for other Russian material. I made a copy and later paved the way for a Russian edition.

Dal's Swedenborgian interpretation of the apocalypse has the form of an analytic dictionary and is derived from Swedenborg's works on the apocalypse, such as *The Apocalypse Revealed* and *The Apocalypse Explained*. It was compiled during the years Dal' spent with Aleksandr Muravyov in the provincial ministry of Nizhniy Novgorod,[15] and this uncollected work shows that Solovyov's view of Dal' was more well-informed than anyone has imagined.

In Search of Robsahm's Memories

$\mathcal{I}$n Martin Walser's contemporary novel *A Runaway Horse*,[1] about two couples who meet at a resort, the name "Swedenborg" suddenly comes up during a mealtime conversation. One of the principal characters, who is blessed with a ravenous appetite, reminds himself, in the presence of his offended spartan and puritanical companions, of Swedenborg's call vision. The great Swedish philosopher was sitting by himself, eating his dinner in a London hotel. "Suddenly he saw a man in the corner of the room who said to Swedenborg, 'Do not eat so much.'"

Now we turn the clock back a hundred years—to Camden, New Jersey, where the aged Walt Whitman is talking with his friend Horace Traubel about everything from heaven to hell. "America's singer" states that his own life experience has confirmed Swedenborg's pronouncements. Much earlier in his life, he had run across Swedenborg's call to be an interpreter of the

Translated from the original Swedish by George F. Dole. "In Search of Robsahm's Memories" was first published in Swedish as an introduction to the annotated critical edition of Robsahm's memorandum, Anders Hallengren, ed., *Anteckningar om Swedenborg* (Skrifter utgivna av Föreningen Swedenborgs Minne: Stockholm, 1989), 5–21. It was first published in English in *Studia Swedenborgiana* 9, no. 1 (October 1994): 27–43.

Bible, "a historic event" that happened in "somewhat comical" fashion, the "most unromantic and vulgar" circumstances: toward the end of a meal in an inn in London. Whitman understood this in terms of himself. Like Ralph Waldo Emerson earlier, he had become aware of the divine presence precisely in the most everyday things.[2]

Now back in time another half century, to the literarily influential German politician and writer Joseph von Görres and his critique of Swedenborg, published in 1827, *Swedenborg, seine Visionen und sein Verhältnis zur Kirche*. Von Görres, an honestly searching Catholic, concedes that this very call vision speaks for Swedenborg's honesty and passion for truth: it gives the impression of authenticity. A charlatan, von Görres asserts, would have come up with a more evocative and dazzling introduction to his visions![3]

This vision has, of course, central importance and, as we can see from these examples, has played a decisive role in the way Swedenborg has been accepted throughout the world. What, however, is the source of this vision, which occurred in London in the spring of 1745? No complete account is found in Swedenborg's own writings, only some memoranda of an accountant, Carl Robsahm, who as a boy lived next door to Swedenborg and became a friend. His father, the banker Christer Robsahm, made Swedenborg's acquaintance in the course of buying property near Zinkensdamm in Stockholm in1736.[4]

Robsahm! The name constantly crops up in international literature about Swedenborg. Carl Robsahm's reminiscences about Swedenborg are a central Swedenborgian document, number five in Rudolf Leonard Tafel's *Documents*.[5] In a German translation by the Lund theologian Achatius Kahl (1794–1888), who owned the original Robsahm manuscript, Robsahm's memoir had been published by Immanuel Tafel in 1842 in his German collection of documents.[6] The previous year, something called "Anecdotes collected by Mr. Robsahm" was published in the English edition of Immanuel Tafel's collection. However, as R. L. Tafel noted, this was not Robsahm's reminiscences, the actual memoirs, but something completely different. The description of Swedenborg is assembled from all over, in part but by no means always in connection with Robsahm. And there are many examples of this sort.[7] We have at the outset, then, to deal with a pseudo-Robsahm as well as an actual one.

Carl Robsahm (1735–1794) was an accountant in the "Loanbank" [*Lån-banquen*][8] in Stockholm.[9] After Swedenborg's death, on the order of the writer Carl Fredrik Nordenskiöld (1756–1828), who was in regular contact with the influential Abbé Antoine-Joseph Pernety,[10] a librarian of Frederick the Great, Robsahm began to write down what he had seen and heard during his dealings with Swedenborg. The eminent miner August Nordenskiöld, who together with his brother was one of the most enthusiastic devotees of Swedenborg in Sweden at that time (and who ended his days as an alchemist and utopian seeker in West Africa), long planned to publish a collection of texts in Swedenborg's memory. A proposed title was *Efterrättelse om Em. Swedenborg och alla hans så väl tryckta som otryckta arbeten, jämte åtskilliga samtida mäns omdömen om honom* [A Guide to Em. Swedenborg and All His Works, Published and Unpublished, Together with Evaluations of Him by Various Contemporary Individuals].

Robsahm is thought to have written down his memoir in 1782.[11] However, the intended publication never appeared, though the Nordenskiöld brothers, and especially Pernety, availed themselves of the material in other contexts, and his own international connections provoked reports from Robsahm circulating abroad—as we saw in the case of von Görres.[12] Until recently, Robsahm's widely discussed memoir about Swedenborg had not been published in book form in Sweden. On the other hand, Tafel's complaint can easily be dismissed: Robsahm's memoir was printed serially shortly afterwards in the first year of *Skandinavisk Nykyrk-Tidning*, published in Stockholm in 1876, from a copy made by Consul Fredrik L. Cöster in London.

Abroad, Robsahm was widely known and cited at that time. Anecdotes from Robsahm recurred in print as early as 1784 in *An Eulogium on the lately deceased Mr. Emanuel Swedenborg . . . to which is added a Variety of Anecdotes and Observations . . .* , published by Robert Hindmarsh in London; and major parts of the memorandum were published in the newly founded *New-Jerusalem Magazine* in London in 1790. When the learned New Churchman David George Goyder brought out *A Concise History of the New Jerusalem Church* in 1827, he quoted Robsahm as a matter of course.

In the United States, the memoir is adduced and cited in Nathaniel Hobart's *Life of Emanuel Swedenborg*.[13] The memoir was the most important biographical source for Hobart's fellow college student Ralph Waldo Emerson in his influential essay, "Swedenborg; or, the Mystic" in *Representative Men* (printed in 1849). In the same year, Emerson's English friend James John Garth Wilkinson published *Emanuel Swedenborg: A Biography*, where Robsahm's recollection is a central document. The same holds true for William White's *Emanuel Swedenborg: His Life and Writings*, vols. 1 and 2, published in London in 1867; and, in German, it is basic to Johann Gottlieb Mittnacht's *Emanuel Swedenborgs Leben & Lehre*, Frankfurt am Main, 1880.

But where did the original manuscript come to rest? It was not among the papers of the former owner Achatius Kahl in the library of Lund University; only the German translation is found in that repository. The Royal Library in Stockholm owns a copy made by the printer and circuit court notary Carl Erik Deleen (1767–1850), acquired from his estate in 1850.[14] The Swedenborg collections in the Royal Academy of Sciences and in the Stockholm University Library also lack further information, and so does the Nordenskiöld Frugårds Archive. In the manuscript collection of the National Archives, splendidly arranged by Helge Almquist, Robsahm's memoir on Swedenborg appears as No. 169, a manuscript acquired from Christian Hammer's famous collection of holographs in 1939. But the handwriting alone excludes any possibility that this was written by a mature official in the 1780s, and in this text many of Robsahm's kinfolk and acquaintances are wrongly named. A marginal entry gives a hint that this is a copy that comes from the eccentric chancellery clerk Johan Erik Dybeck (1806–1853), whose interest in these matters can be seen from, among other things, the Swedenborg volumes that belonged to him.[15] Still, the intriguing question remains: what was Dybeck's version copied from?

Other archival collections give a unanimous answer to this primary question, an answer from our "national register," that is, Otto Walde's register of private archives, where the manuscript's place of storage is indicated with the alarming question, "Where is this memoir?"

One answer is London. In a volume of manuscripts, D/27, in the archives of the Swedenborg Society in Bloomsbury, there is a forty-six-page manuscript signed "Stockholm d. 29 Martii 1782. Carl Robsahm." The manuscript was probably left behind in London after R. L. Tafel's work with the English documentary collection, whose "Memoirs" were not based solely on Kahl's German version. Tafel wrote that, through Kahl, he had access to the Swedish original "in Robsahm's own handwriting." But is this really Robsahm's original manuscript? The archival entry from 1938 asserts that this is the original manuscript and that it was given by Achatius Kahl to R. L. Tafel in connection with the latter's visit to Sweden in 1868, and that it had come into the possession of the Swedenborg Society in this way.

The problem, though, is not so easily solved. A comparison with Robsahm's handwriting in the archives of the Riksbank does not support the premise that the London manuscript was written by Robsahm himself. The possibility that this is a considerably later copy must be kept completely open—many stylistic clues can be interpreted in this way, as can the handwriting. If this were a copy approved by Robsahm himself (which I do not believe) or a later fair copy based on Robsahm's draft, we could regard it as an original. The impression is, though, that it is a manuscript from the 1800s. The odd thing is that this is a document with Robsahm's signature in his own handwriting added to the page. This at least indicates the zeal of the copiers. Further, the London manuscript is the clearest and, for information about names in general, the most reliable in comparison with the copies we have mentioned thus far—the ones that are not copies of the London manuscript or the converse: their mutual variations reveal the existence of an older document. Dybeck's ambitious but unreliable manuscript gives us many hints of an earlier, more old-fashioned *Vorlage*, whose invisible presence we can feel everywhere. However, there are actually only relatively minor differences between the known versions, including the oldest translations. Thus, the contents can be determined with considerable certainty.

Still, there is a serious objection. An eminent scholar of Swedish Swedenborgianism, Harry Lenhammar, has maintained that there must be a still older version than the 1782 manuscript. The memoir is mentioned—in part, Lenhammar thinks, used as well—earlier.[16] It is likely that Robsahm, like others such as Gabriel Beyer, were already searching out material during the years around Swedenborg's death.[17] August Nordenskiöld included the above-mentioned Robsahm material in his plans for his volume, for which he unsuccessfully sought official approval in Sweden, but this does not mean that the definitive copy of the memoir already lay before him. Information was, of course, in circulation, as were promises of written contributions. The fact that Pernety, in his introduction to the French translation *Les Merveilles du Ciel et de l'Enfer* (1782) wrote that he did not have access to Robsahm's Swedish biography[18]—though there are direct borrowings from it—indicates that such details as he used had been delivered to him in translation, probably via the Nordenskiöld brothers.[19] The definitive document was prepared by Robsahm earlier in the same year—as he himself wrote once and for all just for the sake of the French publication. The date "29 March 1782," which appears in all the earlier-mentioned copies, would seem to be Robsahm's, and marks in that case the completion of the writing of the original document—in any case, not older—or possibly the date of an accompanying letter. The memorandum account can have been begun—read by someone else and translated—much earlier.

An interesting solution to the problem just mentioned, though, is offered in the manuscript volume T 96 in Carolina Rediviva, Uppsala, where, in an unsigned and undated eighteenth-century manuscript, in elegant German style, we find Robsahm's memoir in a somewhat shorter version. The handwriting is not Robsahm's, but the wording and the handwriting are definitely contemporary. The text may be a fair copy. Here we may perhaps discern the original version, which may even be older than 1782. The volume of manuscripts, which otherwise contains pure Swedenborgiana from the eighteenth century,[20] was purchased by the library in 1859 at a book sale following the death of Dean Jonas Torin (1781–1855). One feature of interest is the table of contents, probably drawn up by the owner at the time of the binding. The entry gives interesting details concerning the circumstances surrounding the genesis of Robsahm's "article":

> As an old and intimate friend of Swedenborg, Robsahm composed this account at the request of many individuals, the account being revised in English and used by Pernetti [sic] and many others who wrote about Swedenborg. The well known Chastanier was the one who wanted the account. I have seen his letter to Robsahm on this subject at the house of his son-in-law, Professor Pehr Kraft [sic].[21]

This is an indication that it was not only the Nordenskiöld brothers (and Pernety) who encouraged the writing of the memoir. It also sheds light on the way both the English and the French versions spread so quickly. Further, the context suggests that the Uppsala manuscript may have come from Robsahm's family or from circles that were closely connected to it.[22] The connection between England and Chastanier is not farfetched, either. Bénédict Chastanier, a friend and kindred spirit of both Pernety and Nordenskiöld, lived forty years of his life in England and was the greatest collector of Swedenborg manuscripts of his time.

A look at the minutes of the "General Conference" that established the New Church, held in the Great East Cheap in London on April 13, 1789, allows us to make out the background of Robsahm's memoir appearing in print in England so early. Among those signing the minutes we find August Nordenskiöld, Carl Bernhard Wadström, and Bénédict Chastanier. All three were members of the "Theosophical Society" founded in 1783, whose driving force was the printer Robert Hindmarsh. Nordenskiöld and Wadström were style-setting contributors to the *New Jerusalem Magazine,* as is apparent both from its material and from signed articles. August Nordenskiöld's plans for an anthology had not been fruitless: the texts were published in England. From 1784 on, Robsahm is a name that, in an ever-widening circle, brings revolutionary spiritual associations.

Toward the close of his life, Chastanier was reduced to poverty and pawned his collection under miserable circumstances.[23] Did a Robsahm manuscript disappear at this point as well? Or did it disappear when the *Exegetiska och Philantropiska Sällskapet,* founded by C. F. Nordenskiöld and C. B. Wadström on the English model, was dispersed owing to official intervention?[24] Perhaps, but in this case, what is the London manuscript a copy of, if it is in a hand from the 1800s? Many details speak for the thesis that this is an interpretation of the archaic Uppsala manuscript or of a text of identical tenor, possibly a common *Vorlage,* though the dating is not wholly clarified by this. Is the affectionate closing, which is lacking both in the Uppsala manuscript and in a pair of fragmentary copies from the collection of the *"Pro Fide et Caritate"* society (1796–ca. 1840),[25] perhaps a later addition? Is it a coincidence that the close of the memoir is dated so respectfully and aesthetically to March 29, 1782, exactly ten years to the day after the death of Swedenborg, which the introductory proposal describes?[26]

As for the question about an addition in a later hand, this part was probably either prompted or approved by Robsahm himself. The bright tone of devotion that closes the memoir is Robsahm's own. He was involved in the founding of the Exegetical-Philanthropic Society in 1786, which prescribed that its members should "acknowledge and believe in the *Heavenly Truths* of the New Jerusalem" and whose aim was to translate and publish Swedenborg's theological works.

The Uppsala manuscript, written in a German style, as are some of Robsahm's letters, is strikingly reminiscent of the style of an official or office secretary of the 1770s or 1780s. So, for example, there is a kinship with a minute dealing with "inspection at the bank's warehouse" from August 29, 1785 (Rb 658).

Did Robsahm allow a clerk to write out his manuscript? Or did someone around him make a copy? Beyond any doubt, the text is a fair copy or a careful copy, since it is almost entirely free of emendations or signs of hesitation. In the text itself, Robsahm observes explicitly and with some surprise that Swedenborg did not use scribes. Had there perhaps simply never been a manuscript about Swedenborg handwritten by Robsahm, or possibly only one in draft form? In this case, we are perhaps as close to the original as we can come.[27]

If we now have at last certified the real memoir's existence and contents, how much can we trust in its information when much of it cannot be found anywhere else? Unfortunately, we do not know. The truth eludes us, and we peer through a haze of plausibilities. However, it is probably safe to say that what Robsahm himself saw and heard during the latter years of Swedenborg's life happened credibly and reliably, while part of the earlier information has more of a hearsay quality and does not come from Swedenborg himself.

However, just as the powerful von Görres came up against the simple authenticity of the call vision, we can view Robsahm's literarily unpretentious account in the same fashion: this is a bank accountant who, for his book, also calculates as accurately as possible everything he knows indiscriminately in order to be correct. This is most certainly taken down in complete honesty and conscientiousness, to the limit of his ability and understanding.

Now for the calling vision. In the following way, Carl Robsahm relates the experience that changed Swedenborg's life and accordingly gave rise to the worldwide tradition that has extended over the centuries. Robsahm tells the story in Swedenborg's words:

I was in London and had dinner somewhat late in a restaurant [a spirit-vaults] where I used to eat, and then had a chamber by myself, where I amused myself with thoughts on the mentioned subject [the sciences or Scripture, unclear reference]. I was hungry and ate with good appetite. Towards the end of the meal I noticed something like a dimness before my eyes; it darkened and I saw the floor covered with the most hideous crawling animals, like snakes, frogs, and such creatures. I was startled, because I was completely conscious and my comprehension was rational; eventually darkness prevailed, but suddenly it was dispelled and I saw a man sitting in one of the corners of the chamber; since I was then all alone I was quite amazed when he started talking and said to me, "Don't eat so much." Again it darkened before my eyes, but it cleared up as soon and I found my self alone in the room.

Such an unexpected horror hastened my returning home. I did not let the landlord notice anything but considered what had happened, and I could not regard it a random occurrence or as an effect of physical causes. I went home; but in the night the same man appeared before me, and then I was not frightened. He then said that he was the Lord God, the creator and redeemer of the world, and that he had chosen me to explain to humanity the spiritual content of the Scripture, and that he would himself explain to me what I ought to write on the subject. To me was then in the same night convincingly opened *mundus spirituum infernum & coelum* [the spiritual, infernal, and celestial world], where I recognized several acquaintances of all estates: and from that day I left all worldly scholarly endeavor and work *in spiritualibus* [in spiritual matters] from what the Lord commissioned me to write. Daily the Lord rather often opened my bodily eyes, so that right in the middle of the day I could look into the other life and in the most joyful alertness talk with angels and spirits.[28]

The Code of the Ancients

New Church Spirituality and New England Transcendentalism

In New York, as well as in New England, there was, in the era of "Newness" from 1830 to 1850, a freshly built vision of Adam's primal language: the expressive power within things themselves and their inner essence and meaning reborn, revealed. American transcendentalists, from Ralph Waldo Emerson to Walt Whitman, dreamed of reproducing the expressive power of the language of nature. I will, in this essay, approach the very essence of this vision, and later on will address the question of why this occurred in America at that particular time. It was this dream of Eden and the *lingua adamica* that Whitman was later to frame in "A Song of the Rolling Earth":

A SONG of the rolling earth, and of words according,
Were you thinking that those were the words, those upright lines?
    those curves, angles, dots?

This essay was first presented as a paper at the American Academy of Religion, Kansas City, Nov. 23, 1991, entitled "Hermeneutics, Transcendence, and Modernity: The Swedenborg–Whitman Connection." It was first published in the proceedings of the Radcliffe New Church College Summer Seminar of Swedenborg Studies, Manchester, England, July 13–17, 1993.

No, those are not the words, the substantial words are in the ground
   and sea,
They are in the air, they are in you.[1]

Emerson and Whitman belonged to a generation that experienced humanity as liberated from the coils of original sin and as
allowed to return to the lost paradise, now standing face to face
with Nature herself, with responsibility for a world destined to
elevate itself to Eden: "To the garden the world anew ascending,"
Whitman declared.[2] "Here's for the plain old Adam," announced
Emerson; Adam should give things their names again. Every
human being is latently a new Adam. The Adamite era is here
and now, Emerson proclaimed in a poem: ". . . in the new-born
millions, / The perfect Adam lives.[3]

Emerson

In 1803, in Boston, one of the American cities where Swedenborgianism first took root, Ralph Waldo Emerson was born.
While he was growing up, and especially later at Harvard College and its Divinity School, there were many students around
him who were attracted to Swedenborg: Sampson Reed; Thomas
Worcester; Benjamin Peter Hunt; John H. Wilkins; Nathaniel
Hobart; Theophilus Parsons, Jr.; and, not to be forgotten, his
classmate and roommate Warren Burton, who later was to take
part in the Brook Farm collective experiment (at that later time,
in the 1840s, we can include friends like Henry James, Sr., and
James John Garth Wilkinson among Emerson's Swedenborgian
acquaintances).

   In 1818, when Emerson began his studies at Harvard, there
was an active Swedenborgian church in Boston; by 1830, the
Church of the New Jerusalem comprised twenty-eight societies,
with one of its headquarters in Emerson's home city. Sampson
Reed, a slightly older student of divinity (b. 1800), converted to
Swedenborgianism and supported himself as a druggist. He was
the driving force behind the beginning of *The New Jerusalem Magazine* in 1827 and for years was its editor and most diligent con-

tributor. The magazine contained summaries of and extracts from Swedenborg's writings; and Emerson read it for many years after its first appearance, as we can observe from his memoranda and citations. A set for the first year (1827–1828) is complete in the library he left in Concord, Massachusetts, at his death; the rest was destroyed in a major fire at Emerson's house in 1872.[4]

Contact with Sampson Reed had tremendous meaning for Emerson. First, there was a remarkable lecture Reed gave at Harvard in 1821, his "Oration on Genius." This speech echoes with Swedenborg's philosophy of language and with his interpretation of the lost paradise in *Arcana Coelestia* and in his creation drama *De cultu et amore Dei* (On the Worship and Love of God). Reed set the divine understanding of the lost paradise and the living language of Adam in a contemporary perspective:

> Because God is love, nature exists; because God is love, the Bible is poetry. . . . When the heart is purified, . . . the harps which have hung on the willows will sound as the first breath of heaven that moved the leaves in the garden of Eden. . . . There is a unison of spirit and nature. The genius of the mind will descend, and unite with the genius of the rivers, the lakes, and the woods. Thoughts fall to the earth with power, and make a language out of nature.
>
> Adam and Eve knew no language but their garden. They had nothing to communicate by words; for they had not the power of concealment. The sun of the spiritual world shone bright on their hearts, and their senses were open with delight to natural objects. . . . The people of the golden age . . . possessed nothing which evil passions might obliterate; and, when the "heavens were rolled together as a scroll," the curtain dropped between the world and their existence.
>
> Science will be full of life, as nature is full of God. She will wring from her locks the dew which was gathered in the wilderness. By science, I mean natural science. . . .
>
> The time is not far distant. The cock has crowed. I hear the distant lowing of the cattle which are grazing on the mountains. "Watchman, what of the night? Watchman, what of the night? The watchman saith, The morning cometh."[5]

Two decades later, Emerson declared in his journal that Reed had been the "oracle" of his youth. Reed had published a philosophical treatise, strongly influenced by Swedenborg, but also by Wordsworth, entitled *Observations on the Growth of the Mind* (1826). Its prophetic optimism and symbolic thinking, its belief in the indwelling, latent divinity of human beings—the exact opposite, that is, of Calvinism's stress on sinfulness and on a collision course with the prevalent Lockeanism—this was to be a new gospel for Emerson, the Unitarian minister and skeptical son of a minister, especially when his whole world, his whole trust and confidence, had been shattered by his young wife's death from tuberculosis, a sickness that was constantly threatening to bring him to his own grave, as it had one after another of his family and his friends. He resigned his pastorate and tried to find a new basis for his shaken beliefs. He tried to see ahead, and Swedenborgian thought became increasingly a fountain of optimism both for Emerson himself and, to some extent, for the whole transcendentalist movement in New England.

To find a new platform to stand on and to regain his strength, Emerson crossed the surging sea to England and France, where he turned to natural science to find a new foundation. This interest in natural science would deepen his interest in Swedenborg, particularly in his theory of correspondence: the constant repetitions in both the organic and inorganic forms Emerson was studying in museums (especially in the Jardin des Plantes in Paris) led him, in an epiphany in 1833, to intuit a hidden relationship between things of the body and things of the soul, between the spiritual and the material: that forms are expressions and can be likened to feelings and thoughts.

When he returned to America, Emerson delivered a series of lectures on natural science. But when talking about "nature," his subject in reality was human nature, the truth about life and the world. Especially, he had to investigate the relationship between word and object: What are we really talking about? What do words stand for?

In his 1833–1834 lectures, "The Uses of Natural History," "On the Relation of Man to the Globe," and "The Naturalist," and in an 1835 series of lectures on English literature, Emerson sketched the understanding of the relationship between language and reality, which he assembled and summarized in *Nature* (1836). Addressing the question of whether there is material in *Nature* that might appear reminiscent of Swedenborg's thought, we should offer a glimpse of Emerson's new insight. He finds that, when we examine more closely the words we use to express moral or intellectual facts, they have their roots in natural phenomena. "Right" means "straight," "wrong" means "twisted," "spirit" originally means "wind," "transgression" is the crossing of a boundary, "supercilious" is a lifted eyebrow. We say "heart" to mean feeling, "head" to express thinking—in this way applying words for visible things to spiritual things. Words are symbols, but so are things. Every natural fact symbolizes a spiritual fact. Natural phenomena correspond to states of mind, and the state can be described only in terms of the natural phenomena.

For example, the cunning person is a fox, the perseverant person a rock, and the learned man a torch. The lamb stands for innocence, the snake for devious malice, flowers for delicate affections. Light and darkness denote knowledge and ignorance, respectively, as warmth is an expression for love. Directions like backward and forward are images of memory and hope. Who, in the stillness of meditation, can see a stream as anything other than "the flux" of everything? Cast a stone into the river, and the rings give a picture of everything that exerts an influence! This kind of influence is exerted by the universal soul behind and within everything, as humanity has always known—what we call, intellectually, the Reason in the cosmic order, but have thought of in relation to nature: Spirit. "Spirit is the Creator," life itself, and we have incarnated or materialized it in our language as "the Father." These analogies pervade our whole world, for the human being is an analogist, one who looks for relationships. As a result, there is a pervasive "correspondence between visible things and human thoughts," and language is increasingly pictorial as we follow it back to our childhood and natural condition, where from the beginning it is nothing but poetry. The world itself is symbolic of its nature.

According to Emerson, language contains metaphors because nature is an image of our own inner nature. Natural moral laws correspond to the laws of nature like a mirror image. The axioms of physics translate ethical principles. In consonance with this, many expressions have both an ethical and a physical content. Wholes are greater than parts; action and reaction correspond to each other; the smallest weight can lift the greatest, if the difference is compensated for by time, and so forth. Similarly, memorable proverbs often consist of a natural fact, selected "as a picture or parable of a moral truth:" a rolling stone gathers no moss, a bird in the hand is worth two in the bush, a cripple on a straight path gets ahead faster than a racer on a crooked one, make hay while the sun shines, it's hard to carry a full cup without spilling it, vinegar is the son of wine, the last straw broke the camel's back, etc.

Furthermore, Emerson asserts that the analogy between spirit and matter in our world is no invention of poetic imagination, except secondarily. Rather, it arises from the Creator's unfathomable will and providence, leaving us faced with "the standing problem which has exercised the wonder and the study of every fine genius since the world began; from the era of the Egyptians and the Brahmins to that of Pythagoras, of Plato, of Bacon, of Leibnitz, of Swedenborg."

It is possible to read nature's text as a pure discourse if our senses are purified in love for truth and virtue; our prospect, Emerson proclaims, is to be able to understand the original meaning of natural objects, so that "the world shall be to us an open book, and every form significant of its hidden life and final cause."[6]

How was all this understood by the contemporary reader?

When Emerson's *Nature*, published anonymously, reached England, some New Church people there believed that it was a Swedenborgian tract that had come to them from their sympathizers in the West! The learned New Churchman Jonathan Bayley, pastor of the society in Accrington, praised the well-informed account. In his review, published in *The Intellectual*

Repository and New Jerusalem Magazine in April 1840, Bayley wrote of *Nature:*

> This work is, we think, the production of one of our trans-Atlantic brethren, whose name is unknown to us. . . . [The] chapter which is headed "Language," we could have wished to have given entire, had our space permitted. If the Author is not a member of the New Church, it is clear that he has read the writings of Swedenborg, and that his mind is imbued with their truths.

Consequently, when the Rev. David George Goyder in the next year published his theological textbook for the New Church *The Biblical Assistant and Book of Practical Piety* (1841), *Nature* appeared among the suggested reading.[7]

Whitman

Something similar happened to the "Singer of America," Walt Whitman. When his first book *Leaves of Grass* was published in 1855, it was enthusiastically received by *The Christian Spiritualist*, a journal founded by a group of Swedenborgians. *Leaves of Grass* was reviewed as a great work that partly embodied and realized the wisdom of Swedenborg's doctrines.[8]

Whitman's debt to Emerson has been profoundly explored. It has in fact been stated by scholars that "there is no doubt that Whitman was more indebted to Emerson than to any other for the fundamental ideas in even the earliest *Leaves of Grass*."[9] When Emerson delivered his six lectures on "The Times" in 1842 to the Library Society of New York, the editor of the journal *The Aurora*, the still-named Walter Whitman, was on the spot as reporter. In his lecture on "The Poet," Emerson said:

> After Dante, and Shakespeare, and Milton, there came no grand poet until Swedenborg in a corner of Europe, hitherto uncelebrated, sung the wonders of man's heart in strange prose poems which he called "Heaven and Hell," the "Apocalypse Revealed," the "Doctrine of Marriage," "Celestial Secrets" and so on, and

which rivalled in depth and sublimity, and in their power to agitate this human heart, this lover of the wild and wonderful, any song of these tuneful predecessors. Slowly but surely the eye and ear of men are turning to feed on that wonderful intellect.[10]

Focusing on the symbolic, Emerson declared that "all things are symbols. We say of man that he is grass. . . ." Whitman reviewed the lecture on "The Poet:" "The lecture was one of the richest and most beautiful compositions, both for its manner and style, we have ever heard anywhere, at any time."[11]

Whitman's affinity with Swedenborgian thought may have been inspired through various channels. Besides New Church literature and collateral writings, which had a wide circulation in the middle of the nineteenth century, and contacts with Swedenborgians, Whitman may have met with similar ideas in many contemporary works, among them William Fishbough's *The Macrocosm and Microcosm; or, The Universe Without and the Universe Within*, published in New York in 1852—a book where distinct echoes can be heard from Swedenborg's teachings on spheres, on correspondences, spiritual influx, the communication between soul and body.[12]

In *Democratic Vistas*, Whitman approaches the literary pertinence of the mystic. He states that the

culmination and fruit of literary artistic expression, and its final fields of pleasure for the human soul, are in metaphysics, including the mysteries of the spiritual world, the soul itself, and the question of the immortal continuation of our identity. In all ages, the mind of man has brought up here—and always will. . . . [In this sublime literature,] the religious tone, the consciousness of mystery, the recognition of the future, of the unknown, of Deity over and under all, and of the divine purpose, are never absent, but indirectly give tone to all.

Even though these works are sometimes aesthetically defective, they are the highlights of world literature, since such "poetry" towers up to literature's real heights and elevations like great mountains of the earth:

> The altitude of literature and poetry has always been religion— and always will be. The Indian Vedas, the Nackas of Zoroaster, the Talmud of the Jews, the Old Testament, the Gospel of Christ and His disciples, Plato's works, the Koran of Mohammed, the Edda of Snorro, and so on toward our own day, to Swedenborg, and to the invaluable contributions of Leibnitz, Kant, and Hegel.[13]

There are other examples to show that America's most influential and prophetic poet of the nineteenth century valued Swedenborg. At Duke University, there is preserved, among some manuscripts, a newspaper clipping on "The New Jerusalem," together with a page where Whitman, probably in 1857 or 1858, has taken down some of his thoughts regarding Swedenborg. He especially observes how strangely unknown Swedenborg was in his time—neither Voltaire nor Rousseau noticed him. Yet, Whitman claims, Swedenborg's mission was one of major historical significance: "He is a precursor, in some sort of great differences between past thousands of years, and future thousands."[14]

Here we are also faced with the prophetic optimism that is the keynote of Whitman's writings, an ecstatic homage to life, humanity, and the times; the world will be reborn before our eyes, and we will retrieve the divine nature of things—these prospects are open to all of us. Like Sampson Reed and Ralph Waldo Emerson, Whitman believed in the progress of science and society, but he thought the contemporary scientist too intellectual and devoid of the awareness of divine providence and meaning.

A Hieroglyphic Text

Leaves of Grass is a reading in the hieroglyphic text of nature, where man is a part. The grass is "a uniform hieroglyphic," a symbolic writing, that signifies an omnipresence of seething life, among all peoples, in all humans. It means, "Sprouting alike in broad zones and narrow zones, / Growing among black folks as among white." There is a spiritual inflow into all the living, and the grass symbolizes humanity, ultimately the vital force itself.[15]

Echoes may be descried here of the old literary myth of the divine hieroglyphics, which dates back to Plutarch and Iamblichos and became current in Renaissance Neoplatonism and occultism; the history of hieroglyphic Bibles, storybooks, and picture puzzles; Champollion's deciphering of the Rosetta stone in the 1820's; the ancient history of allegory and analogy; but no less Emerson's well-known description of Swedenborg's conception of the world as a "a grammar of hieroglyphs."[16] Emerson's early usage of the word "hieroglyph" gradually was tinged with correspondential vision, originally certainly through his Swedenborgian friend Sampson Reed, whose interest in these matters is obvious from his contributions to the Boston journal *The New Jerusalem Magazine*, where he published a paper on Egyptian hieroglyphics in 1830. Another source of major importance was the French Swedenborgian Guillaume Œgger whose book *The True Messiah* left many traces in the basic outline of Emerson's philosophy in *Nature*. Œgger's remarkable work *Le Vrai Messie, ou l'Ancien et le Nouveau Testaments examinés d'après les principes de la langue de la nature* (Paris 1829) was an attempt to interpret the Bible by means of the "Book of Nature," translating things into thoughts and notions, and vice versa. This interplay of exegetics and ontology was derived from the old idea that the Author had written two books—the Word and the World—in corresponding hieroglyphs. In 1835, Emerson already had read Elizabeth Palmer Peabody's manuscript translation of Œgger's *The True Messiah* (Boston, 1842).[17]

According to Œgger and Swedenborg, God had endowed Adam with the faculty of reading the ideographic names of the creatures from their physical forms, to recognize the significant and realize the meaning from the design. This tongue, which is the nature of things, now once again can be interpreted; Œgger presents a "hieroglyphic key," and later on also a dictionary (*Essai d'un dictionnaire de la langue de la nature*, 1831).[18] He summarizes and exemplifies Swedenborg's doctrine of correspondences, laying claims to its universal applicability. Thus, humanity is the divine written in cipher: "Man is the true hieroglyphic of the Divinity," infinitely detailed even in his corporeal existence, "since his material form itself is but the emblem of his moral being."[19] This approach to the human condition reverberates throughout Emerson's poetical universe, as in the prologue to *Nature*: "Every man's condition is a solution in hieroglyphic to those inquiries he would put."

According to Œgger's "hieroglyphic Key," or grouping of correspondences, the two most important faculties of man are "Goodness" and "Knowledge" (Swedenborg's *bonum* and *scientia*); God is "Love" and "Truth"; the *Sun* in our world is "heat" and "light" (corresponding to the Divine Love and Wisdom of the heavens); the *Wind* announces wherever it advances "the invisible action of a hidden God:" it is "Spirit."

This linguistic insight struck Emerson and was immediately turned into literary imagery. In the prophetic conclusion of *Nature*, the revolutionary impact of the influx of the spirit is described:

> The sordor and filths of nature, the sun shall dry up, and the wind exhale.

Whitman also preaches the new language, the regained Adamic perception, for example, in "A Song of the Rolling Earth":

> I swear I begin to see little or nothing in audible words,
> All merges toward the presentation of the unspoken meanings of
> the earth.
> Toward him who sings the songs of the body and of the truths of
> the earth,
> Toward him who makes the dictionaries of words that print cannot
> touch.

A constant theme in *Leaves of Grass* is the strange connections between the "I" and the World, the outward and the inward:

Locations and times—what is it in me that meets them
All, whenever and wherever, and makes me at home?
Forms, colors, densities, odors—what is it in me that corresponds to
   them.[20]

When writing *Good-Bye My Fancy* (1891), completed on his
deathbed, Whitman was many times over convinced of the con-
current text: "In every object, mountain, tree, and star—in every
birth and life. . . . A mystic cipher waits infolded."

For the same reason, Emerson (like Sampson Reed) could
write, "My garden is my dictionary," "Life is our dictionary";
and in the "Prospects" of *Nature* declare that we are all, poten-
tially, Adam's equals. It is within our power to regain that relation to the birds, the trees, the clouds, and the stars that
the transcendental poet and mystic Jones Very (1813–1880)
prophecized:

For he who with his maker walks aright
Shall be their lord, as Adam was before.[21]

The Trusting Sailor

The errand into the wilderness was a return to the Garden of
the world. The ancient Word was present with the settlers in the
New World, and they felt guided by providence. They had a
special compact or covenant with God. According to Emerson,
man had become a "new Adam in the garden."[22]

"We are to know that we are never without a pilot," Emerson
and the transcendentalists felt assured:

When we know not how to steer, and dare not hoist a sail, we
can drift. The current knows the way, though we do not. When
the stars and sun appear, when we have conversed with naviga-
tors who know the coast, we may begin to put out an oar and
trim a sail. The ship of heaven guides itself, and will not accept a
wooden rudder.[23]

Indeed, the first Puritan poet in America, Anne Bradstreet, "The Tenth Muse," used a similar image in her *Meditations*, written for her son in 1664: "A Christian is sailing through this world unto his heavenly country."[24]

According to this persistent vision, ranging from Sinuhe and Sindbad to Bacon and Bunyan and beyond, to succeed means to trust and obey, whereupon favorable winds accordingly follow. That is basically an ancient conception of Justice, which prevailed in Minoan and Sumerian times, and beyond. The prehistoric Mesopotamian code reads:

> A Ship with good intent sails before the wind,
> Utu [the sungod] finds good harbours for it.[25]

Emerson took down a quotation from Francis Bacon's *De Augmentis Scientiarum* to the same effect: if once the mind has chosen noble ends, then not virtues but deities encompass.[26] At that point the law of nature, divine will, and human efforts make one, and providence becomes *proventus*, or *ventus secundus*, tailwind. That is an ancient idea, and American transcendentalism reestablishes a conception of nature keen to classical antiquity and to archaic and prehistorical times.

We may recall here a remarkable account by Benjamin F. Barrett, who was struck by the marvelous agreements between the beliefs and teachings of Swedenborg and those of William Ellery Channing, the Unitarian leader in Boston (1780–1842). Barrett, who thoroughly researched the matter, was so overwhelmed by the numerous similarities that he felt compelled to scrutinize also the few but significant *differences* between these writers in his book *Swedenborg and Channing* (Philadelphia, second edition 1879.) Gathering an impressive comparison material, where the abundant convergencies apparently bordered on complete congruity, the Swedenborgian scholar Barrett concluded that all these basic similarities were *not* due to any influence of Swedenborg on Channing. All historical evidence contradicted any idea of impact.

Perhaps we have here a forgotten key to a deeper understanding of the connections between New Church spirituality and New England transcendentalism. The remarkable susceptibility to Swedenborgian thought in America was due to the fact that some of the basic tenets were already there, as if drawn from an ancient Word or an archetypal mind, and also due to the special environment and circumstances of the American settlers in the New World.

Accordingly, the language of the "hieroglyphic key" introduced by Swedenborg and his followers Sampson Reed and Guillaume Œgger was very easily accepted when the power of the Puritan tradition was dispelled in the days of secularization, liberalism, and scientific progress in the nineteenth century. The language of nature addressed in the era of "Newness" and on was no new invention, but was given a new significance. "The sun" of our world represented the transcendent warmth and light of divine love and wisdom of the spiritual world, and likewise "the wind" signified the invisible action of a hidden God. We recall Emerson's visionary prospects in 1836: "The sordor and filths of nature, / the sun shall dry up, and the wind exhale."[27]

This imagery fit well in the tradition of Puritan typology, where it had many counterparts and early American predecessors. We may in this context recall the meditations of the Calvinist Edward Taylor (1644–1729):

> The glory of the world slickt up in types
> In all Choise things chosen to typify,
> His glory upon whom the worke doth light,
> . . .
> The glory of all Types doth meet in thee.
> Thy glory doth their glory quite excell:
> More than the Sun excells in its bright glee
> A nat, an Earewig, Weewill, Snaile, or Shell.[28]

The figurative language and its metaphorical *topoi*, even more than the strictly biblical types themselves, may be traced even further and be described in archetypical as well as historical terms. Catherine L. Albanese, in *Religion in America from the Algonkian Indians to the New Age*, challenges the time-honored idea that "civil religion" is the great tradition of American culture, giving prominence to the heritage of nature religion, stressing the importance of natural imagery in writings by (and about) Jefferson and other leaders of the early republic. Albanese suggests that political thought was tied to religious experiences of the American landscape. From the point of view of comparative religion, however, this imagery is also universal, if not commonplace. Ellen Russell Emerson wrote in her book *Indian Myths, or Legends, Traditions, and Symbols of the Aborigines of America*:

> The Egyptian god Re, or Ra, was called the Sun of both worlds . . . , by which the ancients represented the Divine Being as a source of spiritual and physical light. Baron Swedenborg describes a spiritual sun, corresponding to, and source of the natural sun. The Indians describe a fiery substance above the sun, which is the ruler of all things, Wa-cheaud, the maker, or creative spirit.[29]

American imagery, from the Puritans to Emerson, can also be seen against this background. Anne Bradstreet, for instance, in 1664 explained that just as there is "but one sun" in the firmament, from which all things receive their light, "so is it in the church both militant and triumphant: there is but one Christ, who is the sun of righteousness. . . . All receive their luster (be it more or less) from that glorious sun that enlightens all in all. And if some of them shine so bright while they move on earth, how transcendently splendid shall they be when they are fixed in their heavenly spheres!"[30] Consequently, Emerson—the Scholar and the American Man of Letters—always declared he read "for lustres," which at heart meant seeking the sun. Caroline Sturgis Tappan, one of his confidants whom he published in *The Dial*, wrote on the quality of the transcendent light in "Life": "The sunshine of love / Streams all around."[31]

The transcendency appealed to by Bradstreet and Emerson is essentially "Christ's dear love's transcendency" of America's first "bestseller," Michael Wigglesworth's *The Day of Doom* (1662)[32]—that is, in Emerson's version, elevation of mind and society responding to spiritual metamorphoses in interaction: "a correspondent revolution in things" will attend "the influx of the spirit."

The prospect in the age of Newness was one of "an original relation to the universe," a state of mind when the different planes of reality and our awareness once again coincide and everything suddenly becomes "transparent," reveals its inner nature, its truth. The Concord philosophy rings out as hymn and formula in the poem "Correspondences," written by Christopher Pearse Cranch (1813–1892) for Emerson's and Margaret Fuller's *The Dial* at the outset of the 1840s:

> Lost to man was the key of those sacred hieroglyphics,—
>> Stolen away by sin,—till with Jesus restored.
> Now with infinite pains we here and there spell out a letter;
>> Now and then will the sense feebly shine through the dark.
> When we perceive the light which breaks through the visible symbol,
>> What exultation is ours! we the discovery have made!
> Yet is the meaning the same as when Adam lived sinless in Eden
>> Only long-hidden it slept and now again is restored.[33]

An American
Philosophy
of Use

The emergence of the philosophy of utility in the eighteenth century was closely connected with the idea of
progress and its reactions to obstacles posed by old theological
thought. This reaction had a practical, an economic, and an ethical side—a material and a spiritual function. In the Anglo-Saxon
world, utility has been a kind of norm since John Locke wrote
his classic *Essay concerning the Human Understanding* and preached
"the uses of reason" in all fields of thought. Its spirit is alive not
only in technology and business but also in culture. We feel faint
echoes of it in T.S. Eliot's lecture series on "The Use of Poetry
and the Use of Criticism," as well as in Jerome Hamilton Buckley's inquiry into "The Uses of History" in Victorian thought or
Monroe Engel's "Uses of Literature." A German Emerson scholar,
Hedi Hildebrand, saw the connection with a general American
trait, *Nützlichkeitssinn*, the practicality of the American mind intimately connected with a Puritan view of material goods as to-
kens of God's favor, which had paved the way for a positive

This essay appeared in an early version in the collection *Swedenborg and His Influence*
(Bryn Athyn, Penn.: Academy of the New Church, 1988).

lifestyle that is the opposite of detachment: to seize the day and the opportunity.[1]

America was born in a forced shift from otherworldly to this-worldly concerns, from metaphysical and ideological dependence to independence. In this historical context, the practical notion of utility was as central to Thomas Paine as it was to Thomas Jefferson and Benjamin Franklin, who also perceived the economic value of traditional Puritan virtues. In that historical shift, these virtues were more and more appreciated as ways to happiness, and that gave them a utilitarian function quite apart from the traditional goals of salvation or divine enlightenment. Instead, Jefferson saw that nature had "constituted utility to man" as "the standard and test of virtue."[2] This is almost the opposite of traditional Puritan belief, and Jefferson championed Joseph Priestley's book *An History of the Corruption of the Christian Religion* (1782).[3]

As Flower and Murphy point out in the best modern history of philosophy in America, Joseph Priestley accordingly figured importantly in the background of utilitarianism and was credited with the notion of utility by Jeremy Bentham himself, the most famous utilitarian philosopher along with William James and John Stuart Mill.[4] A similar and as seminal view had been taken by William Paley, in his *Principles of Moral Political Thought*, and still earlier by John Gay in a *Dissertation concerning the Fundamental Principle of Virtue or Morality.* That principle was basically the principle of utility, sometimes even a doctrine of expediency, actions evaluated according to their beneficial results, the right act being the one that produces the greatest amount of happiness or pleasure in the world at large. The influential Francis Hutcheson was explicitly utilitarian in this sense.

The main problem, then, was how each self-seeking individual comes to make his or her own good the general good of society, how the best results become known and valued, and how the obvious differences in values in different societies and cultures are accounted for. These problems arose out of opposition to religious dogmatism and legalism, but the utilitarians were also immediately opposed by rational intuitionists, whose belief

in an immanent moral sentiment led them to evade the utilitarian problem. Emerson was among the latter. He also revolted
against the deist view of the world represented by American Enlightenment utilists such as Jefferson and Franklin. Again, even
though Emerson was indeed a philosopher of progress and held
a strong belief in technology, he was also on guard against current notions of utility. His teacher, William Ellery Channing,
had warned against the vulgarity of that notion. In his "Remarks
on National Literature" in 1823, Channing explained, or rather
exclaimed: "There are those who confine this term to the neces-
saries and comforts of life, and the means of producing them."
"Happily," Channing assured his pupil, "human nature is too
strong for the utilitarian. It cannot satisfy itself with the conve-
nient," and Emerson was to agree with this outburst against materialist practicality.[5] Still, the word "use" appears throughout
Emerson's writings. It appears more frequently in his works and
is more central to his philosophy than it does in or is to any
other of the New England transcendentalists.

In Emerson, there is always an emphasis on use: the uses of
natural history, the uses of nature, the uses of great men, and so
forth. The importance of great men to Emerson was the use, or
applied consequence, in his moral thought and practice, of what
they represented. The most important use of natural history was
that it represented moral and supernatural history in another,
spiritual sense. Emerson enumerates numerous other uses—to
the benefit of health, economy, commodity, progress, enthusiasm, self-awareness—to explain human nature to mankind. The
value of anything accords to its potential use; *value* in Emerson's
thought is always at heart a moral value.

We meet the conviction that everything is made to serve and
that our aim is usefulness already in the young clergyman's sermons. In Emerson's secular ideology, however, the concept is
more extensive. It includes also the Enlightenment concept of
utility, but primarily it is adopted in a practical English sense: the
"economical taste or love of utility," which Emerson thought
characterized all English arts.[6] This passion for utility, which
Emerson expressed in his belief in progress in general, is an

English trait, but he rejected its basic amorality. "I know," he wrote in "Aristocracy," "nothing which induces so base and for-lorn a feeling as when we are treated for our utilities, as econo-mists do."[7]

Much more slight is the connection between Emerson's stress on uses and the doctrine of utilitarianism. Indeed, there appears to be no connection at all, and he expresses his negative views of the doctrine clearly. Discussing the two opposite poles of reason and common sense in "Literary Ethics," Emerson observes that, if a person is "defective at either extreme of the scale, his philoso-phy will seem low and utilitarian; or it will appear too vague and indefinite for the uses of life."[8] Consequently, utilitarianism should not be connected with Emerson's concept of use. In 1832, in his private journal, Emerson explicitly states his opinion: "The stinking philosophy of the utilitarian!"[9] Utilitarianism's material-istic intellectualism disgusted him. But, above all, he doubtless dismissed the moral philosophy of Jeremy Bentham and others because of its hedonism. Lust or pleasure is a moral measure alien to Emerson. Indeed, it is one of the seven deadly sins. To him *morality* means *duty*.

The Primacy of Morals

In *Nature* (1836), Emerson explains how nature itself is a disci-pline. The use of nature, he says, includes all other uses as parts of itself. Nature is made to serve. Thus, for instance, "the use of commodity, regarded by itself, is mean and squalid." But, Emer-son underlines, "it is to the mind an education in the doctrine of Use, namely, that a thing is good only as far as it serves." And as "every natural process is a version of a moral sentence" and the "moral law lies at the centre of nature," good is thus identified with useful, which means that it is in accordance with the moral law.[10]

This doctrine is obviously of central importance. Use is the beginning and the end. Use is from God, and use is the end for which man exists, Emerson declares. Useful equals good.[11] To understand what he means by "the doctrine of Use," we must first realize that Emerson is primarily a moralist, and then recall that Sampson Reed was his early "oracle."

There is a primacy of morals in Emerson's thought. "All things are moral," he wrote in *Nature*. "All things are moral," he declared in his essay "Compensation." This assertion by no means implies that nothing is immoral. On the contrary, Emerson emphasizes the degenerate state of humanity and the fallen state of the world. But Emerson was convinced that the universe exists from moral causes for moral ends.[12]

Emerson attacked formal religion. However, he looked forward to a new awakening, a spiritual revival, and was a spokesman for it. According to him, true religious thought arises only from moral sentiment. In "The Sovereignty of Ethics," Emerson declares that "the progress of religion" depends on "its identity with morals."[13] The "fatal trait" of his own times, which he looked upon as a transition period, was the divorce of religion from morality. In the essay "Worship" he describes the present state of society and man:

> In our large cities the population is godless, materialized—no bond, no fellow-feeling, no enthusiasm. These are not men, but hungers, thirsts, fevers and appetites walking. How is it people manage to live on,—so aimless as they are? . . . There is no faith in the intellectual, none in the moral universe.[14]

However, Emerson perceived that a "silent revolution" was under way and was convinced that the "moral" and the "spiritual" are a lasting essence—the one and only!—and that we will certainly bring back the words in their true essence, "age after age, to their ancient meaning."[15] How is the new generation to be edified? Emerson provided the answer: by bringing back the identity between metaphysics and morals. In "The Sovereignty of Ethics," Emerson expressed his hope:

> A new Socrates, or Zeno, or Swedenborg . . . may be born in this age, and, with a happy heart and a bias for theism, bring ascetism, duty and magnanimity into vogue again.[16]

Certainly, Emerson aimed at promoting that new "vogue," or state of affairs, himself.

Barbara Packer and Gertrude Reif Hughes have beautifully shown how conduct, in Emerson's terms, appears as a language of use when the action is right. *Use* and *right* appear as synonymous, and out of this the perception of truth arises.[17] The true and the good make one.

Swedenborg's *Doctrine of Life*, a book purchased by Emerson as a young man, contains the teaching, which was also with his own, that truth and goodness are identical, that a person has the amount of truth equal to his or her amount of goodness. "God," according to Swedenborg's *Divine Love and Wisdom*, "is the very form of all uses, from which all the uses in the created universe derive their origin," and accordingly "the created universe viewed as to uses, is an image of Him."[18] To quote other works Emerson knew very well, "the kingdom of heaven is a kingdom of uses"; this is no utilitarianism since value is intrinsic: "Heavenly love consists in loving uses for the sake of uses or good for the sake of good. . . . This is loving God and loving neighbor," which means that love is identical with performing uses.[19]

Truth, in Emerson's transcendental terminology, was joined to the practical, the ethical. Concerning the "Method of Nature" he wrote: "The one condition coupled with the gift of truth is its use. That man shall be learned who reduces his learning to practice." To illustrate the ephemeral quality of knowledge without virtue, Emerson turns to the metaphysical level of one of Swedenborg's memorabilia: "Swedenborg affirmed that it was opened to him 'that the spirits who knew truth in this life, but did it not, at death shall lose their knowledge.'"[20]

Swedenborg stresses and develops this point throughout his writings: Truth (*veritas*), or Knowledge (*scientia*), or Understanding (*intelligentia*) or Faith, without Good—which is good uses, charity, work in accordance with good uses—is worthless, if not evil. The many different aspects of this doctrine are, for instance, treated at length in *Apocalypse Revealed*, which Emerson bought and first read in 1836, annotated, and quoted many times. This central part of the doctrinal system is treated also, on the moral and social level, in *Heaven and Hell*, and it is the very subject of another book Emerson read, *Angelic Wisdom concerning the Divine Love and the Divine Wisdom*.

In book after book, Swedenborg stated and illustrated that morals are of primary importance, especially in *Arcana Coelestia*, where the use of scientific knowledge is extensively discussed. Good is not merely as important as truth or faith and knowledge; they may not be divorced, but essentially presuppose each other, imply each other. Good (*bonum*) comes first. No justification by faith or truth alone (*iustificatio sola fide* in the Lutheran theology) exists, nor does a justification by knowledge or understanding alone.

Swedenborg's implicit revolt here against his own Protestant Lutheran legacy is expressed in terms that attracted Emerson.[21] As a former clergyman of the Unitarian church, Emerson retained a staunch Puritan moralism in his heart, but revolted against the Protestant Calvinist creed and rejected all empty and choking formalism. Emerson tries to make clear that truth, faith, or knowledge without good degenerates or is fruitless. Science and religion have to be joined to the moral; they can only prosper in their moral dimension. Religion has to be identified with morality to elevate man from his fallen state. Thus, morals become essential again. It was the primacy of morals that appealed to him above all in Swedenborg.

The Love of Use

Jonathan Bishop observed that, among Emerson's representative men, Swedenborg exemplified the moral sentiment, and the moral character of Emerson's notion of utility becomes particularly clear in the influence of Swedenborg.[22] Emerson seems first to have adopted his wording of the "doctrine of Use" from Swedenborg. In one of his notebooks from the late 1830s, "use" is mentioned among doctrines of Swedenborg.[23] But the earliest and principal source is Sampson Reed and his *New Jerusalem Magazine*.[24]

The model *Observations of the Growth of the Mind* by Sampson

Reed is permeated by the doctrine of uses, as is nature. More closely examined, uses is the true subject of Reed's book.[25] Reed writes on the language of things, the use of that language being the manifestation of the mind. Everything expresses the use for which it is designed, and similarly every human being has a particular sphere of usefulness. It is in dialogue with Reed that Emerson tries to cure his fear of death by animating the soul with "love and uses," and finds the essential meaning of life in finding one's correct place in the universal order. We are, according to Reed, created for uses and can realize ourselves by taking every opportunity of being useful, making ourselves perfect members in the body of humanity. This doctrine is an organic conception of the human condition as well as of the moral mission of the individual. The parts contribute to the whole. Love is a form of use. This is the essence of the moral philosophy of Swedenborgianism. The universe is a language of uses, where each individual has his or her own particular contribution to make: this is one's mission.[26] Or, in Swedenborg's own words, what is meant by use "is carrying out one's duty, whether in public service, or in business, or in employment, honestly and justly; when this is being done, the welfare of the general body of people or mankind is being cared for." There is a unity of all uses. "In the Lord's sight the whole human race is as one man. . . . It is the uses with them that do so."[27] This thinking echoes throughout the pages of Swedenborg's works as well as in the early New Church publications in Boston.

The doctrine of uses is a pivotal Swedenborgian philosophy since, according to Swedenborgians, good works are more important than creed. What a person does is more important than what he or she thinks: the function is central. When we do good, we are actually living in truth. And, according to Swedenborg's teachings, all religions and all cultures have some important part to play in the body of humanity. Each simply has different missions. In that way, the relativity of opinion and the eighteenth-century conflict between truth and utility, which was topical to Thomas Jefferson and his generation, are bridged by a notion of providence and an organic conception of human history. Swedenborg in his way matched Jefferson's question regarding moral relativity in space and time this way:

> There is not an atom of our bodies which may not remind us of a truth of constant practical importance, which may not help us to confine our thoughts and efforts to the uses which properly belong to us, to the duties which lie before us and within our reach. Every one has, at every moment, some use which he may then perform, some station in which he is then distinctly placed, some mode of action in which it is well for his neighbours and himself, that he be employed.[28]

Use is identified with duty, that is to say, relative to person and moment. Still, there is always one choice of action that is the best one.

It is beside the point to address the problem of causality here—whether Emerson held these views because of his early reception of Swedenborgian thought, or if he was drawn to these ideas since they expressed his own thought. But the doctrine of uses was perhaps the only one of Swedenborg's doctrines that Emerson accepted at its face value, where he took "the mystic" at his word. This doctrine provided the following wording to Emerson's hard-won optimism: "What is useful will last, what is hurtful will sink." Emerson became convinced, as expressed in this opinion on slavery from 1844, that "a compassion for that which is not and cannot be useful or lovely, is degrading and futile." In "The Fortune of the Republic," he stressed morality, that is, good works. "Use is the end" to which man exists. A democratic aspect of charity is also implied when Emerson describes it in the mid-war lecture "American Civilization": "Use, labor of each for all, is the health and virtue of all beings." Hence, the primacy of morals is expressed in terms of the primacy of use. When we interpret Emerson's "use" this way, a line in his poem "Merlin's Song" may be understood: "The richest of all lords is Use."[29] This poem was used as a motto for "Considerations by the way" in Emerson's *The Conduct of Life*.

Emerson identifies uses with virtue, while to Swedenborg

good consists of uses. Essentially, these mean the same. To both, good affections imply, or correspond to, useful acts. Not surprisingly, one of Swedenborg's "golden sayings," praised by Emerson for its beautiful way of expressing ethical law, reads: "The perfection of man is the love of use."[30]

Emerson's ideas of self-reliance, individual success, and progress thrived in his early dialogue with the doctrines of the New Churchmen. As early as 1831, he pondered in his journal, "Is it not true that every man has before him in his own mind room in one direction to which there is no bound, but in every other direction he runs against a wall in a short time? One course of thought, affection, action is for him—that is his use, as the new men say."[31] One of the origins of this famous idea, fully developed in the essay "Spiritual Laws," is to be found here. It was part of the emergence of his secular faith in the calling and talent of everyone. Our particular use is our special assignment, the task we have to fulfill in life. "Talents supplement each other," Emerson says.[32]

Whereas Emerson dismissed utilitarianism, he subscribed to a moral and practical code of uses, where the progressive, and perhaps even pragmatic, idea of utility formed a subset, making him extol the divine uses of the railroad and other advances of his time. This includes also the intertextual presence of earlier achievements, such as the usable past, the advantage of preceding steps taken by humanity, the accumulation of knowledge and culture that is civilization.[33] The useful sums up all the good and beneficial in a moral, social, and historical sense, where the measure of value in the particular case is the general good of the whole seen as a unit.

The Ancients and the Postmoderns

Notes on the Currency of a Classic

Long ago, during the twelfth-century Renaissance in Europe, *moderni* had fought *veteres*. In late-seventeenth-century France raged "la Querelle des Anciens et des Modernes," the English counterpart of which was "The Battle of the Books." In that battle between the old and the new, Francis Bacon's philosophical optimism was the motive power of "the moderns." In Emerson's time, the American Scholar embodied "The Party of the Future," attacking "the Conservative" of "The Party of the Past." Emerson was as "modern" as Bacon in his time was a "man of good hope."

This essay was first presented in an early form as a lecture at the Guangxi Teachers University, People's Republic of China, July 1993.

In an abstract for discussions in St. Petersburg and Moscow in 1991 on the recovery of Russian philosophy and spirituality in the era of change, my colleague Stephen Lapeyrouse suggested that the idea of the humane expressed in Emerson's American Scholar address has one of its eastern counterparts in the Russian *staretz*, for instance, Zosíma in Dostoevsky's *The Brothers Karamazov*, whose communications sometimes take the shape of Swedenborg's mapping of the beyond. Both certainly represent "Man Thinking" and the independent way of the self to wisdom. However, experience is to Emerson and contemporary Americans of much more vital importance than to the Russian counterpart: there is the beginning and the end of enlightenment. The philosophizing American Scholar leads no sedentary life. Baconian reality never was turned gaseous by Concord philosophy, which persistently tried to permeate idols, the illusions. Emerson's philosophy is down to earth. Without the interplay with the outer world through the course of life, the inner world becomes silent. Wisdom is no layer to be found by excavation. Wisdom is *becoming*, is everywhere. It is a process, displayed in the laws of the dynamics of reality. Truth and wisdom cease when the pathfinder withdraws from the nature of everyday life to build a castle in the air. Far from being an intellectual or a rationalist, Emerson, like Thoreau, never left the attitude of the pathfinder, the confident pragmatist, knowing that the idea must be revised by the turn of the road. The turn, however, might be bent by a grand design; a future surveyor may not find it, since it is no longer there.

Emerson remained, indeed, an endless seeker, in Donald Gelpi's terms. His vision of our uncertain position on the ladder of experience, in his unforgettable wording after the death of his five-year-old son, opens the door to the enigma and existential wonder of the modern and postmodern world:

Where do we find ourselves? In a series of which we do not know the extremes, and believe that it has none. We wake and find ourselves on a stair; there are stairs below us, which we seem to have ascended; there are stairs above us, many a one, which go upward and out of sight. But the Genius which according to the old belief stands at the door by which we enter, and gives us the lethe to drink, that we may tell no tales, mixed the cup too strongly, and we cannot shake off the lethargy now at noonday. Sleep lingers all our lifetime about our eyes, as night hovers all day in the boughs of the fir-tree. All things swim and glitter. Our life is not so much threatened as our perception. Ghostlike we glide through nature, and should not know our place again. . . . We are like millers on the lower levels of a stream, when the factories above them have exhausted the water. We too fancy that the upper people must have raised their dams.[1]

"Life is a dream"; "life is surrounded with a sleep"—with imagery akin to the seventeenth-century outlook of Shakespeare's *The Tempest* and Pedro Calderón de la Barca's *La vida es sueño*, Emerson, as when he wrote "Illusions," explains or exclaims that we wake from one dream into another dream and that to experience every ultimate fact we eventually reach is only the first in a new series. Furthermore, every general law is only a partial fact of some more general law—a similar theme of another major essay, "Circles." In this perpetual cycle or on this stair, the sentimental, the temperamental, or even the passionate—the imaginary point of transition—is the point of support. In "Circles" the perspective is continued:

Step by step we scale this mysterious ladder: the steps are actions; the new prospect is power. Every several result is threatened and judged by that which follows. Every one seems to be contradicted by the new; it is only limited by the new.[2]

There is a definite connection between this experience and the undogmatic nonfoundational character of modern and postmodern philosophy.[3]

Erwin Schrödinger, one of the pathfinders for modern quantum mechanics, tended toward mystical explanatory models and saw parallels to his wave mechanics in the age-old religious sources of the East. However, it occurred to him that we may have reached an era where a traditional worldview—that is, an all-inclusive or a general picture of the universe—is no longer possible. A theory can eventually be falsified, but it can never be proved: it can only seem more probable, more useful. So, theories succeed each other—perhaps without end.

Far from being deconstructive (rather, it is constructive in the Baconian sense, a liberation from the world of idols), Schrödinger's view may make us understand Emerson in a new way. He did not try to destroy either belief or logic. His thought is neither a relativism nor a skepticism, still less a nihilism. There are simply no constraints of the reality principle; his fiends are prejudices and illusions, the idols of the tribe, of the cave, of the marketplace, the idols of the *theatrum mundi*, the blind acceptance of authority or tradition. That is the program of this Baconian scholar: experience and encounters without escape. The metaphysical aspect of the Emersonian attitude corresponds to pure mathematics. Emersonian "logic" may be compared to Kurt Gödel's theorem on the fundamental difficulties in formalizing a consistency proof for a logistic system within that system: "You cannot see the mountain near."[4] For similar reasons humanism may have to resort to transcendence. There is an incompleteness in the logical support for logic since a logical system cannot be proved logically, and likewise democracy cannot be justified by a ballot. From a scientific viewpoint, both morality and ontology are confronted with metaphysics: the immanent and the transcendent, instincts as well as intuitions; and what is right, according to Emerson, as well as to pragmatists like William James, John Dewey, or Charles Sanders Peirce, is, in effect, that which works, even though we are easily deceived and blinded: "Far be from me the despair which prejudges the law by a paltry empiricism;—since there never was a right endeavor but it succeeded."[5] The real is merely provisional, whereas there is a constancy in the laws of change. In this sense, Emerson can be viewed as a pragmatic optimist. He was certainly not an irrational rambler. In Emersonian thought, empiricism, intuitionism, and commonsense philosophy were combined.

Life is not intellectual, but factual. The duty of the American

Scholar is not only to think honestly, but principally to act upon his or her thoughts. The meaning of hermeneutics, the use of reading the riddle of life and becoming a poet, is moral. Even though there are similarities between Emerson and the new pragmatism and the relativistic quagmire of the modern world, as pointed out above, it is typical that Emerson, as well as classical pragmatists like James, Peirce, and Dewey all proposed a normative ethic. They were no relativists. In the forming of Emerson's ethics, as well as of his aesthetics, the notion of analogy and correspondence was instrumental and served the purpose of distinguishing between right and wrong, good and bad, good and evil.

Emerson's philosophy is a kind of holism. The fact that everything may be seen as steps on a stair, be it the great chain of being or the doctrine of series and degrees, yet leveled, affirms order, be it cosmic or random. It also means that everything has its significance, and that each may affect all.

The crucial point is the idea that facts essentially have ethical meaning, that they are never morally neutral. To understand how this notion of reality was developed, we can turn to a portending passage in Swedenborg's magnum opus, the *Arcana Coelestia*, ¶3483.

Wherever in the universe any object appears, it is a representative of the Lord's kingdom; so much so, that there is actually nothing in the atmospheric and starry universe, nothing in the earth and its three kingdoms, that does not, after its kind, represent. Because in nature the whole, and every part of the whole, are ultimate images. From the divine essence are celestial states of goodness, and from these, spiritual states of truth, and, from both of them conjointly, natural objects; and because all things, as well as each thing singly, subsists from the Divine essence— that is, continually exist from Him—and as all their derivatives must of necessity represent those states through which they become extant, therefore, it follows that the visible is nothing else but a theater, representative of the Lord's kingdom, and the kingdom itself is a theater representative of the Lord Himself.

"Books are for the scholar's idle times. When he can read God directly, the hour is too precious to be wasted in other men's transcripts of their readings," Emerson observed in his American Scholar address. He had appreciated a related statement in Swedenborg's "Prologue" to the *Animal Kingdom* (¶22); this book was not written for Emerson: "These pages of mine are written with a view to those only who never believe anything but what they can receive with the intellect," Swedenborg wrote. A contemporary reviewer of Emerson's subsequent Divinity School address focused on the homage Emerson paid to "the spirit of freedom"; however, the reviewer thought Emerson was dangerous, even though he felt it was not likely that Emerson's views would take hold in America since they were "too dreamy, too misty, too vague."[6] That haze was the climate of freedom, however, opposed to any confinement or even to any rigid definition; the two aspects were closely connected. Despite the contemporary forecast, the American climate turned Emersonian.

The commandments echo throughout the illusive and multidimensional *theatrum mundi*. In Emerson's view, it is exactly this ambiguous or contradictory quality of reality that is so convincing and reassuring. Truth can never precipitate except in this dialectic and its transitions. In an essay where these questions are addressed, "Nominalist and Realist," Emerson summarizes: "All things are in contact; every atom has a sphere of repulsion; Things are, and are not, at the same time;—and the like. All the universe over, there is but one thing, this Two-Face, creator-creature, mind-matter, right-wrong, of which any proposition may be affirmed or denied."[7] Indeed, Emerson saw that "there is throughout nature something mocking, something that leads on and on. . . . We live in a system of approximations, not of fulfillment. . . . Every end is prospective of some other end."[8] This is not skepticism or nihilism. It is faith.

Emerson's claims were dependent upon a belief in change, the flux of being. Neither Thoreau's nor Emerson's world was static. Their optimism, the belief in human power, was intimately connected with a belief in humanity's spiritual agent, the force of life, a spiritual influx.[9] Considering the quality of that spiritual element in the world of matter, and its pre-Darwinian facets, we should first of all realize in what way it was linked to the ancient idea of the Great Chain of Being. Arthur D. Lovejoy believed that the rise of romanticism meant a demise of that chain, which is partly wrong since ideas on natural hierarchies, of series and degrees in the creation, during the nineteenth century were combined with natural history, with the science of the day, which inspired Spencer and Darwin. Darwin's constant companion was Milton's *Paradise Lost*, and he certainly never aimed at annihilating the dream of return nor renounced any claims of legacy. The static world was gone long ago; now people were seeking directions, the way everything moved forward. The belief in the great chain survived. We should, then, observe that the chain traditionally is disconnected from evolution, progress, and optimism in one specific and very vital aspect: it had always principally been a static view of the universe, the opposite to changes and transitions. In the Christian tradition, which appropriated this ancient view, this meant a scale between the high and the low, a chain where each and every being was placed, from the Supreme Being to the most inferior beings in the realm of matter. Discussing twentieth-century knowledge of human nature, Page Dubois argues in *Sowing the Body* that the Freudian view of the female as a man bereft of penis, as an incomplete human, draws directly on the hierarchical view of the great chain, which sees emanating as if from God "a series of beings arranged on a ladder of diminishing value and quality, from god to philosopher to master to husband to wife to slave to animal down through the oysters."[10] This pessimistic view of the chain in the nineteenth century had been turned upside down: the particular became central, as Lovejoy rightly pointed out, and the Almighty was in effect dethroned by his earthly substitute. The rise of liberalism meant the demise of hierarchy. The static view had gradually been replaced by a dynamic view, an idea of incompleteness and imperfection: the work of the creator was only half-finished, and was in fact still going on—a view opposite to the Newtonian outlook. At the same time, belief in inspiration or spiritual influx was retained and inflated—inspiration came not from above, but from "within," or it worked "through" the human agent, acting as a mediator. The vital force itself was at the scene with the new Adam, now with the whole garden to sow. The *ladder*, or rather the direction, and still more the ambitions, were turned upstream.

The Swedenborgian focus on the human being as maker of heaven and hell on this earth and accordingly in the beyond, which helped to propel the Emersonian claims, had forerunners in neo-Platonic traditions, such as the philosophy of the Cambridge Platonists. Ralph Cudworth's massive philosophical compilation *The True Intellectual System of the Universe* concludes in the first book that, since "neither all things are produced Fortuitously, or by Unguided Mechanism of Matter, nor God himself may reasonably be thought to do all things" immediately or miraculously, there must be a plastic force of nature itself which executes "that part of His Providence."[11] This idea of a creative force in our world, in both Swedenborg and Emerson (although to different effects) was combined with the notion of spiritual influx or inspiration. In Swedenborg, the vertical hierarchy survives; in Emerson, it is being dissolved. There we touch upon a momentary breaking point between the old world and the new, a discontinuity in the tradition. In the same way, Emerson's idea of originality forebodes the modern idea of intertextuality, which paradoxically dismisses the idea of literary heritage, sources, and influence for one that figures unique new combinations of old elements in a particular space-time, just as oysters are made of the same kind of elementary particles as suns, only in different arrangements. When the hierarchies were dismantled and the shimmer of the past was dying, literary history, quite unlike biological history, lost something of its lineage. Leaving out the stress laid upon the antiquity of elements, as his own house was a "quotation" from woods and mines, Emerson's transcendental theory of aesthetics was not a doctrine of descent, and neither was the thinking of other American transcendentalists. The philosophical tenet that shaped the American mind was an idea of perennial individual ascent in a pluralistic and ever-changing universe.[12] In this scenery, we can perceive Swedenborg's ladder of ascent as if in a galaxy of mirrors.

Symbolism and Modernity

The precondition for any crosswise symbolization or correspondence in the world is some kind of unity or organic structure, common origins, and different levels within that whole, making it a dual (or plural) monism. All these old ideas were revivified in nineteenth-century New England and are the reason for the centrality of the image. The propelling force is the interaction between science and metaphysics, as apparent in Emerson as in Coleridge. Religion could only be saved by adjustment; the old theology was replaced by a focus on the spiritual forces answering to the material move, analogies. Stasis was replaced by dynamics, as Macaulay wrote on the new Baconian thought, for "it is a philosophy which never rests, which has never attained, which is never perfect. Its law is progress."[13] "The philosophy of Bacon began in observations and ended in arts." Nature appeared as increasingly "symbolic" since Being revealed itself as always Becoming, the only fixed points in the universe being invisible laws. Likewise with the state—be it an estate of the realm, a body politic, or simply a manner of standing—is never static but rather a structure in a process of time, if not fictitious: it has an invisible nature. It is, in Carlyle's terms, also a text.

Poetical imagery meant an exchange between or within the material and the spiritual levels. All tropes expressing some similarity, like parables, metaphors, symbols, allegories or personifications, then are of four kinds in our two-faced mid-world of icy hearts and sighing winds, windbags and sunny moods, currents, movements, streams, and revolutions, rock-bottom depressions and storms of anger. It is always an exchange, and upon that perpetual crossing transcendental religion and poetics rested. Observation—the scientific approach, the "naturalist" devotion of Emerson, Thoreau, Melville, and Whitman—was the starting point for a development towards symbolism, a consequence of realist "accuracy" and spiritual observance.[14] The symbolic contribution of Swedenborg was that he "observed and published the laws of nature."[15]

Emerson wanted to "merge religion into literature, and realize theology,"[16] and the origin of transcendentalism and symbolism is partly exegetical: a generalization of ideas concerning scriptural language, as studied by Philip F. Gura in *The Wisdom of Words* and by Richard A. Grusin in *Transcendentalist Hermeneutics*.[17] The starting point for Emerson's now-acknowledged "modernity" was liberal theology, historicist relativism, and "higher criticism" in Unitarian scriptural exegesis. Swedenborg's doctrine of correspondence, which became literarily influential, was originally a mode of interpreting the Bible by means of natural analogy, which attracted much attention in the early-nineteenth century. In this context, both Whitman and Swedenborg belong to an old hermeneutic tradition, where the language of God was stereoscopically read in the *litteræ sacre* and the *liber naturæ*.[18] There are many similarities between Whitman's and Swedenborg's conceptions of the nature of language and the language of nature. The context of the remarkable susceptibility to that kind of thinking in nineteenth-century America was a sustained theological debate over the authority of scriptural language, where the doctrine of correspondences was to represent an allegorical or proto-metaphoric approach from which American symbolism germinated.[19] From the point of view of literary history, this is the reason that Swedenborg, in Perry Miller's terms, became "a pervasive influence upon New England transcendentalism, as fundamental as Coleridge and Carlyle."[20]

Since there is an innate relation between words, images, and things and because the concrete and material must be used to express the abstract and the spiritual, there also appears—in the words of Michel Foucault—"*une symétrie rassurante qui fait de l'inconnu le reflet inversé du connu:*"[21] the original apprehension of correspondences between the mundane things and a supra-mundane reality naturally may arise in the human condition from a linguistic awareness. Angelo Bertocci, in *From Symbolism to Baudelaire*, looks upon nineteenth-century symbolism as the summit of a long tradition that he traces back to antiquity. As has been pointed out by Joseph Anthony Mazzeo in *Renaissance and Seventeenth Century Studies* (1964), Swedenborg served as a bridge-builder between Renaissance and Baroque metaphysics and modern symbolism. Anna Balakian, in her well-known book *The Symbolist Movement*, maintains that this tradition inspired modern symbolism through the agency of Swedenborg and Jean-Paul Sartre (*Baudelaire*, 1947) and Julia Kristeva (*Histoires d'amour*, 1983) on the whole agree on Swedenborg's impact in their country. Viewed also from C.M. Bowra's wide perspective in his classical *The Heritage of Symbolism*, Emerson and Whitman as well as Swedenborg are "symbolists," in a specific modern sense, though. According to them, humanity is no longer fallen and neither is our world, and we have no longer tied a fragile hope to a capricious Grace. Mankind is rising to its full stature, and the possibilities are immense. The Day of Doom is past, and people embrace the world, where they are themselves creators. A modern optimism is being born. In this world, language itself, the interplay between word and object, early offered the great enigma and the great revelation both to Swedenborg and to Whitman: it was a key to the soul. That view was combined with the positive view of life and this world, with the focus on man. The conception of all things as pregnant with transcendent meaning in a world fully at humanity's disposal makes symbolism neighbor to naturalism. Romanticism and realism can be viewed as complementary aspects or two sides of the same coin. As Harry Levin has remarked, "The relationship between the two movements, as we acknowledge more and more, is continuous rather than antithetical. The realism of the romanticists has its dialectical counterpart in the romanticism of the realists."[22] Going one step further, the Mexican poet Octavio Paz, recipient of the Nobel Prize for Literature in 1990, pointed out in his Harvard lectures (published in *Los hijos del limo*, 1986) that modernism is indebted to Swedenborgian doctrines. Historians are aware of this, Paz says, but mostly they suppress this knowledge.

The Moral End

The first American writers to be widely read in Russia were James Fenimore Cooper and Washington Irving. *The Spy* and *Rip Van Winkle* were translated in 1825. Thomas Mayne Reid, Harriet Beecher Stowe, Emerson, and Thoreau were authors favored in the second half of the nineteenth century, very much due to their moral reasoning in the days of the emancipation of the serfs (1861). Thoreau's *Civil Disobedience* influenced Tolstoi. In the early-twentieth century, Whitman also became part of the Russian literary scene, where he was to influence the modernists, especially the futurists, among them Mayakovsky. The literary scholar and essayist Viktor Shklovsky, who was associated with the *Lef* futurists and contributed to their journals, moves very closely to Concordian imagination in his pursuits of the volatile links between reality, language, and mind. Emerson's idea, that language is fossil poetry, in Shklovsky's version corresponds to a petrifaction of reality itself: the use of literary imagination and transformation is to make our commonplace reality visible and the mute metaphors audible by the stairway of estrangement, surprise, and new encounters.

In the field of mediation and transition, poetry and morality coincide. Their fiber, like the physical world of the mind, is riveted to the nexus, the mathematical point. In his early youth, Emerson had concluded that, since there are two natures, the moral and the material, there is also a science of ethics.[23] Emerson apprehended these principles already as a student, as can be seen from his journals. It is important to note that this foundation was set almost from the beginning, long before he began to read Swedenborg, Coleridge, and other such current "unconventional" literature of the time. His thinking was rooted in the seventeenth and eighteenth centuries. But the universal consequences of these thoughts occurred to him only gradually; the greatest leaps forward were taken in his crisis years of the 1830s. The full convergence of moral and poetics was an outcome of his "naturalist" conversion. In the antebellum turbulence, when his moral reasoning was actuated from the very breadth of his mind, all the deep connections surfaced. In 1858, when the land was rocked by the gale of dissension, his lapidarian memoranda appear as syllogisms, as part of an ethic-aesthetic *Tractatus*:

"Use of life is to learn metonymy. All thought is analogizing."
"Metaphysics the transcendency of physics. All thought analogizes."
"Every natural law is a moral law."[24]

For the development of this universal paradigm, which is the basic concept of Concord philosophy, the mechanism behind all writings and endeavors, writers like De Staël, Swedenborg, Jeffrey, Butler, Bacon, and many others supplied Emerson with instrumental examples and incitements. In this way he continued and transformed the moral reasoning of the American Revolution and the constitution, represented by the eighteenth-century scientific approach to morals of Tom Paine and the Anglo-Saxon moral-sense conviction of people like Thomas Jefferson, and through the era of liberalism, independence, secularization, national literature, and Civil War. In Emerson we clearly perceive the connections between the Emancipation Proclamation of 1862 and the Declaration of Independence of 1776, but also the distance traveled. These disconnections, some of which are revealed in the whirl of political and spiritual currents, in effect represent a part of an on-going social and ideological process from the national Bill of Rights to the Declaration of Human Rights.[25] Equal liberty is "a slow fruit," Emerson said. At one and the same time, we face a decisive phase in the making of modern literature and thought. From the point of view of classical metaphysics (as well as of metaphysical classicism), Emerson's own struggle to save his confidence and age-old convictions in an era of science, technology, industrialization, and social change can be seen as one of the last major attempts at a reconciliation between the old world and the new.

The Russian reformer Aleksandr Muravyov, a leader of the Decembrist Conspiracy in 1825 and active in drafting and carrying through the peasant reform of 1861, was, as we have seen in a previous essay in this volume, a devoted Swedenborgian all his mature life and is known for his secret distribution of handwritten copies of Swedenborg's works, a *samizdat* of the era. His attraction to the principles of the New Church was obviously in harmony with his love of freedom and right of all men. His English friend the Reverend Jonathan Bayley thought that was a natural result of teachings that declare "that man should act from liberty according to reason" and that without these two faculties man "cannot be reformed and regenerated." This is a crucial point, since there is no place for any natural right at all unless the moral value of individual freedom is recognized, including an absolute freedom of thought.[26] Freedom was conceived as a condition for amelioration or perennial progress, which would imply a perpetual revision of traditional views and values, and contradict any claims of petrified dogma. In these, in practice relativist terms, a future ascension of humanity was envisoned.

A Mirror
Reflecting a
Higher Reality

Hermetics,
Al-Qur'an, and the
Crisis of Modern Man

In Christendom where is the Christian?
RALPH WALDO EMERSON, "Self-Reliance"

Swedenborg was the last Christian.

EMERSON, *Journals*

*Swedenborg styles himself in the title-page of his books, "Servant of the Lord
Jesus Christ," and by force of intellect, and in effect, he is the last Father in the
Church.*

EMERSON, *Representative Men*

Inspired by Ralph Waldo Emerson's inquiry into the universe of correspondences, the Argentine writer Jorge Luis
Borges, in an essay on Swedenborg, highlighted the centrality of
"things" in the world of man:

From a symbolic reading of the Bible, Swedenborg went on to a
symbolic reading of the universe and of human beings. The sun
in the sky is an image of the spiritual sun, which is in its turn an
image of God: there is not a single creature on earth that does
not owe its continued existence to the constant influence of the
Divine Being. Thomas De Quincey, who was a reader of
Swedenborg's works, writes that the smallest things are secret

mirrors of the greatest. Carlyle says that universal history is a text we must continually read and write, and in which we are also written. The disturbing suspicion that we are ciphers and symbols in a divine cryptography whose true meaning we do not know abounds in the volumes of Léon Bloy, and the Jewish Cabbalists knew of it. . . . In the first chapter of the Scripture we read that God created man according to his own image and likeness. This affirmation implies that God has the shape of man. The Cabbalists who compiled the Book of Creation [Sefer Yetsirah] declare that the ten emanations, or sefiroth, whose source is the ineffable divinity, can be conceived under the species of a tree or of a Man—the primordial man, the Adam Kadmon. If all things are in God, all things are also in man, who is his earthly reflection. Thus, Swedenborg and the Cabbalah both arrive at the concept of the microcosm, that is to say, man as the mirror or compendium of the universe. According to Swedenborg, hell and heaven are in man, as well as plants, mountains, seas, continents, minerals, trees, flowers, thistles, fish, tools, cities, and buildings."[1]

This is an organic facet of both the centrality of humanity and a metaphysical materialism that has some bearing on the development of both realism and symbolism in the middle of the nineteenth century. Glimpses of the cabalistic and hermetic undercurrents in Western traditions of thought have been seen from time to time ever since their appearance in the whirling surfs of the Renaissance. Penetrating into the complex semiotics of correspondential imagery, we may inquire into yet another semitic connection, and turn to Henry Corbin's special survey of Creative Imagination, and Seyyed Hossein Nasr's challenging evaluation of the spiritual standard of modern man.

Searching focal points by means of distant reflections, the world of the Qur'an offers material for comparison. Emerson, when he wrote about Swedenborg, Plato, and Shakespeare, quoted the Qur'an. He referred particularly to Davāni's Persian tract Akhlak-i-Jalāly, "exalted morals," where he found a connection between Mohammed and Plato, between Rumi, Sa'adi and Swedenborg, between the Orient and the Occident.

Seyyed Hossein Nasr, in *The Encounter of Man and Nature*, joins Islamic traditions to Renaissance ideas. In doing so, he describes different levels of meaning. In Islam, the *Logos* or Word of God is the unforfeitable link between man and nature. Revelation to humanity is inseparable from the cosmic revelation, the miracle of nature, which is also a "book" of God. Besides the recorded Qur'an, there is also a "Qur'an of creation," which contains the "ideas" or "archetypes" of all things. "Yet the intimate knowledge of nature depends upon the knowledge of the inner meaning of the sacred text or hermeneutic interpretation (*ta'wil*)." The key to the inner meaning of things lies in penetrating "from the outward (*zahir*) to the inward (*batin*) meaning of the Qur'an"—which roughly corresponds to *sensus externus* and *sensus internus* of Swedenborgian exegetics (although there are higher levels as well).

Nasr recognizes the same search for the roots of knowledge in the esoteric meaning of a sacred text in Middle Age writers like Philo, Hugo of St. Victor, Joachim of Flora, in Hermeticist and neo-Platonic thinkers of the Renaissance, and in Swedenborg in the eighteenth century. This likeness is not only in the form of approach but also in the structure of meaning, and Swedenborg's achievements especially can be understood in Islamic terms. Consonant with the discernible Renaissance or rather Baroque elements of his traditionally tinged philosophy, the anatomy of existence "consisted not only of the physical and the purely intelligible worlds but also of the intermediary world between matter of pure spirit, the 'imaginal world' (*mundus imaginalis*)," which was the immediate principle of nature "and through it the symbolic science of nature was made possible. Among Christian thinkers (albeit distant from the center of theological orthodoxy), even after the Renaissance a man like Swedenborg could write a hermeneutic commentary upon the Bible that was also an exposition of a symbolic science of nature and could rely upon this intermediary world as the meeting ground of spiritual and material forms."

The seventeenth-century Cambridge Platonists, Ralph Cudworth and Henry More foremost among them, spoke of this domain of reality. But "the Cartesian surgical operation," which

separated spirit and matter, closed the shutters to this domain of
meaning, which henceforth remained hidden. The Holy Scripture, like nature itself, became opaque. Nasr tells us that Islam,
however, refusing to separate man and nature, has preserved an
integral view of the universe, similar to that found in Swedenborg. "From the bosom of nature man seeks to transcend nature,
and nature herself can be an aid in this process provided man
can learn to contemplate it, not as an independent domain of reality but as a mirror reflecting a higher reality, a vast panorama
of symbols which speak to man and have meaning for him."[2]

Addressing the crisis of modern man, Nasr hopes to restore
Christian doctrines with the help of Eastern metaphysics: for the
same reason he and other Muslims invoke "Shaykh Swedenborg," the last Christian. In his approaches to Sufism, Henry
Corbin has recognized Swedenborgian characteristics such as
the *mundus imaginalis*, the notion of an *ecclesia spiritualis*, and a
hermeneutics of "the invisible history" of spiritual man.[3]

However, it appears to us that Swedenborg was not "the last
Christian" in Nasr's sense—perhaps even less than in Emerson's
sense.[4] Nor was he the first. Nasr's description of the Islamic art
of deciphering nature is a fair summation of one aspect of Emerson's profoundly influential ideas on the nature of Art and symbolic writing—the intermediary world, the mid-world of
humanity, being the hermeneutic field of activity where the
reader is the writer. This is a key to Emerson's repeated references to "the mid-world," which he extolled: the mid-world "is
best." The idiom of intermediation is indirection. That is also
the reason that Emerson calls the world "a vast trope," a poem
being read and written at the same time, a nexus. It is the transparent mirror of the flood of reality, subject and object; the
scene is the medium. In Concord, Narcissus and Newton com-
bine. In this process of identification between mankind and nature, creator and creation, reader and writer, Swedenborgian
metaphysics served as a catalyst, since it maintained the two opposite angles of incidence, theurgy as well as interpretation, man
as builder and receiver, father and son: the creator in this world
is the maker of heaven and hell. In this spiritual yet secularized

modernism, which we can trace from Emerson to Borges and beyond, the mid-world became the center, the summit.[5]

To understand the heart of this central trait of the westerner, however, we must penetrate even deeper, below the substratum of ideological descent and out of earshot of the racing currents of historical event.

The Theurg of the Middle World

In his essay on William Blake, the Polish Nobel Prize winner Czeslaw Milosz called Swedenborg a "theurgus," indicating a belief in a supernatural agency in human affairs, the doctrine of influx from the spiritual world. Theurgy is an old mystical concept. It was developed as a magical or religious science among Roman Neoplatonists, foremost among them the emperor Julianus Apostata. There was a related thought also in Philo, the "Philonic inspiration" or revelation through the Logos. To grasp Emerson's idea of creativity and inspiration, his sometimes almost-Platonic skepticism towards ingenuity and imagination (fabulism or "divine madness"), his epistemological standpoint that was neither realistic nor idealistic, and his idea of God and man's mission, this concept supplies us with an important key—which also provides an illuminating comparison to something peculiar in his poetical imagery, the asymmetry (or contradiction) he perceived in the symbolic character of our world.

The idea that there is a divine wisdom concealed in the ancient Egyptian language, the ideographic hieroglyphs, containing a key to reality in its images, was developed among Pythagoreans and early neo-Platonists. The idea of a divine hermeneutics was combined with the idea of theurgy. Emerson, for example, owned two copies, one in Latin, of one of the most influential works in this tradition, Iamblichus' *De mysteriis Egyptiorum*.[6] In the English edition, translated by Thomas Taylor, Emerson marked especially the passages on what he calls the "Magic of theurgy."[7] The idea of a divine hermeneutics, a natural language and a language of nature and of the supernatural agency in

133

human affairs, was developed further, in the scientific context of the seventeenth and the eighteenth century, into a comprehensive system by Swedenborg.

In Swedenborg's first, scientifically tuned outline of the doctrine of correspondence, *Clavis hieroglyphica*, and onwards in the bulk of his theosophic writings, the ancient powers of the human species are focused.[8]

Swedenborg's major work *Arcana Coelestia* and a number of supplementary works were a massive effort to interpret the language of the Bible allegorically or symbolically. He did not intend to be bringing in anything new. This was a rediscovery of an ancient language, an inherent relationship between spirit and object, the concrete and the abstract. He even dreamed of a universal dictionary, a key to the hieroglyphs of reality on which he succeeded only in making a start, namely, the work drafted in his period of scientific emphasis, *Clavis hieroglyphica*, "A Hieroglyphic Key," which is in itself a key to Swedenborg's later writings—cast in a rational mold. In this work, we find a distinctive, versatile effort concentrated on rediscovering and reclaiming the ancient language, the primal human language, invented by mankind and consonant with humanity's environment, the mysterious text of the world, an effort originating from an attempt to find a universal mathematics for creation and the nature of its inherent laws. The starting point for this was Swedenborg's developing theory about the sequences or levels of creation, between which—as within which—he found clear analogies or correspondences. In this he believed he had the key to heavenly mysteries, to the unseen that lies behind objects. That was the Adamite language.[9]

The "hieroglyphic key" takes for granted that there are three universal levels that correspond to each other and together pervasively underlie creation. Thus, there exists, in Swedenborg's first example, an interplay between motion and impelling force in the course of nature, just as in the relationship between intention and activity in human beings. These in turn correspond to the fact that divine providence presupposes God's desire for results. There are correspondences between nature, humanity, and

God. According to another example, there is an effort, a principle of activity, and therefore there is also the possibility of realization. The nature of the impelling force determines the motion and its effect. In every individual's inner reaches, in his or her intention, there is a specific underlying tendency or love with some particular purpose. By analogy with the relationship between impelling force, motion, and effect, a person's wishes depend on his or her unique preference, and intention or benevolence depends on the nature of the individual's wishes. All this determines behavior, or as much of his or her intent as the individual can accomplish. Correspondences have to do with the divine, spiritual plan. However, the nature-humanity-God harmony can change into discord: Swedenborg is obviously thinking about the Fall. In the world order and the "representative" or symbolic world, perfection reigns if there is a ruling harmony between divine providence, earthly intentions and goals, and nature's impelling forces and activities.

Between the divine model objects, the *exemplaria*, and the intellectual, moral, and political world of *typi et imagines*, along with the similarly symbolic representations of nature, there should (or "ought to,") rule a complete mutual harmony—"at all costs." God, therefore, does not manage the world all by himself, but according to his image, whose character and intent are of fundamental significance for conditions in the world. God remains in touch with the perceptible world "through" humanity, which is God's *medius proportionalis*, the being in the middle acting as a nexus.

The most striking feature in Swedenborg's writing is the central role humanity is given in the face of everything; God seems powerless in relation to our free will. On the other hand, God is the world-ordering standard with which we must align ourselves in order to attain personal and societal happiness in both the short and long term, and the divine is present in the vital force throughout nature. Precisely as in Emerson, humanity is described as being in the middle of the world, but in the presence of nature, whose standard we can use to measure our self-willed deviation, as Emerson explained in *Nature* (1836). For Emerson too, our role is to be the Creator's deputies: the Highest Essence creates the world around us "through" us, "puts it forth through us." The human being, as the creating deputy, actually has access to God's consciousness, "has access to the entire mind of the Creator, is himself the creator in the finite."[10]

Swedenborg, then, presented an exalted view of humanity from a Christian perspective, remote indeed from both the Calvinist and the Lutheran moods. Only through the agency of the human mind, the divine has access to reality. In this sense, humans are mirrors of God.

Notes

Music, Mysticism, and Modernity, pp. 3–16

1. The chamber organ was restored by Mads Kjersgaard in 1985; he has described this type of instrument in a paper published in the Danish journal *Orglet* 2 (1984): 4–27. The conservator conjectured that the instrument was manufactured (in the mid-1700s) probably at an organ workshop near Swedenborg's estate at Hornsgatan in Stockholm. The organ is item No. 77.233 at Skansen; there are several documents relating to this instrument in the archives of the museum. The chamber organ is described in Einar Erici's and Axel Unnerbäck's *Orgelinventarium* (Propius: Stockholm, 1988). After Swedenborg's death, the organ seems to have been in the possession of one of his early followers, the clergyman Gabriel Rosén (1720–1784), and then his son, the organist Eric Gabriel von Rosén (1775–1866). After them, it was owned by the opera singer Isidor Dannström. Finally, it was among the belongings of the famous collector Christian Hammer, before Skansen bought it at an auction held in 1893.

2. The family name, Svedberg, was changed to Swedenborg in 1719 when the children of Jesper Svedberg were ennobled by Queen Ulrika Eleonora.

3. See E. Liedgren, *Svensk psalm och andlig visa* (Diakonistyrelsens förlag: Stockholm, 1926); and H.W. Tottie, *Jesper Svedbergs lif och verksamhet* (Uppsala, 1885–1886).

4. George Trobridge, *Swedenborg: Life and Teaching* (London: Swedenborg Society, rvd. 1974), 108; cf. the accounts of "Music Appreciation" (series), *The Territorial: Newsletter of the Tuscon Az. Society of the General Church of the New Jerusalem*, 1989. *New Church Life* (January 1914), a journal of the Academy of the New Church, responds to an editorial in *The New York Musical Courier* of November 19, 1913, on "Swedenborg and Music."

5. Cyriel Odhner Sigstedt, *The Swedenborg Epic* (London: Swedenborg Society, 1981), 16; Alfred Acton, ed., *Letters and Memorials of Emanuel Swedenborg*, vol. 1 (Bryn Athyn, Penn.: Swedenborg Scientific Association, 1948–1955), 7–8.

6. R.L. Tafel, ed., *Documents Concerning the Life and Character of Emanuel Swedenborg*, vol. 1 (London: 1875–1877), 203.

7. Acton, vol. 1, 55–59. Cf. *The New York Musical Courier*, November 19, 1913; *New Church Life*, January 1914, 57–58; and *The Territorial*, November 1989, 3–4.

8. Acton, vol. 1, 11, 15–16, 70.

9. Tafel, vol. 1, 20; vol. 2, 5.

10. Tafel, vol. 1, 615–616.; vol. 2, 908.

11. Swedenborg's notion of harmony is related to that expressed in the influential Jean-Philippe Rameau's *Traité de L'harmonie: Reduite à ses Principes naturels* (1722), which set the tone for the world of music in his time.

12. Brussels, August 26, 1736 (Tafel, vol. 2, 89).

13. Turin, April 1738 (Tafel, vol. 2, 105).

14. Trobridge, 60.

15. Verona, April 1738 (Tafel, vol. 2, 109).

16. Swedenborg later reported that he had spoken with the great composer on the day the latter was buried, and even at the very moment of his funeral. See Tafel, vol. 1, 6. General Christian de Tuxen also witnessed the musical side of Swedenborg's character on the last trip (Tafel, vol. 2, 437).

17. Trobridge, 108.

18. For my understanding of Swedenborg's conception of music, I have drawn especially from *Apocalypse Explained*, ¶323–326; 376, 700:28, and 936; *Apocalypse Revealed*, ¶ 276, 279, and 661; *Arcana Cœlestia*, ¶417–424, 457, 1977, 2595, 3880, 3893, 8195, and 8337–8340; *Conjugial Love*, ¶3, 6, 55, 86, and 243; *De Verbo*, ¶ 3; *Divine Providence*, ¶190; *Doctrine of Charity*, ¶189; *Doctrine of Faith*, ¶42; *Last Judgment (Posthumous)*, ¶308; *On the Divine Wisdom*, ¶X:5; *Spiritual Diary*, ¶2090, 2403, 2581, 5603, and 5990; and *True Christian Religion*, ¶353 and 763.

19. String music thus is conceived in the mid-world of the spirits, not in the heaven of the angels.

20. A contemporary counterpart of Swedenborg's notion of the origin of music, as expressed in the *Arcana Coelestia*, is found in, for example, J.A. Scheibe's *Abhandlung vom Ursprunge und Alter der Musik* (1754); cf. Warren Dwight Allen, *Philosophies of Music History: A Study of General Histories of Music* (New York: Dover, 1939; rpt. 1962), 50ff.

21. Cf. Frank Bostock, "Music in the Ritual of Worship," *Journal of Education of the Academy of the New Church* (1947): 167–176; and the musi-

cian Lachlan Pitcairn's views on "The Value of Music," *Performing Arts in the New Church* 2, no. 1 (October 1991): 5–6.

22. Trobridge, 258; William R. Woofenden, *Swedenborg Researcher's Manual* (Bryn Athyn, Penn.: Swedenborg Scientific Association,1988), 7–10.

23. *New Church Life* (1895): 102, 153–155, 184.

24. See the very informative paper by Helen Colley, "The Development of Music in the New Church," *Journal of Education of the Academy of the New Church* (1911): 31–41.

25. *The New Philosophy* 3 (1988): 643–644.

26. Anders Hallengren, "Hôtel du Nord 1874," *Världarnas Möte— Nya Kyrkans Tidning* (Stockholm), nos. 1–2 (1990): 4–6.

27. The latter—"The Influence of Swedenborg on the Music of Richard Yardumian"—was published in Robin Larsen, ed., *Emanuel Swedenborg: A Continuing Vision* (Swedenborg Foundation: New York, 1988), 73–77. The Longstaff article is unpublished, but a copy may be obtained from the Lord's New Church, Bryn Athyn, Penn.

28. *New Church Messenger* (1954): 381; and *Who's Who in Music*.

29. Geoffrey R. Self, *In Town Tonight: A Centenary Study of Eric Coates* (London: Thames Publishing, 1986), 26, 66.

30. In Sweden, as in other countries, both composers of sacred music (such as the hymnwriter Karin Höjer) and musicians and composers of more profane music (such as Sven-Eric Johanson and Tommie Haglund) have been imbued with the spirit of Swedenborg. This fact may seem remarkable, but is rather illustrative, since we are here approaching problems regarding the nature of serious music, where distinctions of this kind basically appear out of place.

31. Friedemann Horn, "Kant's Relationship to Swedenborg and the Consequences" (unpublished, Zürich); letter from Horn of January 5, 1993, on his conversations with Furtwängler's widow, who told him that Furtwängler was especially pleased with Swedenborg's *Conjugial Love;* Gordon Jacobs, "Men of Note," *Outlook* 3 (1992): 1–2. I am indebted to Gordon Jacobs, Norman Ryder, Friedemann Horn, and Olle Hjern for information on pertinent passages in the following works: Paul Griffiths, A *Concise History of Modern Music* (London: Thames & Hudson, 1978); Bernard Grun, ed., *Alban Berg: Letters to His Wife* (London: Faber & Faber, 1971); Hans Moldenhauer, *Anton von Webern* (London: Gollancz, 1978); Willi Schuh, *Richard Strauss: A Chronicle of the Early Years, 1864–1898,* trans. Mary Whittall (Cambridge: Cambridge

University Press, 1982); Arthur M. Abell, *Talks with Great Composers* (New York: Philosophical Library, 1994); Malcolm MacDonald, *Schoenberg* (London: Dent, 1976); Alan Philip Lessem, *Music and Text in the Works of Arnold Schoenberg* (Ann Arbor, Mich.: UMI Research Press, 1979); Walter B. Bailey, *Programmatic Elements in the Works of Schoenberg* (Ann Arbor, Mich.: UMI Research Press, 1984); Jelena Hahl-Koch, ed., *Arnold Schoenberg–Wassili Kandinsky: Letters, Pictures, and Documents* (London: Faber and Faber, 1984); H.H. Stuckenschmidt, *Schoenberg: His Life, World, and Work* (London: Calder, 1977); Willi Reich, *Schoenberg: A Critical Biography*, trans. Leo Black (n.p.: Longman, 1971); Alexander L. Ringer, *Arnold Schoenberg: The Composer as a Jew* (Oxford: Clarendon Press, 1980); and *Schweizer Musiker Lexikon/Dictionnaire des Musiciens Suisses* (1964).

32. Gérard de Nerval, *Aurélia*, in *Oeuvres*, vol. 1, ed. Albert Béguin and Jean Richer (Paris: Gallimard, 1952).

33. Honoré de Balzac, *Séraphita* in *La comédie humaine*, ed. Marcel Bouteron (Paris: Nouvelle revue français, Bibliothèque de La Pléiade, 1937).

34. A. Schönberg, *Style and Idea: Selected Writings*, ed. Leonard Stein (London: Faber and Faber, 1975); Joscelyn Godwin, *Music, Mysticism and Magic: A Sourcebook* (New York: Arkana, 1987); and Dore Ashton, *A Fable of Modern Art* (London: Thames & Hudson, 1980). All these texts comment upon Schönberg's mysticism. Balzac's confession is found in his *Oeuvres posthumes, Lettres à l'Etrangère*, vol. 1, 403.

35. *Offene Tore* 3 (1992): 110–113; Finn Benestad, *Musik och Tanke: Huvudlinjer i musikestetikens historia från antiken till vår egen tid* (Stockholm: Rabén och Sjögren,1978), 296–297. J. Brand, C. Hailey, and D. Harris, *The Berg–Schoenberg Correspondence: Selected Letters* (New York: Norton, 1987); Gordon Jacobs (1992), 1–2.

36. Warren Dwight Allen, *Philosophies of Music History: A Study of General Histories of Music* (New York: American Book Company, 1939; rpt. Dover Books, 1962), 275.

37. Cf. Creda Glenn, "What is New Church Music?" *New Church Music Post* (Newsletter) 3, no. 3 (June 1979): 3–8.

38. The breaking-up of traditional space-time, as in Schönberg's analysis, also corresponded to a development in contemporary physics, the theory of relativity and wave mechanics of the 1910s and the 1920s, according to which "there is no absolute down, no right or left, forward or backward," in Schönberg's words.

39. Even electronic music has been apprehended as supernatural in character, otherworldly, if not dehumanizing—as for example in Simon Parmet's *Con Amore* (1960), 249.

40. See Josepf N. Straus, *Remaking the Past: Musical Modernism and the Influence of the Tonal Tradition* (Cambridge: Harvard University Press, 1990).

41. There is another possible interpretation, which is quite the opposite. It is indicated in *Apocalypse Explained* ¶376c, at the moment when music dies away, when there is no longer any singing in the vineyard; at the moment when heavenly enjoyment of goodness and truth is gone, when the song ebbs out, and silence settles down upon our dwellings. That is, music as representation. Cf. J.O. Urmson's lucid discussion on "Representation in Music," in the series *Royal Institute of Philosophy Lectures*, vol. 6 (1971–72); *Philosophy and the Arts* (London: The Royal Institute of Philosophy/The Macmillan Press Ltd., 1973), 132–146.

The Secret of Magna Tartaria, pp. 17–41

1. August Strindberg, *Inferno*, chapter 6. Cf. Martin Lamm, *Strindberg och Makterna* (Stockholm: Svenska kyrkans diakonistyrelses bokförlag, 1936), 97ff. See also Strindberg's letter to the theosophist Torsten Hedlund, May 15, 1896, in *August Strindbergs Brev*, vol. 10 (Stockholm: Bonniers, 1948–1996), 192. Strindberg's study of Swedenborg has been surveyed by Göran Stockenström in his dissertation "Ismael i Öknen" (Uppsala University, 1972) and in later works.

2. On Swedenborg, Tibetans, Chinese, and "mahatmas" in *The Secret Doctrine*, vols. 1–2 (rpt. 1970), cf. S. B. Liljegren's information on the background in *Bulwer-Lytton's Novels and Isis Unveiled* (Uppsala, Sweden: Lundequistska bokh.,1957).

3. *Strindbergs Brev*, vol. 16, 127–130.

4. The name "Tartary," as well as "Chinese Tartary," for the Central Asian mountain regions has been used into far later times; see, for example, Robert Shaw's famous *Visits to High Tartary* (1871) and Owen Lattimore's *High Tartary* (1975).

5. This final sentence, in Swedenborg's New-Latin, is *"apud illos gubernet qui potest gubernare, et si non potest, dimittatur cum mulcta [multa]."* An alternate translation can be "with them, he governs who is able to govern, and if he is not able, he is dismissed with a fine," which offers a parallel to Plato's reflections on the ideal state, namely, that the best

people will not become involved in governing, and therefore must be compelled to do so by means of threats. Cf. Swedenborg's *Heaven and Hell* ¶213–230, 559, and 564, where it is explained why those who want to rule and oppress others are implacably cast out.

6. W. H. Acton, A. W. Acton, and F. Coulson, *The Spiritual Diary* (London: Swedenborg Society, 1962), ¶6077.

7. *The Last Judgment*, ¶133, tr. John Whitehead, in *Posthumous Theological Works*, 2nd edition (West Chester, Pennsylvania: Swedenborg Foundation, 1996). The Latin text and a facsimile of the manuscript were published by R. L. Tafel (1870). A translation of the same text by the Orientalist Eric Hermelin (1920), the only Swedish version, begins its selection, remarkably enough, with the paragraph that follows immediately *after* the one mentioning the Chinese and the Tartars, i.e., from ¶134.

8. *En Blå Bok*, vol. 2 (1918), 621–624. Cf. Strindberg's research methods as far back as 1897 in *Strindbergs Brev*, vol. 12, 247ff. See also "height" (*altitudo*) and "mountain" (*mons*) in Potts' *Concordance*.

9. Thus it was that, in an Egyptian Christian congregation in Alexandria, I was shown their oldest biblical document, a sealed scroll in a locked display case.

10. See Inge Jonsson, *Swedenborgs korrespondenslära* (Stockholm: Almqvist & Wiksell, 1969), 249–253; Inge Jonsson and Olle Hjern, *Swedenborg* (Stockholm: Proprius, 1976), 94–95; and Inge Jonsson, *Humanistiskt Credo* (Stockholm: Norstedts, 1988), 201, 211.

11. *Kulturhistoriska Studier* (1881), 67.

12. Olle Hjern, *Swedenborg och hans vänner i Göteborg* (Stockholm: Nykyrkliga Bokförlaget Swedenborgsförlaget, 1990), 8ff.

13. The same books occupied Swedenborg, we note parenthetically, as sustained the Abbé Casanova during his infamous long imprisonment in the "lead chambers" of Venice. Wolff, like Leibniz, became widely read in Europe, so even an indirect familiarity with their ideas was common. From a reading of Wolff, perhaps especially his *Theologia naturalis*, it is possible, I believe, to trace Casanova's idea that "morality is the metaphysics of physics" (cf. *Mémoires*, vol. 2), a kind of analogical thinking whose power constitutes the background to the eager reception of the doctrine of correspondences within the romantic and symbolist movements of the nineteenth century. Strindberg is a late and perhaps extreme example, closely connected with theosophical and spiritist currents toward the end of the century.

14. Swedenborg's *Notæ ex Wolfii Psychologia Empirica* is a complete manuscript, one of the sheaves of notes precipitated by his reading of Wolff. Another such is the comparison between his own and Wolff's philosophy, which is to be found in R. L. Tafel's photolithographic edition of his manuscripts, *Autographa*, vol. 3 (1870).

15. Jonsson, *Swedenborgs korrespondenslära*, 251. The dissertation Jonsson referred to is J. Ho, "Quellenuntersuchung zur Chinakenntnis bei Leibniz und Wolff," Zurich, 1962.

16. Tafel, vol. 1, 77–81; vol. 2, 746; Jonsson and Hjern, 95. We also meet Schönström in the *Spiritual Diary* (especially in ¶5887).

17. Carl Robsahm, *Anteckningar om Swedenborg* (rpt. 1989), 42 ff. Goroneskul was inducted in 1764.

18. Alf Åberg, *Stralenberg and Other Swedish Cartographers in the Service of Peter the Great* (Stockholm: MSK, 1991).

19. See further "Ur Anteckningar om De svenska Fångarnas öden efter slaget vid Poltava" in *Kulturhistoriska Studier*, 43 ff.

20. Juri Küttner, "Vassilij Tatisjtjev," *Lychnos* (1990): 109–164.

21. Swedenborg seems to have used one of Tatishchev's maps in his *Opera philosophica et mineralia* (1734).

22. Jonsson, *Swedenborgs korrespondenslära*, 252.

23. Bengt Thordeman's annotated 1982 translation, *Marco Polo's Journeys in Asia, 1271- 1295*, pp. 48, 89–101. I have also partly followed Ronald Latham. Leonardo Olschki is the Marco Polo scholar who has gone most deeply into the legend of Prester John; see *L'Asia di Marco Polo* (Venice, 1957), 376ff.

24. *Das Nord- und Ostliche Theil von Europa und Asien* (1730), 13, 40. This work was translated into Russian, English, French, and Spanish. It is scarcely credible that the assessor and scientist Swedenborg would have been unfamiliar with the work of his cousin Schönström.

25. *Die Zeit*, no. 10, October 1978.

26. This theme is related to the "isle of blessedness"—the tone Eric A. Sutton sets in his biography of Swedenborg, *The Happy Isles* (1938).

27. The mysical attraction of mountains, of the high and the mighty, permeates not only theosophical literature, but even the literature of modern mountain climbing. One may recall the mood in Kurt Diemberger's *Summits and Secrets*, trans. Hugh Merrick, 2d edition (London: George Allen & Unwin, 1991).

28. George N. Roerich, "Studies in the Kalacakra," *Journal of the Urusvati Himalayan Research Institute of the Roerich Museum* 2 (1931): 11–12.

29. Edwin Bernbaum, *The Way to Shambhala: A Search for the Mythical Kingdom beyond the Himalayas,* 2d edition (Los Angeles: Jeremy P. Archer, 1989), chapters 1 and 8.

30. Dalai Lama XIV [Bstan-´dzin-rgya-mtsho], *Freedom in Exile* (London: Hodder & Stoughton,1990), chapters 11–12.

The New Church in the West Indies, pp. 43–60

1. Literature on the history of the New Church in the West Indies is almost completely lacking. This chapter is merely a preliminary sketch focusing on the formation of the society on St. Croix and based on an extensive collection of documents. Printed material consists of notices and reports in contemporary New Church publications, especially *The Intellectual Repository* and other periodicals published by the General Conference in England and the General Convention in the United States. Baron C. Dirckinck-Holmfeld's rare pamphlet, *Den nye-christlige Kirke og dens Menighed paa St. Croix: Med inledning og Notiser om Swedenborg* (Copenhagen, 1853), refers to the application of the West Indian society for official sanction for public worship activity and argues at length in support of it, but unfortunately offers no information about the society. The meeting between John Bigelow and Vibe Kierulff, as surprising as it was significant, is described largely in Bigelow's own terms by Margaret Clapp in Chapter 8 of *John Bigelow: Forgotten First Citizen* (Boston: Little, Brown, 1947). That the Swedenborgian mentioned was actually Procurator Vibe Kierulff is my own (highly probable) conclusion.

This study rests primarily on field interviews and archival studies. I am indebted to many local historians, archivists, and others with special knowledge or interest who were willing to help me in my quest. Foremost among them are Carol Wakefield of the St. Croix Landmarks Society in Whim, St. Croix; Erik and Frits Lawaetz in Christiansted and Fredriksted, St. Croix; Curator William F. Cissel of Christiansvœrn, St. Croix; Louise Woofenden and Jonathan Mitchell of the Swedenborg School of Religion in Newton, Massachusetts, where previously unstudied manuscript material from Jamaica may be found; Carroll Odhner of the Swedenborg Library in Bryn Athyn, Pennsylvania, who provided me with Elijah Bryan's reports; and Nancy Dawson of the Swedenborg Society, London, who granted me access to many of A. C. Birch's letters in the original and in copies. Last but by no means least, I should like to mention the patient and generous staff of the State Archives in Copenhagen, who let me freely handle the immense, handritten *Folketællinger* of the Virgin Islands for the 1840s, which gives information about the people named in this account—their occupations, years of birth, addresses, baptismal faiths, children, and (in some instances) color.

2. In this way, I met in Gustavia the titled restauranteur and cultural ambassador Marius Stackelborough, chairman of the Swedish Friendship Society in the former Swedish possession, St. Barthélemy. A distant descendant of the Finnish-Swedish governor of St. Barthélemy—Bernt Robert Stackelberg, born in the same year that the island became Swedish, 1784—Stackelborough belongs to the number of the French island's colored minority.

3. The 1846 census lists "Mary Lindberg, 42 Queen Cross Street, widow, aged 60, born in St. Thomas, selling goods."

4. We also find members of the Fårhreus family, which was likewise involved in the affairs of St. Barthélemy.

5. See *Världarnas Möte* 4 (1991): 151–152; report from General Convention in Philadelphia, 1817.

6. In Trinidad-Tobago, there is a native adherent by the name of Ishmael Samad, who has started a reading circle, since becoming acquainted with Swedenborg's *Divine Providence*, but he is unaware of his precursors of earlier times.

7. We may find here the background—no coincidence—to the fact that most of the Swedenborgians in the world today are Africans, living in western Africa as well as in South Africa.

8. Pastor Hawley was furious over the dentist Bryan's "theft" of the soul of Mary Johnson, in this instance for eternity. Bryan had reason to fear a physical attack from Hawley; we have already seen Hawley's violent nature in the public attack on the plantation owner Ruan, mentioned earlier.

9. The controversial governor Peter von Scholten had had a lifelong relationship with a woman of color (and, as mentioned earlier, unofficially allowed the Swedenborgians to carry on) and was recalled to Denmark after his 1848 emancipation proclamation. Many Swedenborgians wrote to the Danish king to ask for redress on Scholten's behalf. A copy of the letter can be found in the archives of St. Croix Landmarks Society in Whim, Fredriksted.

10. In 1952, the General Convention branch of the Swedenborgian church had a contact person among the blacks there, Randolph Cruser in Christiansted, of whom I could locate no records after that date.

Revival and Reform in Russia, pp. 61–77

1. Author of *Scenes from the Spiritual World* and similar works, the spiritualist Jung-Stilling is also known for his many accounts of Swedenborg's powers of paranormal perception and communication.

2. A. N. Aksakov, *Animismus und Spiritismus* (Leipzig: 1890); *Ratsionalizm Svedenborga*, [. . .] (Leipzig: 1870), which was reviewed in Kleopatra Shakhovskaya's *Introduction au Journal* (1872), mentioned later in the essay. Aksakov translated Swedenborg's *Heaven and Hell* (*O nebie i adie* [Leipzig: 1860] and *O nebesakh, o mirie dukhov, i ob adie* [On Heaven, on the world of Spirits, and on Hell], [Leipzig: 1863]).

3. Cf. Czeslaw Milosz, "Dostoyevsky and Swedenborg," *Slavic Review* (1975). This essay was also included as chapter 9 of Milosz's *Emperor of the Earth* (Berkeley: University of California Press, 1977).

4. See Lea Goldberg, *Russian Literature in the Nineteenth Century: Essays* (Jerusalem: Magnes Press, 1976), 95.

5. See Alexander Herzen, *My Past and Thoughts*, "Alexander Lavrentevich Vitberg," vol. 1, chap. 16, trans. C. Gernett and H. Higgins (London: 1968), 264–277.

6. N.M. Druzhinin, *Dekabrist Nikita Mikhailovich Muravyov* (Moscow: 1933).

7. Jonathan Bayley, *Dr. Bayley's Observations Made during a Tour through Norway, Sweden, Finland, and Russia in the Summer of 1866* (London: 1867). Bailey knew well what he was talking about. People sharing his own views, church members and followers of Swedenborg, had been fighting chattel slavery and slave trade since the 1790s in England, North America, and Africa. Some radicals and utopists in North America had drawn much from Swedenborg's moral reasoning. Among those, Bayley praised the New England transcendentalist Ralph Waldo Emerson especially.

8. Jonathan Bayley ["J.B."], "Memoir and Obituary of General Alexander Nicolaievitch Mouravieff," *The Intellectual Repository and New Jerusalem Magazine*, May 1, 1865; rpt. in Bayley, *New Church Worthies* (London: 1884).

9. Exactly one year later, the same fate befell his only son, Ioann Muravyov (1831–1864), who is said to have studied and expounded Swedenborgian morality since he was a boy. On his deathbed, it is reported that the younger Muravyov told his doctor, "You know my way of thinking about death and everlasting life, so don't be afraid to tell me

the truth." The doctor, also a reader of Swedenborg, told him the truth, whereupon the young man, shortly passed away, at the age of 33.

10. The pamphlet simply stated that it was printed in "Londres: F. Pitman, 20, Paternoster Row." See Kleopatra Mikhailovna Shakhovskaya, "The East and Swedenborg," *Intellectual Repository* (1872): 285ff, 350–356; "Östern och Swedenborg," *Ett Kristligt Sändebud* 4 (1872): no. 1, 88–91; no. 2, 73–80. See also Shakhovskaya's Russian translation of Swedenborg's *True Christian Religion (Istinno-Christianskaya Religiya,* London: 1872)

11. August Tholander. *Ernste Federzeichnungen,* by "T...r" (Moscow: Commissionsverlag von J. Deubner, 1886).

12. William Mather, "The Late Princess Kleopatra Schahoffskoy," *New-Church Magazine* (1884): 199–201.

13. Bayley, *Observations Made during a Tour,* passim.

14. The eminent literary historian Dmitry Ivanovich Chizhévsky perceived these spiritual overtones or undercurrents in Dal's stories *O prividenijach* and *Posluch (Polnoe sobranie sochinenii,* vols. 5 and 10). See also Pavel Ivanovich Melnikov's illuminating biographical introduction in vol. 1; Dmitry Chizhévsky, *Aus zwei Welten. Beiträge zur Geschichte der slavisch-westlichen literarischen Beziehungen* (The Hague: Mouton & Co., 1956), chap. 17, "Svedenborg bei den Sklaven"; and Chizhévsky's *History of Nineteenth-Century Russian Literature,* 2 vols. (Nashville, Tennessee: Vanderbilt University Press, 1974–76).

15. Before his retirement and departure for Moscow in 1859, Dal', a former seaman and naval cadet of Danish and German descent, had participated as a military physician in the campaigns against Turkey (1828–29) and Poland (1831–32). After having worked for some time at the military hospital in St. Petersburg, he resigned from medical practice and accepted administrative posts with the Ministry of the Interior in the Orenburg Province, and later on in Nizhniy-Novgorod, where he was a friend and colleague of Aleksandr Nikolaevich Muravyov. When Muravyov became governor of Orenburg Province, Dal' wrote the following in the local newspaper, quoted by Bayley:

> I cannot refrain from addressing you on the happiness vouchsafed to us in the person of our new governor, the General Aleksandr Muravyov. He is a sage, such as there are but few. Grant us everywhere such governors, and in ten years we shall have progressed so much that we shall not recognize ourselves. The

governor is mild, sensible, independent, experienced: of a holy life, accessible at all times, and to everyone; fond of justice and order, yet merciful. In short, he is native gold and silver; a treasure of goodness and truth without alloy.

In Search of Robsahm's Memories, pp. 79–88

1. *Ein fliehendes Pferd* (1978); cf. Inge Jonsson, "Swedenborg i Tyskland - Resor, reflexer, reception," in *Humanistiskt Credo* (Stockholm: Norstedts, 1988).

2. Cf. Horace Traubel, *With Walt Whitman in Camden*, ed. Gertrude Traubel, vol. 5 (April 8–September 14, 1889) (Carbondale, Illinois: University of Southern Illinois Press, 1964), 376; Emory Holloway, ed., *The Uncollected Poetry and Prose of Walt Whitman*, vol. 2 (Garden City, NY: 1921; London: Heinemann, 1922), 16–18. See also Anders Hallengren, *Deciphering Reality: Swedenborg, Emerson, Whitman and the Search for the Language of Nature*, The Nordic Roundtable Papers (Minneapolis, Minn.: The Center for Nordic Studies, University of Minnesota, 1992), chapters 9–13.

3. *Swedenborg, seine Visionen und sein Verhältnis zur Kirche* (Strassburg: 1827), 56.

4. Arne Munthe, *Västra Södermalm intill mitten av 1800-talet. En stadsdel och dess kyrkliga liv* (Stockholm: Utarbetad på uppdrag av Sancta Maria Magdalena och Högalids församlingar, 1959), 288.

5. R. L. Tafel, ed., *Documents concerning the Life and Character of Emanuel Swedenborg*, vol. 1 (London: Swedenborg Society, 1875–1890), 30–51. In his introduction, Tafel calls attention to the noteworthy circumstance that Robsahm's memoir had not previously been translated into English (although, as we shall see, he was wrong about this) and had never been published in Swedish.

6. On Dr. Kahl and his collaboration with Immanuel Tafel in Tübingen, see also Alfred Acton, *An Introduction to the Word Explained* (Bryn Athyn, PA: 1927), 7ff.

7. Tafel, *Documents*, vol. I, 30–31. Similarly, *Strödda Anteckningar, hörande till Swedenborgs Lefwerne*, published by J. Söderström in Carlshamn in 1821, very often has been attributed to Robsahm (James Hyde, *A Bibliography of the Works of Emanuel Swedenborg, Original and Translated* [1906]; C. Th. Odhner, *Annals of the New Church*, vol. I [1898]; the Royal Library catalog, etc.). It builds on Robsahm, among others, as anyone can see who reads the text. Two versions of the Söderström edition can be found in copies

in the Swedenborg Library, Academy of the New Church, in Bryn Athyn, Pennsylvania. Concerning them, see Alfred Acton, "Depositories of manuscripts by and relating to Swedenborg," 1929, revised by B. G. Briscoe in 1963. A manuscript in the Uppsala University Library entitled "Herr Assessor Em: Svedenborgs Lefvernes Beskrivning Först Till Efter-värden Lemnad af Herr Banco-Comisarien Robsam" is a later reworking, according to a now-missing note by 'M.B.' (*Manu Propria?*), Söderling's hand; this manuscript probably comes from Director Johan Nikolaus Söderling (1802–1889), a church member from Gothenburg who is mentioned in a letter from Viktor Rydberg to J. J. G. Wilkinson (his obituary is found in *Skandinavisk Nykyrk-Tidning* of 1890). For a critical discussion of Carl Robsahm as the source in regard to the call vision, see Friedemann Horn, "Understanding Swedenborg's Initial Vision" in *The Messenger* 207, no. 1 (February 1987): 24–27.

8. The Loan-bank was a department of the Riksbank. Its immense and valuable archive is in the custody of the Riksarkiv. Robsahm's communications from 1753 on are found in Rb 616 ff plac. 3546.

9. The particulars of Carl Robsahm's life are as follows: Enrolled in the university at Uppsala in 1752, where he studied for one and a half years; accepted on probation at the Riksbank in 1753, given full status in 1754; office clerk (like his brother Anders) in the Treasury Commission in 1755; bookkeeper in 1758; bookkeeper in the discount bank in 1761; accountant in the office of the Exchange Commission in 1762; awarded 900 dalers copper in 1764 for thoroughness in service; assistant to the commissioner in 1770; another award for his fidelity and precision in 1774; accountant in the Loan-bank in 1780; Commissioner Plenipotentiary in 1786; died July 10, 1794, in Stockholm. Married Maria Catharina Hagen (1745–1819) in 1763. One of his daughters, Brita Sofia (1784–1854) married Per Krafft [the younger] (1777–1863). See *Svenska ättartal* (Stockholm: 1889), 404; K. A. Leijon-hufvud, *Ny svensk släktbok* (Stockholm: 1906), 503; *Index över svenska porträtt 1500–1850 i Svenska porträttarkivets samlingar*, vol. 2, 677. "En släk-fläta del 7: Robsahm," written and published by Birgitta Pontén in 1973, covers other family branches and collateral lines, but shows in detail the mining tradition and provides information of social interest. Erik Gustaf Geijer's paternal aunt married Robsahm's coeval second cousin, the miner and metallurgist Carl Magnus Robsahm (1735–1819), appointed to the College of Mines. One of his grand-children married a sister of Verner von Heidenstam's mother.

Robsahm/Robson is a Scottish family that came to Sweden via Germany in the early 1600s; the Swedish ancestor is Robsahm's great grandfather Christian Robsahm (1613–1678). According to Cyriel Odhner Sigstedt (*The Swedenborg Epic: The Life and Works of Emanuel Swedenborg* [London: Swedenborg Society, 1981], 198), Carl Robsahm was "a fellow member of the Academy of Sciences." However, it does not appear from the *Kungl. Svenska Vetenskapsakademien: Person förteckningar 1739–1915* that any Carl Robsahm occurs in the academy in any function—and in any case not as a member. There is, therefore, reason to be skeptical about the information in the Swedenborg biography.

10. Karl-Erik Sjöden, *Swedenborg en France* (Stockholm: Almquist & Wiksell International, 1985), 24ff. When Pernety introduced Swedenborg in France, which came to have immediate meaning for Honoré de Balzac among others, he received information from Robsahm: *Les Merveilles du ciel et de l'enfer et des terres planétaires et astrales* (Berlin: 1782), vol. 1, "Discours préliminaire." One consequence of C. F. Nordenskiöld's French inclinations, among others, was his book *Considérations générales sur le Christianisme actuel, et la lumière que Monsieur Emmanuel Svédenborg répand sur les religions* (Rostock: 1819).

11. For background, see Arne Munthe, *Västra Södermalm*, 288, 313ff; R. L. Tafel, *Documents*; and Harry Lenhammar, "Tolerans och bekännelsetvång. Studier i den svenska swedenborgianismen 1765–1795," dissertation, University of Uppsala, 1966, pp. 181, 185, 269.

12. Robsahm's description of Swedenborg's vision in the inn in London was published by Pernety: cf. Tafel, *Documents*, vol. 1, 68.

13. Published in Boston, 1831, and published *in extenso* in the edition of 1845; finally, a sixth edition appeared in 1866. Robsahm's memoir is dated May 29, 1783, in Hobart.

14. In the catalog of the Royal Library, this work is erroneously ascribed to the foundry manager Carl Magnus Robsahm.

15. On Dybeck's tragic life, see (pseudo.) Lazarus, *Svenska Millionärer*, New Series V (Stockholm: 1904). A copy of *Vera Christiana Religio* (1771) bearing Dybeck's autograph is to be found in the Swedenborg Library in Stockholm.

16. See Lenhammar, *Tolerans och bekännelsetvång*, 365n.

17. Cf. Tafel, *Documents*, vol. 1, 620, n. 20.

18. "N'ayant pu me procurer la vie suivie de Swédenborg écrite en langue suédoise par Mr. Robsahm, . . ." (p. 36).

19. Cf. Tafel, *Documents*, vol. 1, 52–53, a letter from Pernety to C. F.

N., 30 October 1781. This information may also have been compiled in French by Bénédict Chastanier or by Robsahm himself.

20. According to information in large part from a copy by the historian Olof Andersson Knös (1756–1804)—but this comes perhaps partly from his father, the theologian Anders Olofsson Knös (1721–1799).

21. This would be Per Krafft the younger, son of Per Krafft the elder, who painted the familiar portrait of Swedenborg in Gripsholm Castle and who had married Robsahm's youngest daughter in 1808.

22. Did the artist and copyist Brita Sofia Krafft, née Robsahm, inherit the papers that her father left?

23. See Sjödén, *Swedenborg en France*, chapter 3.

24. The Academy member Johan Henric Kellgren's notorious fault-finding with these Swedenborgians gives only a slight hint of the mood.

25. The uncatalogued archive of the Lord's New Church in Stockholm, provisionally designated NKBA 1 and 15. The longer of these copies, now comprising about a third of the text, may have come from the Swedenborgian Johan Adolf Löfving (1770–1843), an alderman and tradesman in Falköping who initiated and carried on an immense copying activity.

26. Achatius Kahl's German translation (Lund ms) lacks the date.

27. A recent critical edition—a carefully annotated version of Robsahm's memoir that forms the major part of the book from which this introductory article was abstracted—builds on the Uppsala manuscript, with firsthand comparison to the London manuscript, but also with the copies of Dybeck and of Deleen and a longer, fragmentary copy from *Pro Fide et Caritate*. So far as possible, the original spelling, punctuation, and paragraph division have been noted and retained. In some ambiguous cases, Robsahm manuscripts in the archives of the Riksbank have provided linguistic guidance. In this critical edition, the persons mentioned in the text are identified and the historical context of various details of Robsahm's account is outlined. Numerous mistakes in earlier editions have also been corrected. See Anders Hallengren, ed., *Anteckningar om Swedenborg* (Skrifter utgivna av Föreningen Swedenborgs Minne: Stockholm, 1989).

28. Translated by Anders Hallengren. This account answers partially to notes taken down by Swedenborg himself, to be found in the *Adversaria*, vol. 2, no. 1956 f. and the *Diarium Spirituale*, no. 397, dated

April 1745, which is probably the time of the experience in London, where Swedenborg was living at the time.

The Code of the Ancients, pp. 89–104

1. The introductory strophe of "A Song of the Rolling Earth" (1856), printed in the edition of *Leaves of Grass* in which Whitman praised and cited Emerson. *The Complete Poetry and Prose of Walt Whitman as Prepared by Him for the Deathbed Edition*, with an introduction by Malcolm Cowley (New York: Pellegrini & Cudahy, 1948), vol. 1, 216.

2. "To the Garden of the World" (1860), first section of "Children of Adam" in *Leaves of Grass*, ibid., 114.

3. Cf. *The Complete Works of Ralph Waldo Emerson*," Centenary Edition (Boston and New York: 1903–1904), vol. 1, 76; vol. 9, 283 ("Promise"); vol. 10, 137. See also Joel Porte, ed., *Emerson in his Journals* (Cambridge, Mass.: Belknap Press, 1982), 99, and chapter "Reorientation 1833–34"; R. W. B. Lewis, *The American Adam: Innocence, Tragedy, and Tradition in the Nineteenth Century* (Chicago: University of Chicago Press, 1955), prologue and chapter I:2, "The New Adam: Holmes and Whitman." For another perspective on the creative mission in the New World's pristine outlying land, see Henry Nash Smith, *Virgin Land* (Cambridge, Mass.: Harvard University Press, 1970), chapter "Walt Whitman and Manifest Destiny." On the first and last Adam—the physical preceding the spiritual—see I Cor 15:45.

4. Also left is a random number of issues of *The New Church Magazine for Children* published between 1843 and 1855.

5. The original text was later published in the significant first and last issue of Elizabeth P. Peabody's *Aesthetic Papers* (Boston: 1849), 58–64, one of the most remarkable of the period's collections of papers. Elizabeth Palmer Peabody (1804–1894), sister-in-law of Nathaniel Hawthorne and Horace Mann, is a central figure in the movement. Her bookshop in Boston was a meeting place of the Transcendental Club.

Emerson's earliest Reed excerpts ("People of the Golden Age . . ."), including the first (indirect) fragment of Swedenborg, are found in Notebook XVIII, 1821, *The Journals and Miscellaneous Notebooks*, ed. Ralph H. Orth (Cambridge, Mass.: Harvard University Press, 1966), vol. 1, 293–294. Reed's oration was presented for the M.A. degree at Harvard, August 29, 1821. Emerson procured a copy of the manuscript.

6. The preceding paragraphs are derived from Nature, "Language" in *Complete Works*, op. cit.

7. Rev. Jonathan Bayley, *The Intellectual Repository and New Jerusalem Magazine*, n.s. 1(April 1840), 188–191; David George Goyder, *The Biblical Assistant, and Book of Practical Piety* (London and Boston: 1841), the "Advertisement" (vi) and the section on the "Religious Philosophy of Nature." Goyder included a text written by an American transcendentalist and Unitarian since it was "so beautifully replete with correspondence."

8. Reprinted, and obviously appreciated by Whitman himself, in "Leaves-Droppings," *Leaves of Grass* (Brooklyn, NY: 1856), 363ff: "rare is it to find any receiver of 'the heavenly doctrines' determined to enter for himself into the very interiors of all that Swedenborg taught—to see, not the mighty reflections that Swedenborg was able to give of interior realities, but their originals, as they stand constellated in the heavens! . . . Ralph Waldo Emerson is the highest type. He sees the future of truths as our Spirit-seers discern the future of man." "Leaves of Grass" is "written, as we perceive, under powerful influxes; a prophecy and promise of much that awaits all who are entering with us into the opening doors of a new Era." See also Roger Asselineau, *The Evolution of Walt Whitman* (Cambridge, Mass.: Harvard University Press, 1960), vol. 1, 75.

9. J.B. Moore, "The Master of Whitman," *Studies in Philology*, 23 (January 1926): 77–89. Bringing that impact to a head, Newton Arvin stated that Emerson was as important to Whitman as Epicurus to Lucretius or Spinoza to Goethe (*Whitman* [New York: Macmillan, 1938]).

10. S. E. Whicher, R. E. Spiller, and W. E. Williams, ed., *The Early Lectures of Ralph Waldo Emerson*, vol. 3 (Cambridge, Mass.: Harvard University Press, 1959–1972), 352, 361: The Times Series "The Poet."

11. Gay Wilson Allen, *Waldo Emerson* (New York: Penguin Books, 1982), 400–401; Joseph Jay Rubin and Charles H. Brown, eds., *Walt Whitman of the New York Aurora, Editor at Twenty-two: A Collection of Recently Discovered Writings* (State College, Pennsylvania: Penn State Press, 1950), 105. The full text of the lecture Whitman reported is contained in *Early Lectures*, vol. 3, 347–365. Some passages from this lecture were later used by Emerson in the essays "The Poet," "Eloquence," and "Poetry and Imagination."

12. See Floyd Stovall, *The Foreground of Leaves of Grass* (Charlottesville, Va.: University of Virginia Press 1974), 154 ff.

13. Whitman, *Complete Poetry and Prose*, vol. 2, 470; 263. *Textual note:* the spelling is that of the Editio Princeps and most later editions. Read "Naçkas," "Snorre," "Leibniz."

14. Manuscript 35, no. 25; see E. F. Grier, ed., *The Collected Writings of Walt Whitman. Notebooks and Unpublished Prose Manuscripts* (New York: 1984), vol. 6, 2034–2035. The clipping is identified by Stovall (*The Foreground*, 156, n. 17) and is no. 278 in Bucke's *Notes and Fragments*.

15. Whitman, *Collected Writings*, vol. 1: 34. Cf. John T. Irwin, *American Hieroglyphic: The Symbol of the Egyptian Hieroglyphics in the American Renaissance* (Baltimore, Md.: Johns Hopkins:1980), 19–20.

16. Irwin, 30 ff.; E. Iversen, *The Myth of Egypt and its Hieroglyphs in European Tradition* (Copenhagen: GAD, 1961); W.A. Clouston, *Hieroglyphic Bibles: Their Origin and History* (Glasgow: 1894); Sampson Reed, "Egyptian hieroglyphics," *New Jerusalem Magazine* 4 ([October] 1830–31): 69. That the world to Swedenborg appeared as only "a grammar of hieroglyphs" Emerson stated in *Representative Men* in 1850, i.e., five years before *Leaves of Grass*; cf. Emerson, *Complete Works*, vol. 4, 142.

17. The excerpts are to be found in his Journal B, 1835, i.e., the year before his first book was published: Emerson, *Journals and Notebooks*, vol. 5, 65–69. On Abbé Œgger, see Karl-Erik Sjödén, *Swedenborg en France* (Stockholm: 1985). On the Middle Age and Renaissance ideas behind this kind of hermeneutics, see Michel Foucault, *The Order of Things: An Archaeology of the Human Sciences*, World Of Man series, ed. R.D. Laing (New York: Random House, 1973), 25ff. and passim.

18. Œgger's list is basically a short dictionary of correspondences, compiled from Swedenborg's exegetical and theosophical works. Swedenborg's own first attempt at an outline and systematization of these ideas was made in a treatise which was typically called *Clavis hieroglyphica* (1744; posthumously published in 1784). The first American edition of that "hieroglyphic key" appeared in 1813 (*Halcyon Luminary*, Baltimore). Thus, the hieroglyphic connection was profoundly Swedenborgian.

19. The entry "God" in "Hieroglyphic Key."

20. This theme is discussed in Christopher Collins, *The Uses of Observation* (The Hague: Mouton, 1971), chap. 4.

21. In his poem "Nature," *The Transcendentalists*, edited by Perry Miller (Cambridge, Mass.: Harvard University Press, 1950; rpt. 1979), 360. Very claimed that his sonnets were communicated to him in visions of the Holy Ghost. He was committed to an asylum for the insane. Emerson thought him "profoundly sane," and edited his *Essays and Poems* (1839). Six hundred poems and a choice selection of his lit-

erary criticism are found in *Poems and Essays*, edited by James Freeman Clarke in 1886.

22. Emerson, *Complete Works*, vol. 10, 137; see also Genesis 2:15,19.

23. Lindeman (ed.), *Basic Selection*, 95.

24. *The American Puritans*, edited by Perry Miller (Garden City, New York: Anchor Books, 1956), 280.

25. See E. J. Gordon, "The Sumerian Proverb Collections: A Preliminary Report," *Journal of the American Oriental Society* 74, no. 2 (April–June 1954): 82–85. [Cf. Thor Heyerdahl, *Tigris*.]

26. Emerson, *Journals and Notebooks*, vol. 3, 267 (1831). Emerson turned this idea into a couplet in "Fragments on Nature and Life," *Complete Works*, vol. 9, 349. Related ideas are discussed much earlier; see, for example, *Journals and Notebooks*, vol. 3, 9–10 (1826): there are "correspondences" between means and ends.

27. See further Anders Hallengren, *Deciphering Reality* (Minneapolis, Minn.: University of Minnesota Press, 1992), 18–22, 41–42.

28. Edward Taylor, *The Poems of Edward Taylor*, edited by Donald E. Stanford, with a foreword by Louis L. Martz (New Haven, Conn.: Yale University Press, 1960), 83. Cf. Ursula Brumm, *Die religiöse Typologie im amerikanischen Denken* (Leiden: Studien zur amerikanischen Literatur und Geschichte, 1963).

29. C. L. Albanese, *Religion in America from the Algonkian Indians to the New Age* (Chicago: University of Chicago Press, 1990); E. R. Russell Emerson, *Indian Myths, or Legends, Traditions, and Symbols of the Aborigines of America* (Minneapolis, Minn.: 1965), 94n.

30. Miller, *American Puritans*, 281.

31. Perry Miller, *Transcendentalists*, 403. Compare the Puritan Samuel Davies' famous sermon on love's transcendence in our world, "God is Love," *Sermons*, vol. 1, 316: "*God is love;* not only love and loving, but love itself; pure unmixed love, nothing but love; love in his nature and his operations; the object, source, and quintessence of all love."

32. Miller, *American Puritans*, 282.

33. Miller, *Transcendentalists*, 388; see also "Correspondence" in the useful index.

An American Philosophy of Use, pp. 105–114

1. Hedi Hildebrand, *Die Amerikanische Stellung zur Geschichte und zu Europa in Emersons Gedankensystem* (Bonn, Germany: Bonner Studien zur Englischen Philologie, 1936), 46–48.

2. "Men living in different countries, under different circumstances, different habits and regimens, may have different utilities; the same act, therefore, may be useful, and consequently virtuous in one country which is injurious and vicious in another differently circumstanced" (letter from Jefferson to Thomas Law, 1814). Barbara MacKinnon, ed. *American Philosophy: A Historical Anthology* (Albany, New York: SUNY Press, 1985), 34f., 58–59. Thomas Jefferson, *The Living Thoughts of Thomas Jefferson*, ed. John Dewey (New York: Longmans & Co., 1943), 87. Elizabeth Flower and Murray G. Murphy, *A History of Philosophy in America* (New York: Capricorn Books, 1977), 337.

3. Utilitarianism originated in opposition to the Puritan view that the good works of sinners are double banned, and one of the first to argue in this direction, i.e., making morality a general principle of benevolence, was Richard Cumberland, writing on the laws of nature, *De legibus naturæ* (1672).

4. Flower and Murphy, vol. 1, 288–289. Cf., on the background, pp. 72–73, 224–225, 236–237, 262–263, and chap. 5:2, "Moral Philosophy."

5. *The Works of William Ellery Channing*, (Boston: American Unitarian Association, 1877), 129.

6. Whicher, Spiller, and Williams, ed., *The Early Lectures of Ralph Waldo Emerson*, vol. 1, 249, lecture on English traits read in 1835, observations continued in *English Traits* (1856), in *The Complete Works of Ralph Waldo Emerson*, Centenary Edition (Boston and New York: 1903–1904), vol. 5, 83.

7. Emerson, *Complete Works*, vol. 10, 56, hereinafter referred to as "W."

8. Ibid., vol. 1 ,182; also Ferguson, Slater, et al, ed., *Collected Works of Ralph Waldo Emerson*, vol. 1, 113, hereinafter referred to as "CW."

9. *The Journals of Ralph Waldo Emerson*, ed. E. W. Emerson and W. E. Forbes (Boston: 1909–1914), vol. 2, 455. Emerson then recalls Cicero's severe criticism of Epicuros, who was a materialist and a hedonist.

10. W, vol. 1, 36–42 (CW, vol. 1, 23-26)

11. Ibid., vol. 11, 136, 144, 542; and vol. 6, 21.

12. Ibid., vol. 1, 40 (CW, I, 25); vol. 2, 102 (CW, II, 60); vol. 7, 300 ("Success"). Cf. Alfred Wilhelm Martin, *Great Moral Leaders* (New York: 1933), chap. 6.

13. Ibid., vol. 10, 208.

14. Ibid., vol. 6, 208. "Worship" was first published in *The Conduct of Life* (1860).

15. Ibid., vol. 4, 215.

16. Ibid., vol. 10, 208.

17. Gertrude R. Hughes, *Emerson's Demanding Optimism* (Baton Rouge, La.: Louisiana State University Press, 1984), 20. Barbara Packer, *Emerson's Fall: A New Interpretation of the Major Essays* (New York: Continuum, 1982).

18. Extract from "The Divine Love and Wisdom," *New Jerusalem Magazine* 8 (August 1835): 440, announcing the new edition of that treatise, published in Boston that year and quoted by Emerson in his journals.

19. The quotations are from Swedenborg's *Heaven and Hell*, ¶557. Cf. "Uses in the heavens are splendid and refulgent" (*True Christian Religion*, ¶661), a wording that seems to echo in the opening of Emerson's Divinity School Address).

20. W, vol. 1, 222 (CW, I, 136). See also *Journals and Miscellaneous Notebooks*, vol. 8, 484. Emerson first came across this teaching—that truth, faith, or understanding without Good (uses) is worthless—in Swedenborg's *Apocalypse Revealed* in a paragraph he especially noted, ¶386, and in ¶337, where it is stated that what is only in the understanding, but not in life, will not be preserved, but rejected. Swedenborg explains that with people who are in evil, even if they are "most fully instructed, the truths of faith enter no further with them than into the memory, and do not penetrate to the affection which is the heart; and therefore in the other life their truths of memory are dissipated, and become null and void" (*Arcana Coelestia*, ¶2590:2).

21. Swedenborg's critical view of Lutheran solifidianism was stated clearly already in the early manuscript *De fide et bonis operibus* , published by J. J. G. Wilkinson in *Opuscula quœdam argumenti philosophici . . .* , (London: 1846), 9–14, a book that is still in Emerson's library.

22. Jonathan Bishop, *Emerson on the Soul* (Cambridge, Mass.: Harvard University Press, 1964), 214.

23. Notebook "Z," (MS, Harvard) 136: "Swedenborg" is written on top of the page, "use" under the heading "Doctrines." See also *Journals and Miscellaneous Notebooks*, vol. 6, 312.

24. After that he read many original works by "the mystic." I have treated the pertinence of Swedenborg to the shaping of the Emersonian ethic in lectures and other publications. For more information on

sources and literature, see, in particular, "The Importance of Sweden-borg to Emerson's Ethics" in *Swedenborg and His Influence*, eds. Erland J. Brock et al (Bryn Athyn, Penn.: Academy of the New Church, 1988).

25. Indeed, Emerson says so himself when he explains that chapters two through five will treat different "classes" of the "multitude of uses." W, vol. 1, 12. In Emerson's words, the topics treated in his subsequent four chapters are four "classes" of "uses."

26. Cf. summaries in Kenneth W. Cameron, *Emerson the Essayist* (Raleigh, N. C.: Thistle Press, 1945), vol. 1, 234, 266–267., 275, 280–281., 290–291; vol. 2, 22–23, 30–31. See also George F. Dole, *Sampson Reed: Primary Source Material for Emerson Studies* (New York: Swedenborg Foundation, 1992), passim.

27. *Divine Love and Wisdom*, ¶¶ 35, 133, and passim; Cf. *Heaven and Hell*, ¶392. A summary of this moral philosophy has been given by Wilson Van Dusen in "Uses: A Way of Personal and Spiritual Growth," *The Country of Spirit* (San Francisco: J. Appleseed & Co., 1992), 61–87.

28. *The New Jerusalem Magazine* for 1827–28, vol. 1, 280. There is much to learn about the conflicting concepts of utility and truth in the Enlightenment from Nils Erik Ryding, *Begreppen nytta och sanning inom fransk upplysningsfilosofi: Studier kring en idékonflikt* (Lund, Sweden: Gleerup, 1951). The centrality of the concept of use in Swedenborg's doctrinal system can be seen from John Faulkner Potts's *The Swedenborg Concordance* (London: Swedenborg Society, rpt.1976), vol. 6, 464–483.

29. W, vol. 9, 219.

30.W, vol. 4 126 (CW, IV, 71). See *Journals and Miscellaneous Notebooks*, vol. 11, 171. The quotation comes from Swedenborg's *Delights of Wisdom concerning Conjugial Love*, ¶183; numerous notations in Emerson's copy. Cf. ¶266 where "use" is explained as the love of the neighbor and the love that holds the heavens together.

31. *Journals and Miscellaneous Notebooks*, vol. 2, 426.

32. "Life and Letters in New England," W, vol. 10, 358.

33. Including, then, the benefits of the Fortunate Fall. Even hell can contribute to human progress, Emerson assures us in very Swedenbor-gian terms, "for nothing is useless in the bone and fibre of nature" (*Journals*, vol. 8, 263).

The Ancients and the Postmoderns, pp. 115–128

1. *The Complete Works of Ralph Waldo Emerson*, Centenary Edition (Boston and New York: 1903–1904), vol. 3, 45–46. Cf. *The Tempest*

IV.1: "We are such stuff / As dreams are made of, and our little life / Is surrounded by a sleep." Not by mere coincidence, this was also one of Thomas Carlyle's favorite quotations. See Augustine Birrell's essays on Carlyle and Emerson in *Obiter Dicta* (London: Macmillan, 1923). See also Donald Gelpi, *Endless Seeker: The Religious Quest of Ralph Waldo Emerson* (Lanham, Md.: University Press of America, 1991).

2. *Essays*, second series in *Works*, vol. 3, 181.

3. For this understanding of American "romanticism," I am much indebted to a lecture delivered by Ihab Hassan at Stockholm University on May 6, 1991: "The New American Pragmatism: Emerson to Rorty."

4. *Works*, vol. 4, 117.

5. *Works*, vol. 3, 85.

6. *Boston Morning Post*, August 31, 1838 (cited in Robert Burkholder and Joel Myerson, ed., *Emerson: An Annotated Secondary Bibliography* [Pittsburgh, Penn.: University of Pittsburgh Press, 1985], 17).

7. *Works*, vol. 3, 144.

8. *Uncollected Writings*, ed. C. C. Bigelow (New York: 1912), 119, the *Dial* essay on "Tantalus."

9. It is this active element Gennády Agyí refers to in the "Foreword" to *Veronica's Book* (1989): "Somewhere in these pages one can sense my recollection of one of the points in Swedenborg's teaching about man, who is created 'incomplete and imperfect' so that in the future he may be 'worked on' by That, of Which it is better not to speak (especially in our so rational age)."

10. Page Dubois, *Sowing the Body* (Chicago: University of Chicago Press, 1988), 16. Compare the acute comments of Dorothy I. Sly, in "Philo's Practical Application of Dikaiosyne," *SBL 1991 Seminar Papers* (Atlanta, Ga.: Scholars Press, 1991), 298–308; and Marion Leathers Kuntz and Paul Grimley Kuntz, eds., *Jacob's Ladder and the Tree of Life* (New York: P. Lang, 1987); and, furthermore, the broad perspectives of David Parkin's anthology, *The Anthropology of Evil* (Oxford: Oxford University Press, 1985), chap. 2.

11. Ralph Cudworth, *The True Intellectual System of the Universe* (London: 1678), 150 (book I, "Nature as Subordinate," § 5.); cf. pp. 121, 146, 648, 895. See especially part 3 on "'Plastic Nature preside over the whole." Typically, Emerson especially marked the passages on "Art" in Cudworth. Cudworth uses the word *correspond* to indicate analogies. The idea of "old Egyptian Theology,"—Emerson marked this idea in his copy!— "That God is All things, is every where insisted

upon in the Trismegistick Writings" (IV:17–18), p. 346–347. This idea, I may add, was to make people in the nineteenth century dispute whether Thoreau and Whitman were pantheists or materialists. From that confusion both realism and symbolism emerged. Interesting also is the notion of "A Scale or Ladder of Perfections in Nature," (Cudworth, 648). (A more curious point here is Cudworth's discussions of "Spermatick" theories of creation, which may as well recur in some of Emerson's wordings. If so, Joel Porter, in one of the striking intimations of his psychological biography, got hold of the wrong end of the stick.) Emerson's excerpts are from the two first volumes of the London 1820 edition of *The True Intellectual System* (I, 334, 336; II, 101, etc.).

12. Cf. Michael W. Stanley, *The Ladder of Ascent* (London: Swedenborg Society, 1976).

13. Jerome Hamilton Buckley, *The Triumph of Time* (Cambridge, Mass.: Belknap Press, 1966), 35; Thomas Macaulay, *Essays and Lays of Ancient Rome* (London: 1893), 402, 414.

14. "'Tis a forgotten maxim that 'accuracy is essential to beauty.'" William Gilman and Alfred Ferguson have traced this maxim to Philo, who stated in *On the Creation*, 28, that "beauty is absent where there is disorder." This is probably (indirectly) derived from Plutarch's phrase in *Pericles*, xiii, 2, *kallous akribeian*, "exactness of beauty." Ralph Waldo Emerson, *Journal and Miscellaneous Notebooks*, ed. Ralph H. Orth (Cambridge, Mass.: Belknap Press, 1966), vol. 3,12. "Accuracy" and *akribeia* are synonymous notions.

15. *Works*, vol. 4, 81.

16. Charles J. Woodbury, *Talks with Ralph Waldo Emerson* (London: 1890), 107–108. Cf. the liberal individualism that shaped the new era: Gustaaf Van Cromphout, *Emerson's Modernity and the Example of Goethe* (Columbia, Missouri: University of Missouri Press, 1990), chap. 7, "The Modern Individual." On Emerson's modernity, see also Richard Poirier, *The Renewal of Literature: Emersonian Reflections* (New York: Random House, 1987). On the short step from transcendentalism to postmodernism and the new pragmatism, see Ihab Hassan, *The Postmodern Turn* (Columbus, Ohio: Ohio State University Press, 1987) and later works.

17. Richard A. Grusin, *Transcendentalist Hermeneutics: Institutional Authority and the Higher Criticism of the Bible* (Durham, N.C.: Duke University Press, 1991), chap. 1–2; Philip F. Gura, *The Wisdom of Words: Language, Theology, and Literature in the New England Renaissance* (Middletown, Conn.: Wesleyan University Press, 1981).

18. Focusing on the Renaissance origins of this mode of thinking, Seyyed Hossein Nasr explained that "Swedenborg could write a hermeneutic commentary upon the Bible which was also an exposition of a symbolic science of nature" because he could rely upon a intermediary world of imagination, *mundus imaginalis*, as "the meeting ground of spiritual and material forms." *The Encounter of Man and Nature: The Spiritual Crisis of Modern Man* (rpt. London: Unwin, 1976), 70, 95.

19. Gura, 81.

20. Perry Miller, ed., *The Transcendentalists* (Cambridge, Mass.: Harvard University Press, 1950; rpt. 1979), 49.

21. Michel Foucault, *Les mots et les choses* (Paris: Editions Gallimard, 1966), chap. "La prose du monde."

22. Harry Levin, "What is Realism?," in *Contexts of Criticism* (Cambridge, Mass.: Harvard University Press, 1969), 72ff.

23. *Journals and Miscellaneous Notebooks*, vol. 1, 255ff., 263, 270. On the currency of similar ideas in the preceding century, see, for instance, A. E. Pilkington, "'Nature' as Ethical Norm in the Enlightenment," in L. J. Jordanova, ed., *Languages of Nature* (London: Free Association, 1986).

24. *Journals and Miscellaneous Notebooks*, vol. 14, 215–218.

25. Compare Emerson's historical outline in the address on the Emancipation Proclamation: "Liberty is a slow fruit." It comes in short periods, in "moments of expansion," in which the events are acts "working on a long future." *Works*, vol. 12, 315–316.

26. Natural right presupposes that there are any moral rights at all, and if there is then such a thing as moral right, the value of individual freedom is recognized and there is an equal right of all men to be free. Cf. H.L.A. Hart, "Are there any Natural Rights?" in: Anthony Quinton, ed., *Political Philosophy* (London: Oxford University Press, 1968).

A Mirror Reflecting a Higher Reality, pp. 129–136

1. Sig Synnestvedt, *Swedenborg: Testigo de lo invisible*, Prologo de Jorge Luis Borges (Buenos Aires: Miramar, 1982). Cf. José Antonio Antón Pacheco, *Un libro sobre Swedenborg* (Seville, Spain: 1991), 89–94, and A. Hallengren, *Tingens tydning* (Stockholm: ÅSAK, 1997), chap. "Nattens vägvisare." The essay by Borges is also available in *Testimony to the Invisible*, ed. James F. Lawrence (West Chester, Penn.: Swedenborg Foundation, 1995), 3–16.

2. Seyyed Hossein Nasr, *The Encounter of Man and Nature: The Spiritual Crisis of Modern Man* (rpt. London: Unwin, 1976), 70, 94–95, and passim.

3. Henry Corbin, *Creative Imagination in the Sufism of Ibn 'Arabi* (Princeton, N.J.: Princeton University Press, 1981), 76–77, 92–93. See further *Swedenborg and Esoteric Islam*, transl. L. Fox, Swedenborg Studies No. 4 (West Chester, Penn.: Swedenborg Foundation, 1995), and A. Hallengren, *Tingens Tydning* (Stockholm: ÅSAK, 1997), chap. "Fåglarnas språk."

4. Ralph Waldo Emerson, *Journal and Miscellaneous Notebooks*, ed. W. Gillman, A. Ferguson, and Ralph H. Orth (Cambridge, Mass.: Harvard University Press, 1966), vol. 11, 12.

5. As expressed in Emerson's second lecture on Shakespeare in 1835: see Whicher, Spiller, and Williams, ed., *The Early Lectures of Ralph Waldo Emerson*, vol. 1 (Cambridge, Mass.: Harvard University Press, 1959), 311.

6. Iamblichus of Chalcis, *De mysteriis Egyptiorum, nunc primum ad verbum de greco expressus. Icolao Scutellio . . . interprete.* (Rome: 1556). An inscription in Emerson's hand tells us that he got the book from Charles Eliot Norton. Emerson quotes Iamblichus [Iamblichos] in a central passage of the essay "The Poet" (*Works*, vol. 3, 13).

7. Iamblichus. *On the mysteries of the Egyptians, Chaldeans, and Assyrians* (Chiswick:1821) Autograph, markings, notes in Emerson's hand, in Emerson's library, Harvard College.

8. *Clavis hieroglyphica arcanorum naturalium et spiritualium per viam representationum et correspondentiarum* (1742), published in London in 1784. English translation by R. Hindmarsh, *A Hieroglyphic Key to natural and spiritual mysteries, by way of representations and correspondences*, London 1792, first published in America as early as 1813 (*Halcyon Luminary*, NY, Vol II), and in a new translation by J. J. G. Wilkinson, under the same title, in London and Boston, 1847. See James Hyde, *A Bibliography of the Works of Emanuel Swedenborg* (London: Swedenborg Society, 1906). There is a thoroughly analytical survey of the twenty-one examples of the work in Inge Jonsson, *Swedenborgs korrespondenslära* (Stockholm: Almqvist & Wiksell, 1969), chap. 2.

9. A case in point of Emerson's focus is the one marking in his copy of Swedenborg's *Principia*, the passage on "Adam." *The principia; or, The first principles of natural things, being new attempts toward a philosophical explanation of the elementary world*, trans. Augustus Clissold (London and Boston: 1845–48).

10. *Works*, vol. 1, 64 (*Nature*, chap. "Spirit").

Bibliography

Aagaard, Johannes. "Dansk Nykirkesamfund." In *Håndbog i verdens reli-gioner*. Copenhagen: Politikens Forlag, 1982.

Abell, Arthur M. *Talks with Great Composers*. New York: Philosophical Library, 1955. Reprinted 1994.

Åberg, Alf. *Stralenberg and Other Swedish Cartographers in the Service of Peter the Great.* 14th International Conference on the History of Cartography. Stockholm: MSK, 1991.

Acton, Alfred. "Depositories of manuscripts by and relating to Swedenborg," Bryn Athyn, Penn.: Swedenborg Library, Academy of the New Church, 1929. Revised by B.G. Briscoe 1963.

———. *An Introduction to the Word Explained: A study of the means by which Swedenborg the scientist and philosopher became the theologian and revelator.* Bryn Athyn, Penn.: Academy of the New Church, 1927.

——— (ed.) *The Letters and Memorials of Emanuel Swedenborg*. 2 vols. Bryn Athyn, Penn.: Swedenborg Scientific Association, 1948–1955.

Acton, W. H., A. W. Acton, and F. Coulson. *The Spiritual Diary*. London: Swedenborg Society, 1962.

Aksakov, Aleksandr Nikolaevich. *Animismus und Spiritismus*. Leipzig 1890. 4th ed. Leipzig: Bibliothek des Spiritualismus für Deutschland, 1905.

——— (trans.) Swedenborg, Emanuel. *O nebie i adie* (On heaven and hell), Leipzig: 1860. New ed. *O nebesakh, o mirie dukhov, i ob adie* (On heaven, on the world of the spirits, and on hell) Leipzig: 1863.

———. *Ratsionalizm Svedenborga*, [. . .] Leipzig: 1870. [Reviewed in Kleopatra Shakhovskaya's *Introduction au Journal*, 1872. See below.]

Albanese, Catherine L. *Religion in America from the Algonkian Indians to the New Age*. Chicago: University of Chicago Press, 1990.

Allen, Gay Wilson. *Waldo Emerson*. New York: Penguin Books, 1982.

Allen, Warren Dwight. *Philosophies of Music History: A Study of General Histories of Music*, New York: American Book Company, 1939. Reprinted New York: Dover, 1962.

Allison, Eric. "The Swedenborgian Church in Mauritius." In *The Messenger* (Newton, Mass.), February 1993 and February 1994.

Alm, Henrik "Emanuel Swedenborgs hus och trädgård." In *Samfundet Sankt Eriks Årsbok*. Stockholm: Samfundet Sankt Erik, 1938.

Ambjörnsson, Ronny. "Änglarnas verkstad." In *Det okända landet: tre studier om svenska utopier*. Stockholm: Gidlunds, 1981.

Anderson, Quentin, and Stephen Railton. *Walt Whitman's Autograph Revision of the Analysis of Leaves of Grass (For R.M. Bucke's Walt Whitman)*. New York: New York University Press, 1974.

Andrzejewski, Boleslaw. *Emanuel Swedenborg: medzy empiria a mistycyzmem*. Poznan: Wydawn. Poznanskiego Tow. Przyjaciól Nauk, 1992.

Antón Pacheco, José Antonio. *Un libro sobre Swedenborg*. Sevilla: Publicaciones de la Universidad de Sevilla, 1991.

————. "Swedenborg y la religiosidad Romantica." *Isidorianum* 4(1993): 99–114. Centro de estudios teológicos de Sevilla, 1993.

Ardouin, Beaubrun. *Études sur l'histoire d'Haïti, suivies de la vie du général J. M. Borgella* [1784-1843]. 11 vols. Paris: 1853–60.

Arvin, Newton. *Whitman*. New York: Macmillan, 1938.

Ashton, Dore. *A Fable of Modern Art*, London: Thames & Hudson, 1980.

Asselineau, Roger. *The Evolution of Walt Whitman*. Cambridge, Mass.: Harvard University Press, 1960.

Assunto, Rosario. *Infinita contemplazione: gusto e filosofia dell' Europa barocca*. Naples: Studi e testi di storia e critica dell'arte, 1979.

Avis. The St. Croix Avis. Christiansted 1848. Xerox copies in the St. Croix Landmarks Society.

Aygi, Gennady. *Veronica's Book*. Trans. Peter France. Edinburgh: Polygon, 1989.

Bailey, Walter B. *Programmatic Elements in the Works of Schoenberg*. Ann Arbor, Mich.: UMI Research Press, 1984.

Balakian, Anna. *The Symbolist Movement: A Critical Appraisal*. New York: Random House, 1967.

Balzac, Honoré de. *Louis Lambert* and *Séraphita*. In *La comédie humaine*. Ed. Marcel Bouteron. X:2, Paris: Nouvelle revue français, Bibliothèque de La Pléiade, 1937.

————. *Oeuvres posthumes. Lettres à l'Etrangère*. Vol. I. Paris: Lévy, 1899.

Barone, Rosangela. "Il poeta della visione e la visione del poeta: Yeats, Swedenborg e l'immaginazione irlandese." *Hyphos* (Lecce, Italia) 1, no. 2: 30–41.

Barrett, Benjamin Fiske. *Autobiography*. Philadelphia: Swedenborg Publishing Association, 1890.

————. *Swedenborg and Channing: Showing the many and remarkable agreements in the beliefs and teachings of these writers.* Philadelphia: Claxton, Remsen & Co., 1879.

Bayley, Jonathan. Dr. *Bayley's observations made during a tour through Norway, Sweden, Finland, and Russia in the summer of 1866.* London: 1867. Also published as *An Account of a recent visit...* Manchester, England: Cave & Sever, 1866.

―――. "Memoir and Obituary of General Alexander Nicolaievitch Mouravieff," [by 'J.B.'] *The Intellectual Repository and New Jerusalem Magazine,* May 1, 1865. Reprinted in Bayley, *New Church Worthies.*

―――. "Nature." *The Intellectual Repository and New Jerusalem Magazine,* n.s. 1 (April 1840): 188–191.

―――. *New Church Worthies, or, Early but little-known disciples of the Lord in diffusing the truths of the New Church.* London: James Speirs, 1884.

Beaumont, L.B. de. "Russia as a sphere of Work for the New Church." *The New-Church Magazine* (1918): 348–357.

Benestad, Finn. *Musik och Tanke: Huvudlinjer i musikestetikens historia från antiken till vår egen tid.* Trans. Nils L. Wallin. Stockholm: Rabén och Sjögren, 1978.

Bercovich, Sacvan, ed. *Typology and Early American Literature.* Cambridge, Mass.: University of Massachusetts Press, 1972.

Berg, Alban. *The Berg-Schoenberg Correspondence: Selected Letters.* Ed. J. Brand, C. Hailey, and D. Harris. New York: Norton, 1987.

Bergquist, Lars. *Biblioteket i lusthuset: Tio uppsatser om Swedenborg.* Stockholm: Natur och Kultur, 1996.

―――. *Swedenborgs drömbok: Glädjen och det stora kvalet.* Stockholm: Norstedts, 1988.

Bernbaum, Edwin. *The Way to Shambhala: A Search for the Mythical Kingdom beyond the Himalayas.* Second Edition. Los Angeles: Jeremy P. Archer, 1989.

Bernheim, Pauline. *Balzac und Swedenborg: Einfluss der Mystik Swedenborgs und Saint-Martin auf die Romandichtung Balzacs.* Berlin: Ebering, 1914.

Bertocci, Angelo Philip. *From Symbolism to Baudelaire.* Carbondale, Illinois: Crosscurrents/Modern Critiques, 1964.

Beyer, Gabriel Andersson. *Index Initialis in Opera Swedenborgii theologica,* published in three parts. Amsterdam: 1779.

Bigelow, John. *The Bible That Was Lost and Is Found.* First edition 1893. Fourth edition, New York: Swedenborg Press, 1979

―――. [Intro] *A Compendium of the TheologicalWritings of Emanuel Swedenborg,* comp. by Samuel M. Warren. Third edition, with a biographical introduction [pp. 50] by John Bigelow. New York: New Church board of publication, 1888.

_____. *Molinos the Quietist*. New York: Scribner's Sons, 1882.

_____. *The Mystery of Sleep*. Memorial ed. New York: New Church Press, 1924 (1897).

_____. *Toleration, and Other Essays and Studies*. New York: New Church Press, 1927.

Birch, Andreas C. Letter from St. Croix, 20th Sept., 1841. *New Jerusalem Magazine* (Boston) 15 (Jan. 1842): 199.

_____. [Letters from A.C. Birch to the English Swedenborg Society, stored in the archives of the Swedenborg House in Bloomsbury, London.]

_____. [Reports from St. Croix]. *Swedenborg Society Annual Report*, Letters from St. Croix August 14, 1841, and September 20, 1841. London: The Swedenborg Society, 1841, 22–24.

Birrell, Augustine. *Obiter Dicta*. London: Macmillan, 1887. Reprint 1923.

Bishop, Jonathan. *Emerson on the Soul*. Cambridge, Mass: Harvard University Press, 1964.

Blavatsky, Jelena Petrovna. *The Secret Doctrine . . .* Verbatim with the original edition, 1888. 2 vols. Pasadena, Cal.: Theosophical University Press, 1970.

Block, Marguerite Beck. *The New Church in the New World: A Study of Swedenborgianism in America*. With a new introduction and epilogue by Robert H. Kirven. New York: [Octagon Books, 1968 (1932)] Swedenborg Publishing Association, 1984.

Bloom, Harold, ed. *Ralph Waldo Emerson*. New York: Chelsea House Publishers, 1985.

Blyden, Edward Wilmot. "The African's Past, Present, and Future." An address delivered by the Liberian minister to England at the annual meeting of the Swedenborg Society in London 1892, published in *Morning Light* (1892): 261–265. "Afrikanens historia," *Världarnas Möte* (Stockholm) 4/94 (1995): 116–124. Trans. and notes: A. Hallengren.

Borel, Jacques. *Séraphîta et le mysticisme balzacien*. Paris: J. Corti, 1967.

Borges, Jorge Luis. *Borges Oral*. Barcelona: Libro Amigo, 1980 (Buenos Aires, 1979).

_____. "Prólogo," in Sig Synnestvedt, *Swedenborg: Testigo de lo invisible*. Buenos Aires: Ediciones Marymar, 1982. The essay by Borges is also available in *Testimony to the Invisible*, ed. James F. Lawrence. West Chester, Penn.: Swedenborg Foundation, 1995.

Born, Eric von. *Nya Kyrkans väg genom världen*. Stockholm: Nya Kyrkans Svenska Församling, 1937.

Bostock, Frank. "Music in the Ritual of Worship." *Journal of Education of the Academy of the New Church* (1947): 167–176.

Bowra, Cecil Maurice. *The Heritage of Symbolism*. London: Macmillan & Co., 1943.

Brandt, Alex., P.T. Lutheran Minister. "Letter of the Danish Minister." Letter to Elijah Bryan, Cristiansted (Bassin), January 21, 1854. *New Church Repository* (July 1854): 328.

Brock, Erland J., et al, eds. *Swedenborg and His Influence*. Bryn Athyn, Penn.: The Academy of the New Church, 1988.

Brown, William Edward. *A History of Russian Literature of the Romantic Period*. Vol 3. Ann Arbor, Mich.: Ardis, 1986.

Bruhn, Siglind, ed. *Encrypted Messages in Alban Berg's Music*. New York: Garland, 1998.

Brumm, Ursula. *Die religiöse Typologie im amerikanischem Denken: ihre Bedeutung für die amerikanische Literatur- und Geistesgeschichte*. Leiden: Studien zur amerikanischen Literatur und Geschichte, 1963.

Bryan, Elijah. "Dr. Bryan's reply." Letter of February 2, 1854, to the Lutheran Minister in Christiansted, St. Croix. *New Church Repository* (July 1854): 328–329.

———. "From our West India Correspondent." Letter to George Bush, dated St. Thomas, May 18, 1854, with documentary supplements. *New Church Repository* (July 1854): 327–332.

———. "Intelligence from the West Indies." Letter from E. Bryan, dated New York, November 27, 1846. *New Jerusalem Magazine* (Boston) 20 (January 1847): 209–211.

———. Letter to Prof. George Bush on the "Progress of the New Church in Santa Cruz and St. Thomas." *New Church Repository* (New York) 3 (September 1850): 433–435.

———. "New Church in Bassin, Santa Cruz." Letter from E. Bryan to Thomas Worcester, August 17, 1852. "Intelligence and Miscellany." *New Jerusalem Magazine* (Boston) 25 (November 1852): 499–500.

———. "Obituary." "Departed this life, on the 20th of Nov, 1846 . . . Mr. Andreas Birch." *The Intellectual Repository and New Jerusalem Magazine* (1847): 358–359.

———. "On the Progress of the New Church in Santa Cruz." Letter to George Bush, January 8, 1853. *New Church Repository* (New York) 6 (February 1853): 86–89.

———. "Our New Church Society in this Island does not appear to be increasing, owing to the restrictions. . . ." Notice in the *New Jerusalem Messenger*, July 21, 1855.

———. "Progress of the New Church in Santa Cruz and St. Thomas." Letter from St. Thomas, July 16, 1850. "Intelligence and Miscellany." *New Jerusalem Magazine* (Boston) 23 (September 1850): 381–383.

———. "Progress of the New Church in Santa Cruz, W.I." Letter to George Bush dated St. Thomas, August 1, 1851. *New Church Repository* (New York) 4 (October 1851): 469–473.

———. "The New Church in Santa Cruz." Letter to George Bush, New York, Jan. 8, 1853. *The New Jerusalem Magazine* (Boston) 26, no. 306 (March 1853): 141–144.

———. "The New Church in Santa Cruz, W.I." *New Church Repository* (December 1855): 552–553.

———. "The Progress of the New Church in the West Indies." *New Church Repository* (New York) 3 (January 1850): 39–42.

———."New Church in the West Indies." (Extract from the Anglo-American *New Church Repository* of January 1850). "Intelligence and Miscellany." *New Jerusalem Magazine* (Boston) 23, no. 270 (April 1850): 141–144.

Bryant, Barry. *The Wheel of Time . . . : Visual Scripture of Tibetan Buddhism.* Foreword by the XIV Dalai Lama. Published in cooperation with Namgyal Monastery. San Francisco: Harper, 1992.

Bucke, Richard Maurice. *Walt Whitman.* New York: Belles lettres in English. Philadelphia: David McKay, 1883. Reprint 1970.

Buckley, Jerome Hamilton. *The Triumph of Time: A Study of the Victorian Concepts of Time, History, Progress, and Decadence.* Cambridge, Mass.: Belknap Press of Harvard UP, 1967 (1966).

Burkholder, Robert E., and Joel Myerson, eds. *Emerson: An Annotated Secondary Bibliography.* Pittsburgh, Penn.: University of Pittsburgh Press, 1985.

Cameron, Kenneth Walter. *Emerson the Essayist: An Outline of his Philosophical Development Through 1836. . . .* Vols. 1–2. Raleigh, North Carolina: Thistle Press, 1945.

————. "Emerson's *Nature* and British Swedenborgism." *ESQ* [Emerson Society Quarterly] 10 (1958): 14–20.

Canby, Henry Seidel. *Walt Whitman an American: A Study in Biography.* New York: Literary Classics, 1943.

Carlander, Christopher. *Resan till S:t Barthélemy: dr. Christopher Carlanders resejournal 1787–1788.* Ed. Sven Ekvall and Christer Wijkström. Stockholm: Vetenskapsakademien, 1979.

Carlén, Octavia. *Stockholms kyrkor och deras historiska minnen.* Stockholm: Louise Söderqvist, 1864.

Castelli, Enrico, ed. *Retorica e barocco: Atti del III congresso internazionale di studi umanistici.* Rome: Fratelli, 1955.

Césaire, Aimé. "La tragedie du roi Christophe." *Oeuvres complètes.* Collection réalisée sous la direction de Jean Paul Césaire. Paris: Editions Désormeaux, 1976 (Théâtre).

Channing, William Ellery. *The Works of William Ellery Channing, D.D. With an Introduction. New and Complete Edition, Rearranged.* Boston: American Unitarian Association, 1877.

Chevrier, Edmond. *Histoire sommaire de la Nouvelle Église chrétienne fondée sur les doctrines de Swedenborg: Par un amie de la nouvelle Église.* Paris: Librairie, 1879.

Chizhevsky, Dmitry. "Svedenborg bei den Sklaven." Chap. 17 in *Aus zwei Welten. Beiträge zur Geschichte der sklavisch-westlichen literarischen Beziehungen.* Slavistic Printings and Reprintings edited by Cornelis H. van Schooneveld, Leiden University. The Hague: Mouton & Co., 1956.

————. *History of Nineteenth-Century Russian Literature.* 2 Vols. Nashville, Tenn.: Vanderbilt University Press, 1974–76.

Ciesielski, Zenon. "Czesław Miłosz i Emanuel Swedenborg." *Studia Scandinavica* (Gdańsk) 10 (1988): 89–104.

————. *Historia literatury szwedzkiej.* Warsaw, Poland: Wroclaw, 1990.

————. "Miedzy racjonalizmem a mistycyzmem: O Emanuelu Swedenborgu." *W Drodze* (Poznań, Wroclaw, Gdańsk) 5–6 (1986): 153–154; 171–177.

Clapp, Margaret. "From Agnostic to Believer [1850–1854]." Chapter 8 in *John Bigelow: Forgotten First Citizen.* Boston: Little, Brown, 1947.

Clouston, W.A. *Hieroglyphic Bibles: Their Origin and History.* Glasgow: 1894.

Colley, Helen, II. "The Development of Music in the New Church." *Journal of Education of the Academy of the New Church* (1911): 31–41.

Collins, Christopher. *The Uses of Observation: A Study of Correspondential Vision in the Writings of Emerson, Thoreau, and Whitman.* The Hague: Mouton, 1971.

Comitas, Lambros. *The Complete Caribbeana 1900-1975: A Bibliographic Guide to the Scholarly Literature.* Vol. 2. New York: KTO Press, 1977.

Corbin, Henry. *Imagination in the Sufism of Ibn 'Arabi.* Bollingen Series XCI, Princeton, N.J.: Princeton University Press, 1981 (*L'Imagination créatrice dans le Soufisme d'Ibn 'Arabî,* Paris 1958).

————. *Swedenborg and Esoteric Islam.* Trans. Leonard Fox. West Chester, Penn.: Swedenborg Foundation, 1995.

Cudworth, Ralph. *The True Intellectual System of the Universe.* London, 1678.

Cullberg, Johan. *Skaparkriser: Strindbergs inferno och Dagermans.* Stockholm: Natur och Kultur, 1992.

Curtius, Ernst Robert. *Europäische Literatur und lateinisches Mittelalter.* 11th ed., Tübingen: Francke, 1993. English trans. by Willard R. Trask: *European Literature and the Latin Middle Ages.* Princeton, N.J.: Princeton University Press, 1990.

Dahlgren, Erik Wilhelm, ed. *Kungl. Svenska Vetenskapsakademien: Person-förteckningar, 1739–1915.* Stockholm: The Royal Academy of Sciences, 1915.

————. "Carl Bernhard Wadström: hans verksamhet för slafhandelns bekämpande och de samtida kolonisationsplanerna i Västafrika. Bibliografisk sammanställning." *Nordisk tidskrift för Bok- och Biblioteksväsen,* 2. Stockholm:1915.

Dal', Vladimir Ivanovich. *Polnoe sobranie sochinenii.* 10 vols., 1897–98. Published with an introduction by Pavel Ivanovich Melnikov (Andrei Pechersky, native of Nizhny Novgorod).

Dalai Lama XIV [Bstan-'dzin-rgya-mtsho]. *Freedom in Exile: the Autobiography of His Holiness the Dalai Lama of Tibet.* London: Hodder & Stoughton, 1990.

Davāni, Jalal al-Din Muhammed ibn As'ad. *Practical Philosophy of the Muhammadan People . . . being a Translation of the Akhlāk-i-Jalāly . . . by W. F. Thompson.* London: 1839.

David, Hans Theodore, and Arthur Mendel. *The Bach Reader.* New York: W.W. Norton, 1966.

"Den nye christlige Menigheds Ansøgning om Anerkjendelse." Petition to the Danish governor for the acknowledgement of the New Church, from citizens of St. Croix, with a list of those who signed up. The Danish version, presented to the goverment in Copenhagen, quoted in Dirckinck-Holmfeld (1853): 30–38, with an official reply: 39ff. For a later reply, see Feddersen (1854).

Derrida, Jacques. "Cogito and the History of Madness." In *Writing and Difference* [*L'écriture et la différence*]. Trans. Alan Bass. Chicago: Routledge, 1978.

Diemberger, Kurt. *Summits and Secrets.* Trans. Hugh Merrick. Second edition. London: George Allen & Unwin, 1991.

Dirckinck-Holmfeld, Baron C. *Den nye-christlige Kirke og dens Menighed paa St. Croix: Med inledning og Notiser om Swedenborg.*Copenhagen: Gyldendal, 1853.

————. *Visite à Petersbourg. Remarques sur le principe réformateur du gouvernment russe et sur la question religieuse, du point de vue de l'Eglise Chrétienne en Russie.* Altona: 1867.

Dookhan, Isaac. *A History of the Virgin Islands of the United States.* St. Thomas: College of the Virgin Islands, 1974.

Dostoevsky, Fyodor Mikhailovich. *Complete Letters.* Edited and translated by David Lowe and Ronald Meyer. Ann Arbor, Mich.: Ardis, 1988–1991.

————. *F.M. Dostoevsky: novye materialy i issledovaniya. Literaturnoe Nasledstvo,* 86. Moscow: Nauka, 1973.

Dubois, Page. *Sowing the Body: Psychoanalysis and Ancient Representations of Women.* Chicago: University of Chicago Press, 1988.

Duckworth, Julian. "The New Church in Eastern Europe." *The Plough* (Summer 1990): 14–19.

Duina Pasquali, Elisabetta. "Blake/Swedenborg." [Thesis], Università degli Studi di Milano, Facultà di Lettere e Filosofia, Anno Accademico 1992/1993.

Dumas, père, Alexandre. *Joseph Balsamo (Mémoires d'un médecin).* Paris: 1953 (1846).

Dzimbinov, Stanislaw. "Daniil Andréev: 'Roza Mira'—Fragmenti Russkii Swedenborg." *Novyi Mir* ['New World', Moscow] 2 (1989): 176–179.

Eby, S.C *The Story of the Swedenborg Manuscripts.* New York: The New-Church Press, 1926.

Edmisten, Leonard Martin. "Coleridge's Commentary on Swedenborg." A Dissertation Presented to the Faculty of the Graduate School, University of Missouri, June 1954. (UMI facsimile, Ann Arbor 1992.)

Ehrenborg, Anna Fredrika. *Tjugufyra Bref från Frankrike, Tyskland och Sweitz.*1-2. Uppsala: 1856–1857.

Elgenstierna, Gustaf, ed. *Den introducerade. Svenska Adelns Ättartavlor.* 9 vols. Stockholm: Norstedts, 1925–1936.

Elliott, John E., ed. *Small Theological Works and Letters of Emanuel Swedenborg.* London: Swedenborg Society, 1975.

Emerson, Ellen Russell. *Indian Myths, or Legends, Traditions, and Symbols of the Aborigines of America: Compared with those of other countries, including Hindostan, Egypt, Persia, Assyria and China.* Reprint Minneapolis, Minn.: 1965 (Boston 1884).

Emerson, Ralph Waldo. *Collected Works.* Edited by Alfred R. Ferguson, Joseph Slater, et al. Cambridge, Mass: Harvard University Press, 1971–).

————. *The Complete Works.* Centenary edition. Edited by E.W. Emerson. 12 vols. Boston: Houghton, Mifflin and Company, 1903–1904.

————. *The Early Lectures . . . 1833–1842,* I-III (EL). Edited by Stephen E. Whicher, Robert E. Spiller, and Wallace E. Williams. Cambridge, Mass: Harvard University Press, 1959–1972.

————. *Ensayos.* Trans. Juan Angel Cotta, with an introduction by Erly Danieri. Buenos Aires: Estrada, 1943.

————. *The Journals and Miscellaneous Notebooks.* Edited by William H. Gilman, Alfred R. Ferguson, Ralph H. Orth, et al. 16 vols. Cambridge, Mass.: Harvard University Press, 1960–1982.

————. *The Journals of Ralph Waldo Emerson.* Edited by E. W. Emerson and W. E. Forbes. Boston: 1909–1914.

————. *Uncollected writings.* Edited by C.C. Bigelow. New York: 1912.

Engell, James. *The Creative Imagination: Enlightenment to Romanticism.* Cambridge, Mass.: Harvard University Press, 1981.

Erici, Einar *Orgelinventarium: bevarade klassiska kyrkorglar i Sverige.* New ed. by R. Axel Unnerbäck, Stockholm: Proprius, 1988.

Evans, Frederick H. *James John Garth Wilkinsson: An Introduction.* Reprinted by . . . Mrs Frank Claughton Mathews. Edinburgh :1936 (1912).

Fargeaud, Madeleine. *Balzac et La Recherche de l'Absolu.* Dissertation, Paris, 1968.

Feddersen, Hans Dittmar Frederik, Governor of the Danish West India Possessions 1851–55. "To Dr. Ruan and the rest of the signers of the several petitions for the acknowledgement of the New

Church." St. Croix, March 17, 1854. Letter published in *New Church Repository* (July 1854): 329–330.

Filosofskaya entsiklopedia, gen. ed. Fyodor Vasilevich Konstantinov. 5 vols. Moscow: Sovetskaia Entsikopedia, 1960–1970. Vol. 4, Moscow 1967.

Fishbough, William. *The Macrocosm and the Microcosm; or the universe without and the universe within; being an unfolding of the plan of creation. . . .* New York: 1852.

Flower, Elizabeth, and Murray G. Murphy. *A History of Philosophy in America.* New York: Capricorn Books, 1977.

Folketællingslister St. Croix 1846. (MSS) Tabelkommisionen, Folketælling 1846, Sankt Croix, Christansted, Vest-Indien. A. Frie, B. Ufrie. Rigsarkivet, Copenhagen; census from the Danish Virgin Islands.

Foucault, Michel. *Les mots et les choses.* Paris: Editions Gallimard, 1966. English translation in *The Order of Things: An Archeology of the Human Sciences.* New York: Random House, 1973 (1971).

Furness, Clifton Joseph, ed. *Walt Whitman's Workshop: A Collection of Unpublished Manuscripts.* Cambridge, Mass: Harvard University Press, 1928. Reprint New York, 1964.

Gardiner, William. *The Music of Nature, or, An attempt to prove that what is passionate and pleasing in the art of singing, speaking, and performing upon musical instruments is derived from the sounds of the animated world.* London, 1832.

Garrett, Clarke. "The Spiritual Odyssey of Jacob Duché." M.A. thesis, Dickinson College, n.d. (Copy in the Swedenborg Library, Bryn Athyn, Penn.)

Gelpi, Donald L. *Endless Seeker: The Religious Quest of Ralph Waldo Emerson.* Lanham, Md.: University Press of America, 1991.

Gladish, Robert W. *Swedenborg, Fourier, and the America of the 1840's.* Bryn Athyn, Penn.: Swedenborg Scientific Association, 1983 (1979).

Glenn, Creda. "What is New Church Music?" *New Church Music Post* (Newsletter) no. 3 (June 1979): 3–8.

Glenn, E. Bruce. "Gleanings from Emerson's Study." *New Church Life* (March 1955): 123–127.

Godwin, Joscelyn. *Music, Mysticism and Magic: A Sourcebook.* New York: Arkana, 1987 (1986).

Goldberg, Lea. *Russian Literature in the Nineteenth Century: Essays.* Jerusalem: Magnes Press, 1976.

Gordon, E.J. "The Sumerian Proverb Collections: A Preliminary

Report." *Journal of the American Oriental Society* (New Haven) 74, no. 2 (April–June1954): 82–85.

Goyder, David George. *The Biblical Assistant, and Book of Practical Piety, designed for the use of young persons . . . classes in Sabbath Schools.* London: J.S. Hodson, 1841.

Gratzer, Wolfgang. *Zur "wunderlichen Mystik" Alban Bergs.* Wien: Böhlau, 1993.

Grier, E. F., ed. *The Collected Writings of Walt Whitman: Notebooks and Unpublished Prose Manuscripts.* 4 vols. New York: New York University Press, 1984.

Griffiths, Paul. *A Concise History of Modern Music from Debussy to Boulez.* London: Thames & Hudson, 1978.

Grun, Bernard, ed. *Alban Berg: Letters to His Wife.* London: Faber & Faber, 1971.

Grusin, Richard A. *Transcendentalist Hermeneutics: Institutional Authority and the Higher Criticism of the Bible.* Durham, N.C.: Duke University Press, 1991.

Gura, Philip F. *The Wisdom of Words: Language, Theology, and Literature in the New England Renaissance.* Middletown, Conn.: Wesleyan University Press, 1981.

Görres, Joseph von. *Swedenborg, seine Visionen und sein Verhältnis zur Kirche.* Strassburg, 1827.

Götschl, Johann, ed. *Erwin Schrödinger's World View: The Dynamics of Knowledge and Reality.* Dordrecht, Netherlands: Kluwer, 1992.

Hagen, Ellen. *En fribetstidens son, Carl Bernhard Wadström: Bergsvetenskapsman, forskningsresande, filantrop.* Stockholm: 1946.

Hahl-Koch, Jelena, ed. *Arnold Schoenberg–Wassily Kandinsky: Letters, Pictures and Documents.* London: Faber and Faber, 1984.

Hallengren, Anders, ed. [Carl Robsahm.] *Anteckningar om Swedenborg.* Skrifter utgivna av Föreningen Swedenborgs Minne, I. Stockholm: 1989.

——. *The Code of Concord: Emerson's Search for Universal Laws.* Acta Universitatis Stockholmiensis, Stockholm Studies in History of Literature 34. Stockholm: Almqvist & Wiksell International, 1994.

——. *Deciphering Reality: Swedenborg, Emerson, Whitman, and the Search for the Language of Nature.* The Nordic Roundtable Papers, Center for Nordic Studies. Minneapolis, Minn.: University of Minnesota Press, 1992.

——. *Tingens tydning: swedenborgstudier.* Stockholm: ÅSAK, 1997.

———. *What is National Literature?: Lectures on Emerson, Dostoevsky, Hemingway, and the Meaning of Culture.* Stockholm: Current History, 1996.

Hart, H.L.A. "Are there any Natural Rights?" In *Political Philosophy.* Edited by Anthony Quinton. Oxford: Oxford University Press, 1967.

Hasler, Christopher. "Will Ye No' Come Back Again." *The Plough* (Bolton) (Winter 1990): 5–8.

Hassan, Ihab Habib. *The Postmodern Turn: Essays in Postmodern Theory and Culture.* Columbus, Ohio: Ohio State University Press, 1987.

Heimert, Alan. *Religion and the American Mind: From the Great Awakening to the Revolution.* Cambridge, Mass.: Harvard University Press, 1966.

Heimert, Alan, and Andrew Delbanco, eds. *The Puritans in America: A Narrative Anthology.* Cambridge, Mass.: Harvard University Press, 1985.

Hellström, Jan Arvid. *"Åt alla christliga förvanter": en undersökning av kolonial förvaltning, religionsvård och samfundsliv på St. Barthélemy under den svenska perioden 1784–1878.* Uppsala: Erene, 1987.

Hempel, Charlie Julius. *The True Organization of the New Church, as indicated in the writings of Emanuel Swedenborg, and demonstrated by Charles Fourier.* New York and London: 1848.

Herzen [Gercen], Aleksandr Ivanovich. *My Past and Thoughts: The Memoirs of Alexander Herzen.* 4 vols. Trans. Constance Gernett and Humphrey Higgins, with an introduction by Isaiah Berlin. Vol. I, chap.16, "Alexander Lavrentevich Vitberg," 264–277. London: 1968.

Hildebrand, Hedi. *Die Amerikanische Stellung zur Geschichte und zu Europa in Emersons Gedankensystem.* Bonner Studien zur Englischen Philologie, XXIX. Bonn, Germany: 1936.

Hindmarsh, James, et al, eds. *A Dictionary of Correspondences, Representatives, and Significatives, Derived from the Word of the Lord. Extracted from the Writings of Emanuel Swedenborg.* Boston 1847 (1841).

Hindmarsh, Robert. *Rise and Progress of the New Jerusalem Church.* London: Hodson & Son, 1861.

Hjern, Olle. "Det latinska Ordet i svenska Amerika," and "Tidig svensk nykyrklighet i Amerika." *Världarnas Möte* (Stockholm) 4 (1991): 146–152.

———. *Swedenborg och hans vänner i Göteborg.* Stockholm: Nykyrkliga Bokförlaget Swedenborgsförlaget, 1990.

_____. "Swedenborgs religiösa betydelse i världen." *Parnass* (Stockholm) 2, no. 4 (1994): 22–27.

_____. "Swedenborg till Anders von Höpken." *Nya Kyrkans Tidning* (Stockholm) 99, no. 3–4 (1974): 26–28.

Ho, John. "Quellenuntersuchung zur Chinakenntnis bei Leibniz und Wolff." Dissertation. Zürich, 1962.

Hobart, Nathaniel. *Life of Emanuel Swedenborg: with some accounts of his writings.* Third edition. New York: John Allen; Boston: Otis Clapp, 1850 (1831).

Hofstadter, Douglas R. *Gödel, Escher, Bach: An Eternal Golden Braid.* New York: Vintage Books/Random House, 1989 (New York: Basic Books, 1979).

Holloway, Emory, ed. *The Uncollected Poetry and Prose of Walt Whitman: much of which has but been recently discovered.* Garden City, New York: 1921; London: Heinemann, 1922.

Honour, Hugh, ed. *The Image of the Black in Western Art.* Vol. 4. "From the American Revolution to World War I." Cambridge, Mass.: Harvard University Press, 1989.

Horn, Friedemann. "Arnold Schönberg." *Offene Tore* (Zurich) 3 (1992): 110–113.

_____. "Understanding Swedenborg's Initial Vision." *The Messenger* (San Francisco) 207, no. 1 (February 1987): 24–27.

Hotson, Clarence Paul. "Emerson's biographical sources for 'Swedenborg'." *Studies in Philology* 26, no. 1 (January 1929).

_____. "Prof. Bush's reply to Emerson on Swedenborg." *The New-Church Magazine* 51, no. 506 (Oct.–Dec.1932): 213–223.

_____. "Sampson Reed, A Teacher of Emerson." *New England Quarterly* (Boston) 2, no. 2 (1929). [Other works by Hotson are listed in: H.A. Pochman and A.R. Schultz. *Bibliography of German Culture in America to 1940.* Madison, Wis.: 1953. p. 171.]

Howe, Irving. *The American Newness: Culture and Politics in the Age of Emerson.* Cambridge, Mass.: Harvard University Press, 1986.

Hughes, Gertrude Reif. *Emerson's Demanding Optimism.* Baton Rouge, La.: Louisiana State University Press,1984.

Hulting, Johan. "Förbundet i Norrköping 1779." *Historisk Tidskrift.* Stockholm: 1899.

Hutchison, William R. *The Transcendentalist Ministers: Church Reform in the New England Renaissance.* New Haven, Conn.: Yale Historical Publications, 1959.

Hyde, James. *A Bibliography of the Works of Emanuel Swedenborg, Original and Translated.* London: Swedenborg Society, 1906.

Hyde, Martha M. *Schoenberg's Twelve-Tone Harmony: The Suite Op. 29 and the Compositional Sketches.* Ann Arbor, Mich.: UMI Research Press, 1982.

Iamblichus Chalcidensis. *On the mysteries of the Egyptians, Chaldeans, and Assyrians.* Tr. from the Greek by Thomas Taylor. Chiswick, 1821. Reprint London 1895.

"Il caso Swedenborg." *Hyphos: estetica, letteratura, arti, scienze. Periodico semestrale* (Lecce, Italia)1, no. 2.

"Intelligence, Notices, &c.: *St. Thomas, W.I.*" *New Jerusalem Magazine* 3 (July 1830): 349.

Irwin, John T. *American Hieroglyphics. The Symbol of the Egyptian Hieroglyphics in the American Renaissance.* Baltimore, Md.: Johns Hopkins, 1983 (1980).

Iversen, Erik. *The Myth of Egypt and its Hieroglyphs in European Tradition.* Copenhagen: GAD, 1961; Princeton, N.J.: Mythos, 1993.

Jackson, Robert. "Jamaica: Eight Representatives in 1st Conference 13/4/1789." Reference note (MS), Archives, Swedenborg School of Religion, Newton, Mass.

Jacobs, Gordon. "Men of Note." *Outlook* (Cambridge, Mass.) 3 (1992): 1–2.

James, Dennis M. Letter from Montego Bay, Jamaica, April 15, 1897 (MS). Archives, Swedenborg School of Religion, Newton, Mass.

James, Henry, Sr. *The Secret of Swedenborg: Being an Elucidation of His Doctrine of the Divine Natural Humanity.* Boston 1869; facsimile: New York: AMS Press, 1983).

Jefferson, Thomas. *The Living Thoughts of Thomas Jefferson.* Presented by John Dewey. New York: Longmans & Co., 1940. Reprint 1943.

Jones, Richard Foster. *Ancients and Moderns: A Study of the Rise of the Scientific Movement in Seventeenth-Century England.* New York: Dover, 1961.

Jonsson, Inge. *Emanuel Swedenborg.* New York: Twayne, 1971.

———. *Humanistiskt Credo.* Stockholm: Norstedts, 1988.

———. *I symbolens hus: Nio kapitel litterär begreppshistoria.* Stockholm: Norstedts, 1983.

———. *Swedenborgs korrespondenslära.* Acta Universitatis Stockholmiensis. Stockholm Studies in History of Literature 10. Stockholm: Almqvist & Wiksell, 1969.

————. *Swedenborgs skapelsedrama De cultu et amore Dei: En studie av motiv och intellektuell miljö.* (Diss.) Stockholm: Natur och Kultur, 1961.

Jonsson, Inge, and Olle Hjern. *Swedenborg: Sökaren i naturens och andens världar. Hans verk och efterföljd.* Stockholm: Proprius, 1976.

Jordanova, Ludmilla J., ed. *Languages of Nature: Critical Essays on Science and Literature.* London: Free Association, 1986.

Kahl, Achatius. *Den Nya Kyrkan och dess inflytande på theologiens studium i Swerige.* 4 Vols. Lund, Sweden: 1847–1864.

Kaplan, Justin. *Walt Whitman: A Life.* New York: Simon and Schuster, 1980.

Kjersgaard, Mads. "Orgelns ABC (XIII): Orgelpositivet." *Orglet,* Medlemsskrift for Det Danske Orgelselskab (Vanløse, Denmark) 2 (1984): 4–27.

Klitgaard, C. *Kjærulfske Studier: Bidrag til en vendsysselsk bondeæts genealogi og historie.* Ålborg, Denmark: Magnus A. Schultz, 1914–1918.

Knox, John P. *A Historical Account of St. Thomas, W.I.* New York: Negro Universities Press, 1970.

Kristeva, Julia. *Histoires d'amour,* Paris: Denoël, 1983.

————.*Tales of Love.* Trans. Leon S. Roudiez. New York: Columbia University Press, 1987.

Kuntz, Marion Leathers, and Paul Grimley Kuntz, eds. *Jacob's Ladder and the Tree of Life: Concepts of Hierarchy and the Great Chain of Being.* New York: P. Lang, 1987.

Kurtz, Benjamin P. "Coleridge on Swedenborg: with unpublished marginalia on the 'Prodromus'." In *Essays and Studies,* Vol. 14, pp. 199–214. Berkeley, Cal.: University of California Publications in English, 1943.

Kylén, Hjalmar. *Swedenborgsreformation i Sverige under 1800-talets första decennier?* Stockholm: Askerberg, 1910.

Küttner, Juri. "Vassilij Tatisjtjev." *Lychnos: Annual of the Swedish History of Science Society,* (Uppsala) (1990): 109–164.

Lacroix, James Huggins. "Rise and Progress of the New Jerusalem Church in Trinidad." *New Jerusalem Magazine* (Boston), letter from President Lacroix to Joseph Andrews, Boston. "Intelligence," 543–545. (On the black preacher Maisonneuve, etc.)

Lagercrantz, Olof. *Dikten om livet på den andra sidan: En bok om Emanuel Swedenborg.* Stockholm: Wahlström & Widstrand, 1996.

Lamm, Martin. *August Strindberg.* Second edition. Reprint Stockholm: Hammarström & Åberg, 1986 (1948).

―――. *Strindberg och Makterna: Olaus Petriföreläsningar vid Uppsala univer-sitet.* Stockholm: Svenska kyrkans diakonistyrelses bokförlag, 1936.

―――. *Swedenborg: en studie över hans utveckling till mystiker och andeskådare.* Reprint Stockholm: Hammarström & Åberg, 1987 (1917).

―――. *Upplysningstidens romantik: den mystiskt sentimentala strömningen i svensk litteratur.* 2 Vols. New ed., with a preface by Inge Jonsson. Stockholm: Hammarström & Åberg, 1981 (1918–1920).

Larsen, Kay. *Dansk Vestindien 1666–1917.* Copenhagen: C.A. Reitzels Forlag, 1928.

―――. *Guvernörer, Residenter, Kommandanter og Chefer* . . . Copenhagen: 1940. (Copy in Det Kongl. Bibliothek, Copenhagen.)

―――. Slip catalog (MS) of West Indian biography at the Royal Li-brary, Copenhagen, Denmark.

Larsen, Robin, ed. *Emanuel Swedenborg: A Continuing Vision.* With an intro-duction by George Dole. New York: Swedenborg Foundation, 1988.

Lattimore, Owen. *High Tartary.* Reprint, with a new introd. by the au-thor. New York: AMS Press, 1975 (Boston: Little, Brown, & Co., 1930).

Lawaetz, Erik J. *St. Croix: 500 years, Pre-Columbus to 1990.* Christiansted, U.S.V.I., and Herning, Denmark: Poul Kristensen, 1991.

Lawaetz, Eva. *Free Colored in St. Croix 1744–1816.* Christiansted, St. Croix: 1979.

Lawaetz, Hermann. *Peter v. Scholten: Vestindiske Tidsbilleder fra den sidste Gen-eralguvernørs dage.* Copenhagen: 1940.

Lazarus [Carl Fredrik Lindahl]. *Svenska Millionärer: minnen och anteckningar.* 10 vols. Stockholm 1897–1905. Ny följd, V. Stock-holm: 1904.

Leijonhufvud, Karl A. K:son. *Ny svensk släktbok.* Med register af G. Eric-son. Stockholm, 1901–1906.

Lenhammar, Harry. "Sällskapet Pro fide et caritate." In *Kyrkohistorisk Årsskrift.* Uppsala: Svenska kyrkohistoriska föreningen, 1970: 119–141. Reprinted (without notes) in *Världarnas Möte* (Stock-holm) 4 (1993): 160–180.

―――. "Tolerans och bekännelsetvång. Studier i den svenska sweden-borgianismen 1765–1795." Acta Universitatis Upsaliensis, Studia Historico-Ecclesiastica Upsaliensia. Diss., Uppsala: 1966.

Lessem, Alan Philip. *Music and Text in the Works of Arnold Schoenberg: The Critical Years, 1908–1922.* Ann Arbor: UMI Research Press, 1979.

Levin, Harry. "What Is Realism?" In *Contexts of Criticism*. Cambridge, Mass.: Harvard University Press, 1969 (1957).

Lewis, R.W.B. *The American Adam: Innocence, Tragedy, and Tradition in the Nineteenth Century*. Chicago: The University of Chicago Press, 1955.

Liedgren, Emil. *Svensk psalm och andlig visa*: Olaus Petri-föreläsningar i Uppsala. Stockholm: Diakonistyrelsens förlag, 1926.

Liljegren, S. Bodvar. *Bulwer-Lytton's Novels and Isis Unveiled*. Uppsala: Lundequistska bokh., 1957.

Lindberg, Henning Gottfried. "Extracts from a letter of H. G. Linberg" to John Hargrove, dated St. John's, February 27th, 1826. *New Jerusalem Magazine* (Boston) (Jan. 1841): 188–190.

_____. "*Introduction to the History of Philosophy*. By Victor Cousin . . . Translated from the French by Henning Gottfried Linberg. Boston. Hillard, Gray, Little, & Wilkins. 1832." After this announcement, Linberg's Preface is reprinted. *New Jerusalem Magazine* (Boston), (April 1832): 288–293.

Lindeman, Eduard C., ed. *Basic Selections from Emerson*. New York: The New American Library of World Literature, 1954.

Logvinovich, E.G. "Marine Ground-Effect Machine." In *Great Soviet Encyclopedia*, vol. 25, Moscow.

Longstaff, Rachel Odhner. "Richard Yardumian." (Photocopy). Bryn Athyn: The Lord's New Church, 1988.

Lovejoy, Arthur Oncken. *The Great Chain of Being: A Study of the History of an Idea*. Cambridge. Mass: Harvard University Press, 1936. (The William James Lectures, 1933). Reprints.

Lundeberg, Axel. *Emanuel Swedenborg och hans inflytande i Amerika*. Minneapolis, Minn.: 1911.

Macaulay, Thomas B., Baron. *Essays and Lays of Ancient Rome*. London: Longmans & Co., 1892. Reprint 1893.

MacDonald, Malcolm. *Schoenberg*. London: Dent, 1976.

MacKinnon, Barbara, ed. *American Philosophy: A Historical Anthology*. Albany, N.Y.: State University of New York Press, 1985.

Manby, C.J.N. *Swedenborg och Nya Kyrkan*. Stockholm: Nykyrkliga Bokförlaget, 1906.

"Mantal over de frifarvede mænd og kvinder i Christiansted jurisdiktion 1831."(MS) DVI, St. Croix, Christiansted: Rigsarkivet, Copenhagen.

Marielle, Pierre, ed. *Dictionnaire des Sociétés Secrètes en Occident*. With a preface by Louis Pauwels. Paris: Culture, Art, Loisirs, 1971.

Martz, Erin C. "Dostoyevsky's Christianity: Emanuel Swedenborg's Contribution." *The New Philosophy* (Bryn Athyn) XCL, no. 4 (1988): 669–682.

———. "The Writings in Russia." *New Church Life* (Bryn Athyn) (February 1989): 77–82.

Mather, William. "The Late Princess Kleopatra Schahoffskoy." *New-Church Magazine* (1884): 199–201.

Matsevich, A.A. "Emanuel Swedenborg," *Great Soviet Encyclopedia*, vol. 23. Moscow.

Mazour, Anatole Grigorevich. *The First Russian Revolution, 1825: The Decembrist Movement. Its Origins, Development, and Significance*. Stanford, Cal.: Stanford University Press, 1961. (Berkeley: University of Calif. Press, 1937.)

Mazzeo, Joseph Anthony. *Renaissance and Seventeenth Century Studies*. New York: Columbia University Press, 1964.

Memorial to the King of Denmark, St. Croix, Christiansted, October 28, 1848, on behalf of the restoration of the governor Peter von Scholten [signed by a number of citizens of Christiansted]. Copy in St. Croix Landmarks Society, Fredriksted, U.S.V.I.

Mihajlov, Mihajlo. "Dostoevsky and Mysticism." In *Russian Themes*. Trans. Marija Mihajlov. London: 1968.

Miller, Perry, ed. *The American Puritans: Their Prose and Poetry*. Garden City, New York: Anchor Books, 1956.

———, ed. *The Transcendentalists: An Anthology*. Cambridge, Mass.: Harvard University Press, 1950; rpt. 1979.

Milosz, Czeslaw. "Dostoyevsky and Swedenborg." *Slavic Review* 1975; *Roczniki humanistyczne*. Lublin: 1976. Also published in *Emperor of the Earth: Modes of Eccentric Vision*. Berkeley: Univ. of California Press, 1977.

Mittnacht, Johann Gottlieb. *Emanuel Swedenborgs Leben & Lehre*. Frankfurt am Main: 1880.

Moldenhauer, Hans. *Anton von Webern: A Chronicle of His Life and Work*. London: Gollancz, 1978.

Moore, Henry. *The Immortality of the Soul*. Ed. Alexander Jacob. Dordrecht, Netherlands: M. Nijhoff, 1987.

Moore, J.B. "The Master of Whitman." *Studies in Philology* 23 (January 1926): 77–89.

Moskovskii Nekropoli III, (St. Petersburg, 1908): 332.

Munthe, Arne. *Västra Södermalm intill mitten av 1800-talet: En stadsdel och dess kyrkliga liv.* Utarbetad på uppdrag av Sancta Maria Magdalena och Högalids församlingar. Stockholm: 1959.

Muravyov, I. *Kratkaya biographiya Em. Swedenborga.* A short introduction originally published in St. Petersburg in 1847. Reprint Leipzig and London, 1870.

"Music Appreciation" (series) published in: *The Territorial: Newsletter of the Tucson, Arizona, Society of the General Church of the New Jerusalem*, 1989.

Myslivchenko, Aleksandr Grigorevich. *Filosofskaya mysl'v Shvetsii.* Moscow: Nauka, 1972.

Nagel, Ernest, and James R. Newman. *Gödel's Proof.* London: Routledge, 1989 (1958).

Nasr, Seyyed Hossein. *The Encounter of Man and Nature: The Spiritual Crisis of Modern Man.* Reprint London: Unwin, 1976.

Nerval, Gérard de [Gérard Labrunie]. *Aurélia.* In *Oeuvres*, vol. 1. Ed. Albert Béguin and Jean Richer. Paris: Gallimard, 1952.

New Jerusalem Magazine (London) 1, no. 1 (1790).

Nicholson, George. *A Dictionary of Correspondences, Representatives and Significatives* [. . .]. Boston: 1841 (1800).

Nikitenko, Aleksandr. *Dnevnik.* 3 vols. Leningrad: Chudozestvennaja literatura, 1955–1956. *The Diary of a Russian Censor.* Abridged ed. and trans. Helen S. Jacobson. Amherst, Mass.: University of Massachusetts Press, 1975.

Nordenskiöld, August. *Församlings formen uti det Nya Jerusalem.* Copenhagen: Johann Rudolph Thiele, 1790.

Nordenskiöld, August, and Carl Bernhard Wadström. "Plan for a free community upon the coast of Africa [. . .] entirely independent of all European Laws and Customs." London 1789, quoted in *New Jerusalem Magazine* (London) (1790): 142ff., 171ff. and passim.

Nordenskiöld, Carl Fredrik. *Considérations générales sur le Christianisme actuel, et la lumière que Monsieur Emmanuel Svédenborg répand sur les religions.* Rostock:1819/28.

"Obituary" [John Carr Chambers, Lucea, parish of Hanover, Jamaica]."Miscellaneous." *Intellectual Repository* (London) (1871): 54–55.

"Obituary: Died in the Island of Cuba . . . [Alexander] Leslie." *The Intellectual Repository for the New Church* (1821), 468.

Odhner, Carl Theophilus. *Annals of the New Church.* Vol. 1, 1688–1850. Bryn Athyn, Penn.: Academy of the New Church, 1898.

_____. *The Correspondences of Egypt: A Study in the Theology of the Ancient Church.* Bryn Athyn, Penn.: The Academy Bookroom, 1914.

_____. "The Princess Kleopatra Schakoffsky." *New Church Life* (May 1884): 65.

_____. "The Russian Nation." *New Church Life* (May 1904): 268–270.

Œgger, Guillaume. *Essai d'un dictionnaire de la langue de la nature.* Paris: 1831.

_____. *Le Vrai Messie, ou l'Ancien et le Nouveau Testaments examinés d'après les principes de la langue de la nature.* Paris: 1829.

_____. *Rapports inattendus établis entre le monde matériel et le monde spirituel, par la découverte de la langue de la nature . . . .* Paris: 1834.

_____. *The True Messiah.* Tran. by Elizabeth P. Peabody. Boston: 1842.

Oldendorp, C.G.A. *Geschichte der Mission der evangelischen Brüder auf den caribischen Inseln S. Thomas, S. Croix und S. Jan.* Leipzig: Barby, 1777.

Olschki, Leonardo. *L'Asia di Marco Polo: introd. alla letteratura e allo studio del Milione.* Venice: Civiltà veneziana, Studi, 1957.

Örnberg, V., ed. *Svenska ättartal.* Stockholm: Wadstena, 1889–1908.

Packer, Barbara. *Emerson's Fall: A New Interpretation of the Major Essays.* New York: Continuum, 1982.

Parkin, David, ed. *The Anthropology of Evil.* Oxford, England: Blackwell, 1985.

Parmet, Simon. *Con Amore: essäer om musik och mästare.* Helsinki: Söderströms, 1960.

Paz, Octavio. The Charles Eliot Norton Lectures at Harvard University, 1972. In *Los hijos del limo: del romanticismo a la vanguardia.* Second edition. Barcelona: Seix Barral, 1974 (New ed. 1986).

Peabody, Elizabeth Palmer, ed. *Aesthetic Papers.* Vol. 1 (I). Boston: 1849. "The Peace Movement." *New Church Life* (Sept. 1898): 142.

"Perhaps the first in the West Indies." *SPI* (Bryn Athyn, Penn.) 3, no. 4 (Dec. 1992): 2. [communication on Trinidad-Tobago]

Pernety, Antoine-Joseph, Abbé. Emanuel Swedenborg, *Les Merveilles du ciel et de l'enfer et des terres planétaires et astrales.* I, "Discours préliminaire." Berlin, 1782.

Perrelli, Franco. "Con Swedenborg verso Borges." *Hyphos* (Lecce, Italia)1, no. 2: 16–19.

Pettersson, Jakob. "Filonegros Wadström." *Världarnas Möte*(Stockholm) 4 (1991): 126–131.

Pitcairn, Lachlan. "The Value of Music." *Performing Arts in the New Church* 2, no. 1 (Oct. 1991): 5f.

Pociej, Bohdan. *Bach—Muzyka i Wielkość*. Kraków: Polskie Wydawnictvo Muzyczne, 1972.

Poirier, Richard. *The Renewal of Literature: Emersonian Reflections*. New York: Random House, 1987.

Polo, Marco. *Le livre de Marco Polo, citoyen de Venise, conseiller privé et commissaire impérial de Khoubilai-Khaân, rédigé en français sous sa dictée en 1298 par Rusticien de Pise, publié pour la première fois d'après trois manuscrits inédits . . . présentant la rédaction primitive du livre . . .* par G. Pauthier. Paris: Librairie de Firmin Didot Frères, 1865.

———. *Le livre de Marco Polo: Fac-simile d'un manuscrit du xiv:e siècle conservé à la Bibliothèque royale de Stockholm*. Ed. Adolf Erik Nordenskiöld. Stockholm, 1882.

———. *Marco Polo—Il Milione*, edizione del testo toscano ("Ottimo"): Ruggero M. Ruggieri. Biblioteca dell' "Archivum Romanicum," ser. 1: 200. Firenze: Olschki, 1986.

———. *Marco Polos resor i Asien 1271–1295*. Trans. and notes by Bengt Thordeman, Stockholm: Forum, 1982.

———. *The Travels of Marco Polo*. Trans. with an introd. by Ronald Latham. Harmondsworth, England: Penguin Classics, 1958.

Pontén, Birgitta. "En släktfläta del 7: Robsahm" (photostat copy). Stockholm: 1973.

Porte, Joel, ed. *Emerson in His Journal*. Cambridge, Mass.: Belknap Press, 1982.

———. *Representative Man. Ralph Waldo Emerson in His Time*. 2nd edition. New York: Oxford University Press, 1988.

Potts, John Faulkner. *The Swedenborg Concordance*. 4 vols. London: Swedenborg Society, 1888–1902. New ed. London: Swedenborg Society, 1978.

Practical Ideals 24 (Sept. 1912): 17–18.

"Prospects in Denmark." Letter to George Bush from a New Church friend in St. Croix on Søren Kierkegaard's denouncement of the Danish Lutheran clergy. "The foundation of his argument is that of the New Church . . . I have therefore written two long letters to him." *New Church Repository* (Dec. 1855): 553.

Rameau, Jean-Philippe. *Traité de L'harmonie— Reduite à ses Principes naturels*. Paris: 1722. Facsimilie: New York: Broude Brothers, 1965.

Rasmussen, R.H. Vestindien, Dressel. "Personhistorisk Samling." (Handwritten catalog), Rigsarkivet, Copenhagen.

Reed, John A., Capt. "Communication from St. Thomas, W.I." *Convention Report 1830*, Report from the Twelfth Convention 1830, The General Convention (USA), "Selections from letters, &c," p. 17.

Reed, Sampson. "Egyptian hieroglyphics." *New Jerusalem Magazine* (Boston) 4 (1830–31): 69.

———. *Sampson Reed: Primary Source Material for Emerson Studies*. Compiled by George F. Dole. With a Preface by Sylvia Shaw. West Chester, Penn.: Swedenborg Foundation, 1992.

Reich, Willi. *Schoenberg: A Critical Biography*. Trans. Leo Black. London: Longman, 1971.

Richardson, Robert D. *Emerson: The Mind on Fire*. Berkeley: University of California Press, 1995.

Ringer, Alexander L. *Arnold Schoenberg—The Composer as Jew*. Oxford, England: Clarendon Press, 1990.

Robinson, David M. *Emerson and the Conduct of Life: pragmatism and the ethical purpose in the later work*. Cambridge and New York: Cambridge University Press, 1993.

Roerich, George N. [Rerikh, Iurii Nikolaevich] "Studies in the Kalacakra." *Journal of Urusvati Himalayan Research Institute of Roerich Museum* (Naggar Kulu, Urusvati Himalayan Research Institute) 2 (1931): 11–22.(Copy in the British Library.)

———. *Tibetsko-russko-angliiskii slovar's Sanskritimi paralleliami*. Moscow: Nauka, Glavnia redaktsiia vostochnoi literatury, 1983—.

Roos, Jacques. *Aspects littéraires du mysticisme philosophique et l'influence de Boehme et de Swedenborg au début du Romantisme . . .* Strasbourg, France: P.H. Heitz, 1951.

Rorty, Richard. *Philosophy and the Mirror of Nature*. Second edition. Princeton, N.J.: Princeton University Press, 1980.

Rose, Donald L. Editorial: "George Bush." *New Church Life* CIX, no. 5 (May 1989): 233ff.

Ruan, William H. "Dr W.H. Ruan's Reply to Governor Feddersen's Letter." *New Church Repository* (July 1854): 330–332.

Rubin, Joseph Jay, and Charles H. Brown, eds. *Walt Whitman of the New York Aurora: Editor at Twenty-two: A Collection of Recently Discovered Writings*. State College, Penn.: Penn State University Press, 1950.

Rune, Staffan. "'Strindbergs asiatiska horisont': En studie i August

Strindbergs kartografiska forskningar." *Lychnos, Annual of the Swedish History of Science Society* (1975–1976): 157–210.

Rusk, Ralph L. *The Life of Ralph Waldo Emerson.* New York: Charles Scribner's Sons, 1949.

"Russia." *New Church Life* (June 1887): 96; (Aug.–Sept. 1905): 531; (May 1912): 259–260; (April 1917): 236–237; (Jan. 1918): 54–55.

"Russia." *The Intellectual Repository and New Jerusalem Magazine* (1872): 267–268.

"Russia and the New Church." *The New-Church Magazine* (1917): 494–498.

"Russia's New Day-Dawn." *The New-Church Magazine* (1917): 188–190.

"Russian Translation of the Treatise on the Divine Love." *Intellectual Repository* 11(1864): 137–138.

"The Russians in the Spiritual World." *New Church Life* (Feb., 1918): 117ff.

Russkii biograficheskii slovar' (St. Petersburg) 29 (1905).

Russkii Portreti XVIII i XIX Stoletij. (St. Petersburg) 4 (1908):1, 85.

Ryding, Nils Erik. "Begreppen nytta och sanning inom fransk upplysningsfilosofi: Studier kring en idékonflikt." (Diss.) Lund: Gleerup, 1951.

Saabye, H.G. "Swedenborgianerne." In *Sekterne i Danmark med særligt Hensyn til deres Afvigelser i Læren fra den evangelisk-lutherske Kirke*, 307–331. Copenhagen: Andr. Schous Forlag, 1884.

Saint-Martin, C.L. de. *Le Nouvel Homme.* Lyon and Paris: 1796.

Samins, Julius M. Rev. Letters (MSS) of Nov. 25 and Dec. 4, 1925, to Paul Sperry, Washington, D.C., from Pastor J.M. Samins, New Jerusalem Church, St. Michael, Dalkeith Road, Barbados, B.W.I.(auxiliary of the General Convention). Archives, Swedenborg School of Religion, Newton, Mass.

Samlingar för Philantroper. 4 vols. Stockholm: Anders Jac. Nordström, 1787.

Sanct Thomæ Tidende. Newspaper of St. Thomas, V.I., 1852–1853.

Sartre, Jean-Paul. *Baudelaire.* With a foreword by Michel Leiris. Les Essais XXIV. Paris: Gallimard, 1947.

SBL 1991 Seminar Papers. Published by the Society of Biblical Literature. Atlanta, Georgia: Scholars Press, 1991.

Scheibe, Johann Adolph. *Abhandlung vom Ursprunge und Alter der Musik, insonderheit der Vokalmusik . . .* Altona: Kortische Buchh., 1754. Facsimile. Munich: Saur, 1987.

Schlegel, Johan Frederik, Governor of the Danish West India Possessions 27/4/1855-31/05/1860. Letter to the Swedenborg Society in St. Croix, Aug. 20, 1855. Quoted by Elijah Bryan, *New Church Repository* (Dec. 1855): 552–553.

Schmidt-Häuer, Christian. "Reports from a Buddhist Congress in Soviet." *Die Zeit: Wochenzeitung für Politik, Wirtschaft, Handel und Kultur,* Hamburg, No. 1032, 1978.

Schrödinger, Erwin. *My View of the World.* Trans. Cecily Hastings. Woodbridge, England: Ox Bow Press, 1983.

Schuh, Willi. *Richard Strauss: A Chronicle of the Early Years, 1864–1898.* (cop. 1976.) Trans. Mary Whittall. Cambridge: Cambridge University Press, 1982.

Schyberg, Frederik. *Walt Whitman.* Copenhagen: Gyldendal, 1933.

Schönberg, Arnold. *Style and Idea: Selected Writings.* Ed. Leonard Stein. London: Faber and Faber, 1975.

Sealts, Merton M, Jr., and Alfred R. Ferguson, eds. *Emerson's 'Nature': Origin, Growth, Meaning.* Carbondale, Ill.: Southern Illinois University Press, 1979.

Sechrist, Alice Spiers. *A Dictionary of Bible Imagery.* New York: Swedenborg Foundation, 1981 (1971).

Self, Geoffrey. *In Town Tonight: A Centenary Study of Eric Coates.* London: Thames Publ., 1986.

Servanté, Henry. "Epistolary Correspondence of the Earlier Members of the Church, Letter VII." Letter to Alexander Leslie, with remarks by the editors. *Monthly Observer* (London) 5 (1861): 26–28.

Shakhovskaya, Kleopatra Mikhailovna. "The East and Swedenborg." *Intellectual Repository,* (1872): 285ff, 350–356.

_____. *Introduction au Journal: "Orient et Swedenborg."* London: F. Pitman, 1872.

_____. "Östern och Swedenborg," *Ett Kristligt Sändebud* (Uppsala) 4, no. 1 (1872): 88–91; no. 2: 73–80.

Shaw, Robert. *Visits to High Tartary, Yarkand and Kashgar.* London: John Murray, 1871.

Shklovsky, Viktor Borisovich. *O teorii prozy.* Moskva: Krug, 1925.

_____. *Theory of Prose.* Trans. Benjamin Sherwith, and with an intro. by Gerald L. Bruns. Elmwood Park, Ill.: Dalkey Archive Press, 1990.

Sigstedt, Cyriel Odhner. *The Swedenborg Epic: The Life and Works of Emanuel Swedenborg.* London: Swedenborg Society, 1981.

Silver, R.K. "The Spiritual Kingdom in America: The Influence of

Emanuel Swedenborg on American Society and Culture, 1815-1860." Ph.D. diss., Stanford University, May 1983 (Ann Arbor, Mich.: University Microfilms International).

Sjödén, Karl-Erik. "Ett århundrade av den Nya Kyrkans historia i Frankrike." Reprint from *Nya Kyrkans Tidning* (Stockholm) 3–4 (1977).

———. *Swedenborg en France*. Acta Universitatis Stockholmiensis, Stockholm Studies in History of Literature 27. Stockholm: Almqvist & Wiksell International, 1985.

Smith, Henry Nash. *Virgin Land*. Cambridge, Mass: Harvard University Press, 1970.

Solovyov, Vladimir Sergeevich. "E. Svedenborg." *Brockhaus-Ephron Encyclopedia*, 1900.

SPI Swedenborg Publishers International Newsletter (1990–).

St. Croixian Pocket Companion. Copenhagen 1780. (Copy in St. Croix Landmarks Society, Fredriksted, U.S. V.I.)

Stanley, Michael W. *The Ladder of Ascent*. Transaction (No. 6) of the Swedenborg Society. London: 1976.

Stockenström, Göran. "Ismael i öknen: Strindberg som mystiker." Diss.: Uppsala University. Historia litterarum, 5, Uppsala 1972.

Stovall, Floyd. *The Foreground of Leaves of Grass*. Charlottesville,Va.: University of Virginia Press, 1974.

Stralenberg, Philip Johan von. *Das nord- und ostliche Theil von Europa und Asia*, Stockholm 1730. Also available in Russian, English, French, and Spanish translations. Facisimile with an intro. by J. R. Krueger. Studia Uralo-Altica 8, Szeged: Univ. Attila József, 1975.

Straus, Joseph N. *Remaking the Past: Musical Modernism and the Influence of the Tonal Tradition*. Cambridge, Mass.: Harvard University Press, 1990.

Strindberg, August. *August Strindbergs brev*. 20 vols. Stockholm: Bonniers, 1948–1996. Vols. 11 (1896), 12 (1897), 16 (1907–1908).

———. *August Strindbergs samlade verk*. National Ed., publ. by Dept. of Literature, Stockholm University, 1981–, general ed. Lars Dahlbäck. Vol. 37: *Inferno*. Annotated ed.: Ann-Charlotte Gavel Adams. Stockholm: Norstedts, 1994. Vol. 65:1-, *En blå bok*, ed. Gunnar Ollén. Stockholm: Norstedts, 1997-.

———. *En Blå Bok*. 4 vols. Stockholm: Björck & Börjesson, 1907–1912.

———. *Kulturhistoriska Studier*. Stockholm 1881. (*Samlade Skrifter* IV, Stockholm 1987.)

Strödda Anteckningar, börande till Swedenborgs Lefwerne. Carlshamn, Sweden: J. Söderström, 1821.

Strömbom, Sixten, ed. *Index över svenska porträtt 1500–1850 i Svenska porträttarkivets samlingar.* Stockholm: Nationalmuseum, 1935–1943.

Stuckenschmidt, H.H. *Schoenberg: His Life, World, and Work.* London: Calder, 1977.

Sullivan, James. Letter to Paul Sperry from J. Sullivan, St. James Main Road, Trinidad, B.W.I., 8th October 1925. (Copy.) Archives, Swedenborg School of Religion, Newton, Mass.

Surkov, Aleksej Aleksandrovich, gen. ed. *Kratkaya literaturnaya entsiklopedia.* 9 vols. Moscow: Sovetskaia Entsikopedia, 1962–75.

Sutton, Eric A. *The Happy Isles: The Story of Swedenborg.* London: 1938.

Swank, Scott Trego. "The Unfettered Conscience: A Study of Sectarianism, Spiritualism, and Social Reform in the New Jerusalem Church, 1840–1870." University of Pennsylvania, Ph.D.diss., 1970. (Ann Arbor, Mich.: University Microfilms)

Swedenborg, Emanuel. (a) *Angelic Wisdom Concerning the Divine Love and the Divine Wisdom.* Boston:1847 [*Sapientia angelica de divino amore et de divina sapientia.* Amsterdam: 1763]. (b) *Divine Love and Wisdom.* Trans. John C. Ager. Second edition. West Chester, Penn.: Swedenborg Foundation, 1995.

———. *Angelskaya premudrost* [. . .] Karlsruhe: 1864; "Angelic Wisdom concerning the Divine Love and Wisdom." Trans. Stepan E. Dzhunkovskoi. (Copy in the Royal Library, Stockholm.)

———. *Animal Kingdom.* Trans. James John Garth Wilkinson. Boston 1843–44.

———. *Apocalypse Revealed.* (a) Boston: 1836. [*Apocalypsis revelata* . . . Amsterdam: 1766.] (b) Trans. John Whitehead. 2 vols. Second edition. West Chester, Penn.: Swedenborg Foundation, 1997.

———. *Arcana Cœlestia.* London: 1749–56. (a) English trans. Boston: 1837–47. (b) Trans. J. Clowes. Revised J. F. Potts. Second edition. West Chester, Penn.: Swedenborg Foundation, 1995–1998.

———. *Camena Borea.* Edited, with an introduction . . . by Hans Helander. Uppsala Univ., Studia Latina Upsaliensia, 20. Stockholm: Almqvist & Wiksell International, 1988.

———. (a) *Charity* [*DeCaritate,* 1766]. Trans. F. Coulson. London: Swedenborg Society, 1947. (b) *Charity: The Practice of Neighborliness.* Trans. W. R. Wunsch. Second edition. West Chester, Penn.: Swedenborg Foundation, 1995.

_____. *Clavis hieroglyphica arcanorum naturalium et spiritualium per viam repre-sentationum et correspondentiarum* (1742), published in London in 1784. English translation by R. Hindmarsh, *A Hieroglyphic Key to Natural and Spiritual Mysteries, by Way of Representations and Correspondences*. London 1792.

_____. *De cultu et amore Dei*. London: 1745. [Worship and Love of God.] Trans. A. H. Stroh and F. Sewall. Fourth printing. West Chester, Penn.: Swedenborg Foundation: 1996.

_____. *De Equo Albo de quo in Apocalypsi, cap: XIX. Et dein de Verbo et ejus Sensu Spirituali seu Interno, ex Arcanis Cœlestibus*. London: 1758. Crit. ed., London: Swedenborg Society, 1934. including Swedenborg's explanatory appendix from 1769. Swedish ed. *Om vita hästen*, trans. and notes by Anders Hallengren, Stockholm: Skrifter utgivna av Skandinaviska Swedenborgssällskapet, 2. Stockholm and Ann Arbor, Mich.: 1994.

_____. "De fide et bonis operibus," published by J.J.G. Wilkinson in *Opuscula quædam argumenti philosophici*. London: 1846.

_____. *De sensu communi* . . . (1744), published as *The Animal Kingdom*, Part 3. Trans. Enoch S. Price. Philadelphia: Swedenborg Scientific Association, 1914.

_____. *De ultimo judicio* (1762, post.).

_____. *De ultimo judicio*. London 1758. (a) Third English trans.: *On the Last Judgment*. London 1830.

_____. *De Verbo* (1762, post.). Trans. *Concerning the Sacred Scripture* . . ., J. Whitehead. New York: Swedenborg Foundation, 1914.

_____. *Delights of Wisdom concerning Conjugial Love*. (a) Boston, 1843 (1833). [*Delitiae sapientiae de amore conjugiali*. Amsterdam: 1768]. (b) Trans. S. M. Warren. Second edition. West Chester, Penn.: Swedenborg Foundation, 1998.

_____. *Diarium Spirituale*. Ed. J.F.I. Tafel, London: Wm. Newbery, 1843–47. New critical ed. J. Durban Odhner, *Experientiae spirituales*. 6 vols. Bryn Athyn, Penn.: Academy of the New Church, 1983–1997.

_____. *The Divine Love and Wisdom*. Trans. J. Whitehead. New York: Swedenborg Foundation, 1912; 2nd ed. 1995.

_____. *Divine Providence*. Trans. W. F. Wunsch. Second edition. West Chester, Penn.: Swedenborg Foundation, 1996.

_____. *Doctrina Novae Hierosolyma de Fide*. Amsterdam: 1763. Trans. J.

Potts, revised by W. Dick. In *Four Doctrines of the New Jerusalem*. London: Swedenborg Society, 1954.

_____. *The Doctrine of Charity*. Trans. J. Whitehead. New York: Swedenborg Foundation, 1914.

_____. *Doctrine of Life for the New Jerusalem*. Boston: 1831.

_____. *Doctrine of the New Jerusalem concerning the Lord*. Boston: 1833.

_____. *Doctrine of the New Jerusalem concerning the Sacred Scripture*. Boston: 1838.

_____. *Economy of the Animal Kingdom*. Translated and edited by Augustus Clissold. London: 1845–46.

_____. Eman. Swedenborgii *Adversaria in libros Veteris Testamenti*. Tübingen and London, 1847–54. Engl. trans. Alfred Acton: *The Word of the Old Testament Explained*. 9 vols. Bryn Athyn, Penn.: Academy of the New Church, 1928–1951.

_____. *Heaven and Its Wonders and Hell* [Heaven and Hell]. Trans. J. C. Ager. Second edition. West Chester, Penn.: Swedenborg Foundation, 1995.

_____. *Istinno-Christianskaya Religiya;* extracts from "The True Christian Religion" published as Izbrannyia sochineniia [. . .], London 1872. [Swedenborg's exposition of the Ten Commandments, most probably translated by Kleopatra Shakhovskaya.] (Copy in the Royal Library, Stockholm.)

_____. *The Last Judgment (Posthumous)* . . . . Trans. J. Whitehead. New York: Swedenborg Foundation, 1914.

_____. *The Last Judgment in Retrospect*. Trans. George F. Dole. West Chester, Penn.: Swedenborg Foundation: 1996.

_____. Life in Animals and Plants. London: Swedenborg Society, 1981.

_____. *Miscellanea observata circa res naturales* . . . . 4 vols. Leipzig and Hamburg: 1722.

_____. *Nosmertnoe tvorenie Apokalipsis* (Apocalypse Explained, vol. 1). St. Petersburg: 1906. (Copy in Biblioteka Jagiellonska, Kraków.)

_____. *O nebesakh, o mirie dukhov, i ob adie*. Trans. Aleksandr Aksakov. New edition annotated by Aleksandr Dobrokhotov and Anders Hallengren. Moscow: Mirovoe derevo, 1993.

_____. *O Novum Gerusalimie* [. . .]. London: 1904; "Of the New Jerusalem and its Heavenly Doctrine." Another Russian translation of this work: *Novyj Ierusalim i ego nebesnoe uchenie*, transl. Igor

Edomskij. London and Riga: 1938 (Copy in the Royal Library, Stockholm).

———. *O Pasliednem (Strashnom) Sood* (On the Last [Terrible] Judgment). St. Petersburg: 1906. (Copy in the Swedenborg Library, Bryn Athyn, Penn.)

———. *O saabshchénii dushi i tela* (On the Communication of Soul and Body). St. Petersburg: 1910. (Cited in the Great Soviet Encyclopedia.)

———. *Of the New Jerusalem, and Its Heavenly Doctrine.* 1758. 4th American ed. Boston: 1835.

———. *On the Divine Love and the Divine Wisdom* (Posthumous). [*De Divina Sapientia*, 1763]. Trans. E. Mongredien. rev. ed. London: Swedenborg Society, 1963. (Previously published as *Doctrine of Uses.*)

———. *On the Intercourse Between the Soul and the Body, Which Is Supposed to Take Place Either by Physical Influx, or by Spiritual Influx, or by Pre-Established Harmony.* Translation of *De commercio animae et corporis* (1769), first published in London 1812 and reprinted in Boston 1828. (First American edition of this work appeared in the journal *Halcyon Luminary* (Baltimore) 2 [1813].)

———. *Opera philosophica et mineralia.* Leipzig and Dresden: Friedrich Hekel, 1734.

———. *Opera poetica.* London and Uppsala: Swedenborg Society and Uppsala University, 1910.

———. *Opera quaedam aut inedita aut obsoleta de rebus naturalibus.* 3 vols. Stockholm: Royal Academy of Sciences, 1907–1911.

———. *Posthumous Theological Works.* Ed. John Whitehead. New York: Swedenborg Foundation, 1928. Second edition, 1996.

———. *Principia.* Tr. Augustus Clissold. London and Boston: 1845–46.

———. *Resebeskrivningar af Emanuel Swedenborg under åren 1710–1739.*(Itineraria.) Stockholm: Royal Academy of Sciences, 1911.

———. *Responsum ad Dr. Ernesti* (1771). Published in: Jon E. Elliot's critical ed. of the *Small Theological Works and Letters of Emanuel Swedenborg,* 197ff. London: 1975.

———. *Sapientia angelica de Divina Providentia.* Amsterdam: 1764.

———. *A Treatise concerning Heaven and its Wonders, and also concerning Hell.* London:1823. [*De caelo et ejus mirabilibus, et de inferno.* London, 1758].

———. *True Christian Religion.* (a) Boston: 1843 (1833). [*Vera Christiana Religio.* Amsterdam: 1771.] (b) Trans. J. C. Ager. 2 vols. Second edition. West Chester, Penn.: Swedenborg Foundation, 1996.

_____. *Uveselniya premudrosti* [. . .], Moscow 1914. "The Delights of Wisdom concerning Conjugial Love." (Located at the Swedenborg Library, Bryn Athyn, Penn.)

_____. *Wisdom of Angels Concerning the Divine Providence.* Boston 1796 (First American edition).

_____. "Works translated into Russian." Lists compiled by Leonard Fox and Nancy Dawson, 1990, (Mss.). In Swedenborg Society Archives, London.

Tafel, Immanuel. "Letter from Dr. Tafel" [Paris, July 31, 1857], *New Jerusalem Magazine* (Boston) (Oct. 1857): 214ff; and Nov. 1858 [Tübingen Sept. 8, 1857]: 264ff.

_____. [Tübingen, 17th April, 1862]. "Miscellaneous." *Intellectual Repository* 9 (1862): 239–240.

Tafel, Rudolf Leonard. [Emanuel Swedenborg] *Autographa.* Photolithographic edition of Swedenborg's manuscripts. (The Royal Library, Stockholm)

_____. *Documents Concerning the Life and Character of Emanuel Swedenborg,* collected, translated, and annotated. 2 vols. London: British and Foreign Swedenborg Society, 1875–1890.

_____. "Equilibrium." Papers read before the Swedenborg Reading Society: Sessions 1879–1884. London 1880–85 (Copy in Swedenborg Library, Bryn Athyn.)

Taylor, Charles E. *Leaflets from the Danish West Indies.* Westport, Conn.: Negro Universities Press. Reprint 1970 (1888).

Taylor, Edward. *The Poems by Edward Taylor.* Ed. Donald E. Stanford, with a foreword by Louis L. Martz. New Haven, Conn.: Yale University Press, 1960.

Tholander, August. *Ernste Federzeichnungen,* by "T . . . r." Moscow: Commissionsverlag von J. Deubner, 1886.

Tigerstedt, E.N. "The Poet as Creator: Origins of a Metaphor." *Comparative Literature Studies* 5, no. 4 (1968).

Tottie, Henry William. *Jesper Svedbergs lif och verksamhet: Bidrag till svenska kyrkans historia.* 3 vols. Uppsala, Sweden: Akdemiska Boktr. Edv. Berling, 1885–1886.

Transactions of the International Swedenborg Congress [. . .]London, July 4–8, 1910. London: Swedenborg Society, 1912. Page 367 lists exhibited photographs of Russian adherents of the New Church, most of them of the Muravyov and Shakhovskoí families.

Traubel, Horace. *With Walt Whitman in Camden.* (Vol. 5.) April 8–Sept

14, 1889. Ed. Gertrude Traubel. Carbondale, Illinois: University of Southern Illinois Press, 1964.

Trobridge, George. *Swedenborg: Life and Teaching*. London: Swedenborg Society, 1974.

Trungpa, Chögyam. *Shambhala: The Sacred Path of the Warrior*. Boston: Shambhala/Random House, 1984.

Urmson, J.O. "Representation in Music." In the series "Royal Institute of Philosophy Lectures": Vol. 6, 1971/72: *Philosophy and the Arts*. London: The Royal Institute of Philosophy/The Macmillan Press LTD, 1973: 132–146.

"Utdrag af ett bref dat. New York d. 22 Maj 1817." Report from 'Garf-vare Lundgren' on king Christophe, S. Domingo [MS]. Schöherrs Samling, NKBA vol. 47, collections of Nya Kyrkans Bekännare, Stockholm, now deposited in the Royal Library, Stockholm.

Van Cromphout, Gustaaf. *Emerson's Modernity and the Example of Goethe*. Columbia, Mo.: University of Missouri Press, 1990.

Van Dusen, Wilson. "Uses: A Way of Personal and Spiritual Growth." In *The Country of Spirit*, 61–87. San Francisco: J. Appleseed & Co., 1992.

Very, Jones. *Essays and Poems*. Ed. Ralph Waldo Emerson. Boston: 1839.

Viatte, Auguste. *Les sources occultes du romantisme: illuminisme-théosophie*, 1770–1820. Paris: Bibliothèque de la Revue de littérature comparée, 1969 (Diss. 1928).

Vicq, Rigmor de, ed. "A list of the names on inhabitants. The Danish Westindian Islands (The Virgin Islands) from 1650—ca 1825 compiled by Hugo Ryberg (genealog) of Copenhagen (Denmark) from the sources in the Royal Danish Statearchiv," Copenhagen 1945. (MS) St. Croix Landmarks Society, Fredriksted, U.S.V.I.

Wadström, Carl Bernhard. *An Essay on Colonization, Particularly Applied to the Western Coast of Africa, with Some Free Thoughts on Cultivation and Commerce* [1794]. Reprint New York: Augustus M. Kelley Publishers, 1968.

――――. *Observations on the Slave Trade*. London: 1789.

Wahlström, Lydia. *Revolution och Religion: ur den franska revolutionens själsliv*. Stockholm: Hugo Gebers Förlag, 1936.

Walicki, Andrzej. "Russia, Poland and France in the Paris Lectures of Mickiewicz." In *We and They: National Identity as a Theme in Slavic Cultures*, 38–47. Ed. Kristine Heltberg. Copenhagen: Rosenkilde and Bagger.

Walser, Martin. *Ein fliehendes Pferd* (1978). In *Werke*, vol. 5. Ed. Helmuth Kiesel. Frankfurt am Main: Suhrkamp, 1997.

West Indies. "Corresponding with Theosophical Society 1785." Reference note (MS). Archives. Newton, Mass.: Swedenborg School of Religion.

Westin, Gunnar. *Lutheraner Anglikaner Reformerta: Kyrkohistoriska uppsatser.* Uppsala, Sweden: J.A. Lindblads Förlag, 1935: 23–52.

White, William. *Emanuel Swedenborg: His Life and Writings.* 2 vols. London: 1867.

Whitman, Walt. *The Complete Poetry and Prose of Walt Whitman as Prepared by Him for the Deathbed Edition.* With an introduction by Malcolm Cowley. New York: Pellegrini & Cudahy, 1948.

———. *The Complete Writings.* 10 vols. Ed. R.M. Bucke. New York: G.P. Putnam's Sons, 1902.

———. *Democratic Vistas.* Washington, D.C.: 1871. See also *Democratic Vistas, and Other Papers.* London: W. Scott; Toronto: W.J. Gage, 1888.

———. *Leaves of Grass.* Second edition. Brooklyn, New York: 1856.

———. *Notes and Fragments . . . .* Ed. Richard Maurice Bucke. Printed for private distribution. London, Ont.: 1899.

Wilkinson, James John Garth. Letters to Ralph Waldo Emerson 1847–1874 (MSS). London: Swedenborg Society Archives.

Wilkinson, Lynn R. *The Dream of an Absolute Language: Emanuel Swedenborg and French Literary Culture.* Albany, N.Y.: SUNY Press, 1996.

Wilson Moore, Rachel. *The Journal of Rachel Wilson Moore.* Philadelphia, Penn.: 1867.

Wolff, Christian. *Gesammelte Werke*, Abt. 3, Bd. 36: Bd. 1. (*Theologia naturalis*). Hildesheim: Olms, 1996.

Woodbury, Charles J. *Talks with Ralph Waldo Emerson.* Reprint New York: Baker and Taylor Co., 1890.

Woofenden, William Ross. *Swedenborg Researcher's Manual.* Bryn Athyn, Penn: Swedenborg Scientific Association, 1988.

Worcester, William L. *The Language of Parable: A Key to the Bible.* New York: Swedenborg Foundation, 1984 (1892).

Worden, Ethelwyn. "The Influence of Swedenborg on the Music of Richard Yardumian." In Robin Larsen, ed., *Emanuel Swedenborg: A Continuing Vision.* New York: Swedenborg Foundation, 1988.

Wunsch, W. F. *A Practical Philosophy of Life, as gathered from the Writings of Swedenborg.* New York: Swedenborg Foundation, 1937.

Yates, Frances A. *Giordano Bruno and the Hermetic Tradition*. Reprint London: Routledge; Chicago: Univ. of Chicago Press, 1978 (1964).

Zeszyty Naukowe Wydzialu Humanistycznego /Studia Scandinavica, 10, Wydawnictvo Uniwersitetu Gdańskiego, Gdańsk 1988. Papers presented at the Polish-Swedish conference "Emanuel Swedenborg and his significance for the European culture" Warsaw, June 3–5, 1986. Ed. Zenon Ciesielski.

Index

Adam, Max, 11
Adamite era, 89–90, 100, 122, 130
Africans, spirituality of, 45
Aksakov, Aleksandr, 18, 63–64, 75
Aleksandr I, 62, 64–65
Almqvist, Carl Jonas Love, 11, 27
"American Civilization" (Emerson),
    113
American philosophy of uses,
    105–114
"The American Scholar" (Emerson),
    115–116, 118–120
Ancient Church in Asia, 17–41
Ancient Word, 34
Angelus Silesius (Johannes
    Scheffler), 62
Animal Kingdom (Swedenborg), 7,
    115, 120
Apocalypse. *See* Book of Revelation
Apocalypse Explained (Swedenborg),
    77, 141 (n. 41)
Apocalypse Revealed (Swedenborg),
    8–9, 19–22, 24, 29–30, 77, 110,
    157 (n. 20)
Arcana Coelestia (Swedenborg), 8, 13,
    54, 90, 111, 119, 134
Asia. *See* Great Tartary
atonal music, 11–15

Bach, Johann Sebastian, 6–7, 14–15
Bacon, Francis, 94, 101, 115–116,
    118, 123
Balakian, Anna, 125
Balzac, Honoré de, 11–13, 17–19
    a declared Swedenborgian, 13

baroque style, 15, 131
    and polyphony, 6
Barrett, Benjamin F., 101
Barthélémon, Francis Hippolythe, 10
Bayley, Jonathan, 66–67, 75, 94–95,
    128, 146 (n. 7)
Bentham, Jeremy, 106, 108
Benzelius, Eric, Jr., 5, 32–33
Berch, Carl Reinhold, 30
Berg, Alban, 11, 13, 15
Bernbaum, Edwin, 39
Bertocci, Angelo, 124
Beyer, Gabriel, 72, 84
Béyú ("Hidden Country"), 38
Bible
    interpreting allegorically, 134
    references in to older writings,
        20–21
    as song, 8
Bigelow, John, 54
Biörner, Eric Julius, 33
Birch, Andreas, 45–47, 49
Bishop, Jonathan, 111
Björck, Albert, 18–19
Boehme, Jakob, 62–63
Book of Revelation, 34
    Asia in, 20
Borges, Jorge Luis, 129, 133, 161 (n.
    1)
Bowra, C.M., 125
Bradstreet, Anne, 101, 103
Brenner, Henrik, 33
Brenner, Sophia, 5, 33
Brown, Pastor Solyman, 46
Bryan, Elijah, 46–47, 49, 53–55

Buddhism, 27–28, 37–41
Bureus, Johannes, 31
Burke, Francis, 49
Burton, Warren, 90
Busch, Corporal Heinrich, 30

Calvinism, 111, 136
Cambridge Platonists, 122, 130
Camena Borea (Swedenborg), 5
Capell, Daniel, 31
Carleson, Edvard, 30
Carlyle, Thomas, 123–124, 130, 159
    (n. 1)
Carpani, Giovanni, 27, 29
Césaire, Aimé, 51
Chambers, Alexander, 49
Chambers, John Carr, 49
Channing, William Ellery, 101, 107
Charles XII, Swedish king, 26
Chastanier, Bénédict, 72, 85–86
China. See Great Tartary
Christophe, Haitian King Henri,
    50–51
"Circles" (Emerson), 117
Clavis hieroglyphica (Swedenborg),
    134–136, 154 (n. 18), 162 (n. 8)
Coates, Eric, 11
Coleridge, Samuel Taylor, 123–124,
    126
Collijn, Nicholas, 49–50
Columbus, Christopher, 44
composers, inspired by spirit, 9
The Conduct of Life (Emerson), 113
Conjugial Love (Swedenborg), 21, 54
Corbin, Henry, 130, 132
Coronis (Swedenborg), 23
correspondences, 74, 93–94, 98–99,
    135
    to musical instruments, 8
Cranch, Christopher Pearse, 104
Cronhamn, Jöns Peter, 10
Cudworth, Ralph, 122, 131,
    159–160 (n. 11)

Cullberg, Johan, 17–20

Dal', Vladimir, 76–77, 147 (n. 15)
Dalai Lama, 37–38, 41
Darwin, Charles, 121
Davāni, Jalal al-Din Muhammed ibn
    As'ad Akhlak-i-Jalāly, 130
De Anima (Swedenborg), 7
Decembrist society, 62, 65, 127
De cultu et amore Dei (Swedenborg), 91
Deleen, Carl Erik, 82
De sensu communi (Swedenborg), 7
Dewey, John, 118–119
De-yúng , 38
The Dial, 103–104
Dillard, Donald, 10
Divine Love and Wisdom (Swedenborg),
    54, 110–111
Divine Providence (Swedenborg), 54
Doctrine of Life (Swedenborg), 66, 110
The Doctrine of the Sacred Scripture
    (Swedenborg), 8, 20
dodecaphony, 11–15
Dostoevsky, Fyodor, 63–66, 71, 75,
    116
    The Brothers Karamazov, 63–64, 116
Drews, Sir Arthur, 34
Dubois, Page, 121
Dybeck, Johan Erik, 82–83

Eastern orthodoxy, 69–72
emancipation of the serfs (Russian),
    61
Emerson, Ellen Russell, 103
Emerson, Ralph Waldo, 59, 80, 82,
    89–95, 100–104, 107–126,
    132–133, 135–136, 162 (n. 9).
    See also individual works.
Ernesti, Johann August, 6
Exegetiska och Philantropiska Sällskapet
    (Exegetical Philanthropic
    Society), 43, 86

Fishbough, William, 96
Fontenelle, Bernard Le Bouvier de, 27
"The Fortune of the Republic" (Emerson), 113
Foucault, Michel, 124
Franklin, Benjamin, 106–107
freemasonry, 50, 61, 65
free will, 135
Furtwängler, Wilhelm, 11, 139 (n. 31)

Gay, John, 106
Gelpi, Donald, 116–117
Genghis Khan, 31, 36
Gödel, Kurt, 118
Goroneskul, Joaniki, 30, 72–73
Görres, Joseph von, 80, 81, 87
Goyder, David George, 82, 95
The Great Chain of Being, 121
Great Tartary, Word in, 17–41
Great Wall of China, 21, 24, 36
Grusin, Richard A., 124
Gura, Philip F., 124

Haglund, Tommie, 11, 139 (n. 30)
Händel, Georg Friedrich, 15
Hänschell, Hother (Lutheran pastor), 53
harmonies, 15
   of the heavens, 9
Harvard College and Divinity School, 90
Hawley, Pastor F. L., 48, 53–54, 145 (n. 8)
Heaven and Hell (Swedenborg), 11, 76, 111, 142 (n. 5)
   French translation of, 84
Hedin, Sven, 19, 25
Hellström, Jan Arvid, 50
Henderson, James G., 56
hermeneutics, 119, 124, 130–131
Herzen, Aleksandr, 64–65

Heyliger, Anna Caroline (Krause), 58
hieroglyphics, divine, 97–100
   key to, 98–99, 102, 134–136
Hildebrand, Heidi, 105–106
Hindmarsh, Robert, 85
Hobart, Nathaniel, 82, 90
Höpken, Anders Johan von, 43, 60
Hughes, Gertrude Reif, 110
human rights reform, basis in Swedenborg's writings, 52
Hunt, Benjamin Peter, 90
Hutcheson, Francis, 106
hymns, effect on spirits, 8–9

Iamblichus, 133, 162 (n. 6)
"Illusions" (Emerson), 117
Innocent IV, Pope, 27–28
The Intellectual Repository, 54, 69, 94–95
"Ioan Khan." See Prester John
Islam, 130–132

Jamaica, 49
James, Henry, Sr., 90
James, William, 118–119
Jefferson, Thomas, 106–107, 112–113, 127, 156 (n. 2)
Johansén, Anders, 52
Johanson, Sven-Eric, 11, 139 (n. 30)
Johnson, John Meyer, 46–47
Johnson, Mary, burial of, 53
Jonsson, Inge, 26, 29, 34
Jung-Stilling, Johann Heinrich, 62, 146 (n. 1)

Kabbalah, 63, 130
Kahl, Achatius, 60, 80, 82–83
Kalachakra, 40–41
Kangyur, 38
Kierulff, Carl Andreas, 45–50, 52–53, 59
Kierulff, Cathrine Rebekka, 58

Kierulff, Emanuel Swedenborg, 47, 58

Kierulff, Jakob Elias, 47

Kierulff, Rosamunde Vibe, 58

Kierulff, Vibe, 45–47, 58

Knight, R. G., 56

Krause, Gustavus Adolphus, 44

Kristeva, Julia, 125

Küttner, Juri, 32

ladder metaphor, 122–123, 160 (n. 11)

Lange, Lorens, 19, 31

Lao Tzu, 38

Lapeyrouse, Stephen, 116

The Last Judgment (Swedenborg), 24

Leeward Islands, 44–45

Leibniz, Gottfried Wilhelm von, 28–29, 63, 94

Lenhammar, Harry, 84

Levin, Harry, 125

Linberg, Henning Gotfried, 46, 49, 58–59

Linberg, Mary (Mac Lachland), 46–47, 58–59

Lindberg, Supreme Court Justice Jacob, 58

Linköping, manuscripts found at, 18, 25

love, 15
  agape, 71
  like a melody, 8
  between man and woman, 21

Lovejoy, Arthur D., 121

Lutheranism, 47, 53, 111, 136

Macaulay, Thomas Babington, 123

Magna Sina. *See* Great Tartary

Matérn, Johan Anton, 31

Mather, William, 73–75

Mazzeo, Joseph Anthony, 125

"Merlin's Song" (Emerson), 113

Messerschmidt, Daniel Gottleib, 30–31

Mill, John Stuart, 106

Miller, Perry, 124

Milosz, Czeslaw, 64, 133

minimalist music, 16

Miscellanea Observata (Swedenborg), 6

Mittnacht, Johan Gottlieb, 82

modernism, 125

Molin, Lieutenant Ambjörn, 30

monism, organic, in music, 14

Moore, Rachel Wilson, 56–58

morals, primacy of, 108–111

Moravian church, 48, 55

More, Henry, 131

Müller, Johan Bernhard, 30

Muravyov, Aleksandr Nikoláevich, 65–69, 77, 127–128, 146 (n. 9), 147 (n. 15)

Muravyov, Nikita Mikhailovich, 65

Muravyov-Apostol, Sergei Ivanovich, 65

music
  connection with spirit, 9
  minimalist, 16
  other-worldly, 15
  point of crisis in Western, 13–14
  pure, return to, 15

musical instruments, correspondences to, 8

musicians influenced by Swedenborg, 10–16

mystical epiphanies, 7–8

Nasr, Seyyed Hossein, 130–132, 161 (n. 18)

"The Naturalist" (Emerson), 92

Nature (Emerson), 93–95, 99–100, 108–109, 135

neo-Platonic traditions, 122, 131, 133

Nerval, Gérard de, 11–12, 15

Nestorians, 27, 33, 35–36

New Church, 70–71

New Church composers, 10–11

New England transcendentalism, 89–104, 107

New Jerusalem Magazine, 10, 52, 54, 82, 86, 90, 95, 98, 111

"newness," sense of, 89–104

"Nominalist and Realist" (Emerson), 120

Nordenskiöld, August, 52, 59, 81, 84–86

Nordenskiöld, Carl Fredrik, 81, 86

Nordenskiöld Frugårds Archive, 82

Novikov, Nikolai Ivanovich, 62

Odóevsky, Prince Vladímir, 62–63

Œgger, Guillaume, 98–99, 102
  list of correspondences, 154 (n. 18)

Oetinger, Friedrich Christoph, 62

Of the New Jerusalem and Its Heavenly Doctrine (Swedenborg), 73–74

Old Church Slavonic texts, 32

"On the Relation of Man to the Globe" (Emerson), 92

Opera Philosophica et Mineralia (Swedenborg), 6, 73

Oronoskow. *See* Goroneskul, Joaniki

Packer, Barbara, 110

Paine, Thomas, 106, 127

Paley, William, 106

Paracelsus, 63, 65

Parsons, Theophilus, Jr., 90

Paz, Octavio, 125

Peabody, Elizabeth Palmer, 98, 152 (n. 5)

Pernety, Antoine-Joseph, 81, 84–85

Pierce, Charles Sanders, 118–119

Pietist movement, 27

Plato, 25, 94, 130, 141–142 (n. 5)

"The Poet" (Emerson), 95–96

Polhem, Christopher, 33

Polo, Marco, 34–36
  stories from the time of, 32

polyphony
  Baroque, 6
  and the sound of truth, 9
  universal, 14

Prester John, legends about, 25, 31, 34–36

Priestley, Joseph, 106

Principia (Swedenborg), 162 (n. 9)

Pro Fide et Caritate, 50, 86

Pushkin, Aleksandr Sergeevich, 63

Pythagoras, 94, 133

Qur'an, 130–131

Raich, Semyon Egorovich, 62

Rajalin, Salomon Mauritz von, 50

Rameau, Jean-Philippe, 138 (n. 11)

"Rational Psychology" (Swedenborg), 7

Reed, Sampson, 90–92, 98, 102, 109, 111–112

Representative Men (Emerson), 82, 111, 129

Robsahm, Carl, 72, 79–88
  life of, 149–150 (n. 9)

Rosenstein, Herman Rosén von, 50

Ruan, Dr. William Henry, 46–48, 53

Rubricus. *See* Ruysbroeck, Wilhelm van

Rudbeck, Olof, Sr., 31
  followers of, 27, 29, 31, 33

Rudolph, Duke Ludwig, 6

Russia, 61–77
  American writers read in, 126
  breaching isolation of, 62

Ruysbroeck, Wilhelm van, 28, 31, 34

St. Croix, 44, 47–49, 52–59
  literature on New Church in, 144
    (n. 1)
  persecution on, 52–55
St. Petersburg Academy of Sciences,
  32, 73
Sartre, Jean-Paul, 125
Schmidt, Wilhelm, 34
Schmidt-Häuer, Christian, 37
Scholten, Peter von, 47, 145 (n. 9)
Schnitzker, Christopher, 30
Schönberg, Arnold, 11, 13–16.
  breaking up traditional space-
    time, 140 (n. 38)
  "Composition with Twelve
    Notes," 13
  Moses and Aaron, 13
  "realism" of, 15
  Style and Form, 13
Schönström, Peter, 25, 27, 29–31,
  33, 35
Schrödinger, Erwin, 117–118
Schulman, Carl Gustaf, 31
"Self-Reliance" (Emerson), 129
Shakhovskaya, Princess Kleopatra
  Mikhailovna, 69–71, 73–75
Shakhovskoí, Prince Mikhail
  Aleksandrovitj, 69
Shambhala, 38–41
Shangri-la, 38
Shklovsky, Viktor, 126
Sinzheimer, Max, 10–11
Society of Wisdom-Lovers
  (Obshchestvo lyubomudriya),
  62–63
Solovyov, Vladimir, 18, 63, 76
"The Sovereignty of Ethics"
  (Emerson), 109
Spiritual Diary (Swedenborg), 23–24
"Spiritual Laws" (Emerson), 114
Stralenberg, Philip Johan von, 19,
  25–27, 29, 31, 33, 37

An Account of Travels in Russia . . . ,
  26
Strauss, Richard, 11, 14
Strindberg, August, 17–20, 24–27,
  37
  En Blå Bok, 19, 26
  Inferno, 17–18
  Kulturhistoriska Studier, 26
  Legender, 17–18
  "The Sources of the Bible," 24–25
Svedberg, Jesper, 4
Swedenborg, Emanuel, 63, 94, 130.
  See also individual works.
  baroque interests of, 6, 131
  bridge across cultures, 48
  as "Buddha of the North," 18, 41
  chamber organ of, 3–4, 137 (n. 1)
  exegesis of music, 7–9, 138 (n.
    18)
  family tree of, 29
  influence on musicians, 10–16
  influence on philosophy, 125
  influence on writers, 63–64
  interest in the hidden Word in
    the Far East, 17–41
  as the last Christian, 132
  poetry of, 5, 33
  pre-Israelitish Word, 23
  as "Shaykh," 132
  spiritual worlds opened to, 8,
    12–13, 88
  summer house preserved, 3
  travels of, 5–7
  youthful interest in music, 4–5
"Swedenborg; or, the Mystic"
  (Emerson), 82
Swedenborgian groups
  black, 45, 55, 57
  in Jamaica, 49
  in the Leeward Islands, 44–45
  persecution of, 52–55, 59
  in the Virgin Islands, 45–48,
    52–59

in West Africa, 51–52
in the West Indies, 43–60
Swedenborg Society (London), 10, 46, 76, 83
Swedish East India Company, 28

Tafel, Immanuel, 80
Tafel, Rudolf Leonard, 80, 83
Tappan, Caroline Sturgis, 103
Tartary, 141 (n. 4). *See also* Great Tartary
Tatishchev, Vassiliy, 29, 32–33
Taylor, Edward, 102
Tegnér, Esaias, 56
Tengyur, 38
Theosophical Society, 10
theosophy, 18, 25, 39, 61, 85, 143 (n. 27)
theurgy, 133
Tholander, August, 71
Thoreau, Henry David, 116, 120, 123, 126
"The Times" (Emerson), 95
Tolstoi, Count Leo, 63–64, 66, 126
Ton-spiele, return to, 15
transcendental philosophy, 62, 89–104
Traubel, Horace, 79–80
True Christian Religion (Swedenborg), 14, 22–24, 40, 45, 48, 54, 76
twelve-tone technique, 11–15
Tyboni, Carl Oscar, 10

Union of Welfare, 62
Un Khan, 35–36
uses, 105–114
"The Uses of Natural History" (Emerson), 92
utilitarianism, 156 (n. 3). *See also* uses

Vale, A., 10
Very, Jones, 100
Virgin Islands, 45–48
Vitberg, Aleksandr Lavrentevich, 64–65

Wadström, Carl Bernhard, 51, 85–86
Warner, Thomas Shirley, 49
Weber, Friedrich Christian, 31
Webern, Anton, 11, 13–16
  Dead, 14
West Indies, 43–60
  literature on New Church in, 144 (n. 1)
White, William, 82
The White Horse (Swedenborg), 39
Whitman, Walt, 79–80, 89–90, 95–100, 123, 125
  Democratic Vistas, 96–97
  Good-Bye My Fancy, 100
  Leaves of Grass, 95–100, 153 (n. 8)
  "A Song of the Rolling Earth," 89–90, 99
Wigglesworth, Michael, 103–104
Wilkins, John H., 90
Wilkinson, James John Garth, 82, 90
Wittington, Carl J., 10
Wolff, Christian von, 28, 142 (n. 13)
Worcester, John, 10
The Word
  of Creation, 15
  meaning of opened, 8
  originating in Great Tartary, 17–41
  receiving celestial music, 8–9

Yackes, Susanna Kerney, 58
Yardumian, Richard, 10, 14
Yurkevich, Pamphil Danilovich, 63